# Ride Pennsylvania

## Horse Trails

### Part I – The Eastern Half of Pennsylvania

# 50+ Horseback Riding, Hiking, & Biking Trails

*By*
*Carolyn B. Cook*

*Hit The Trail Publications, LLC*
*Pennsylvania*

Ride Pennsylvania Horse Trails
50+ Horseback Riding, Hiking, & Biking Trails
Part I- The Eastern Half of Pennsylvania
By Carolyn B. Cook

**Note to the Reader:** Trails are always changing. If you find any of the described trails have significantly changed or new trails have opened, please notify the publisher and author at the below address. Any comments will be considered in the future editions of this book and are appreciated.

Published by:
Hit The Trail Publications, LLC
P.O. Box 970
Cherryville, PA 18035

Editor: Connie Bloss

ISBN 0-9729080-0-5
Library of Congress Control Number 2003101498

Cover photos: John Spotts on Moonshine (a Fun-E-Farm Mountain Horse), Wyoming State Forest (top); the author on Tabasco (of Willow Brook Farms Quarter Horse breeding) (bottom)
Back photos: Steve Luoni on DJ (Tennessee Walking Horse) and John Spotts on Moonshine on the Heritage Rail-Trail (left); the author on Tabasco at Jacobsburg Environmental Education Center (right)
Other photo courtesies: Connie Bloss, Larry Bloss, Barbara Cook, Jan Huffman, Steve Luoni, and John Spotts

Additional courtesies: Listed in individual chapters

Website: www.ridepennsylvania.com

# DISCLAIMER!
## READ AND UNDERSTAND PRIOR TO USING THIS BOOK!

Please note: This book is a reference source and information book only. The author, publisher, and all others, directly or indirectly associated with this book, do not make any recommendations or guarantees regarding any place, person, animals, service, directions, conditions, environment, or other item mentioned in this book, nor are they responsible for any errors in this book. This book is not all-inclusive. The author may indicate a good personal experience or a favorite personal preference but does not mean the reader or user of the information in this book will have the same positive experience upon their visit to the location or use of the facilities.

Horses (mules included) and horseback riding can be, and is, a dangerous sport. Trail riding can present all sorts of unpredictable or predictable hazards and risks. Circumstances, obstacles, weather, terrain, places, people, attitudes, horses, behavior, trails, traffic, crowds, wildlife, experiences, theft, multiple-uses, hunting seasons, permitted uses, improper usage, surroundings, etc. change. Call the trail administrator in advance; check on the conditions of the trails, changes in the trails, obstacles, concerns, or any other info the office or source of information on the trail can provide. Even if no fees or permits are listed, check for changes or exceptions, such as for large, organized group rides. Obtain maps; ask for recommendations and comments. If water is listed as accessible on a trail, check that the water quality is good and that horses are permitted to drink from the water source. Large rigs should check accessibility and grade. Use common sense and caution. Bring a cell phone, first-aid kit, and be prepared in case of an emergency.

The reader or user of information in this book assumes their own risks and agrees the reader or user of information in this book is responsible for their own health and safety. The author, publisher, and all others, directly or indirectly associated with this book, expressly disclaim any and all liability against any and all claims, causes of action, liabilities of any nature, damages, costs and expenses, including, without limitation, attorney fees, arising because of any alleged personal injury, property damage, death, nuisance, loss of business or otherwise, by the reader or user arising from or in any way connected to the information contained in this book.

# Table of Contents

Introduction                                                    vi
About the Author                                                vii
Dedication and Thanks                                           viii
What is the Difference between State Forests,
State Parks, National Parks, State Gamelands, etc.              ix
The Pennsylvania Equine Council (PEC)                           xiii
Map                                                             xvi


1   Green Lane Park                                             1
2   Valley Forge National Historic Park & The
    Betzwood Rail-Trail                                         6
3   Perkiomen Trail                                             13
4   Evansburg State Park                                        17
5   Wissahickon Trail System                                    21
6   French Creek State Park                                     27
7   Marsh Creek State Park                                      31
8   Ridley Creek State Park                                     34
9   Pennypack Park                                              38
10  Tyler State Park                                            43
11  White Clay Creek Preserve                                   46
12  Blue Marsh Lake                                             52
13  The Central Park Equestrian Trail System                    57
14  Money Rocks                                                 62
15  The Conewago Recreation Trail                               66
16  Lebanon Valley Rail-Trail                                   70
17  Lehigh Parkway                                              73
18  Stony Creek Rail-Trail                                      76
19  The Horse-Shoe Trail                                        81
20  Bucks County Horse Park                                     84
21  Nockamixon State Park                                       86
22  Delaware Canal State Park                                   91
23  Susquehannock Creek State Park                              95

| | | |
|---|---|---|
| 24 | Jacobsburg Environmental Education Center | 101 |
| 25 | Rocky Ridge County Park | 105 |
| 26 | William Kain County Park | 108 |
| 27 | Spring Valley County Park | 113 |
| 28 | Heritage Rail-Trail County Park | 116 |
| 29 | Gifford Pinchot State Park | 121 |
| 30 | Codorus State Park | 124 |
| 31 | Gettysburg National Military Park | 127 |
| 32 | Tuscarora State Forest & The Iron Horse Trail | 133 |
| 33 | Cumberland Valley Rail-Trail | 141 |
| 34 | Michaux State Forest | 145 |
| 35 | Big Pocono State Park & The Old Railroad Trail | 150 |
| 36 | Pohopoco Tract Recreation Area | 153 |
| 37 | Promised Land State Park | 156 |
| 38 | Conashaugh View Trail, Delaware Water Gap Equestrian Trail | 159 |
| 39 | D&H Rail-Trail | 163 |
| 40 | O&W Rail-Trail | 169 |
| 41 | Lackawanna State Park | 172 |
| 42 | Ricketts Glen State Park | 177 |
| 43 | The Tiadaghton State Forest & The Black Forest | 182 |
| 44 | Tioga State Forest, Home of The Grand Canyon of PA, & The Pine Creek Rail-Trail | 188 |
| 45 | Bald Eagle State Forest | 199 |
| 46 | Wyoming State Forest | 206 |
| 47 | Trails in Progress & Possible Future Equestrian Trails | 215 |
| 48 | State Gamelands Trail Information | 217 |
| 49 | Our Trail & Horse Camping Questionnaire | 218 |
| 50 | Our Travel Check List | 219 |
| 51 | Useful, Interesting, or Informative Websites | 221 |
| 52 | Other Helpful Sources of Information & Publications of Interest | 222 |
| 53 | Book Ordering Information | 225 |

# Introduction

I, along with my fiancé John Spotts (and superb trail guide), have ridden and camped with our horses throughout the Northeast for many years. At one time there was very little information available on trails, and they were difficult to research. Now with the surging popularity of trails and the Internet, much more information is available. But that still requires research and the data is not in one place. Having journeyed to so many other states, we often felt there wasn't much material available in a handy, organized, "at your fingertips" form on Pennsylvania trails. We felt Pennsylvania trail riders would like a book that had lots of info available in one location that could be brought along while traveling.

Until I performed the research on Pennsylvania trails, we were under the very mistaken impression that Pennsylvania did not have many trails to offer. But Pennsylvania does have lots of beautiful trails, rich with history and scenery, and more are being added. Due to the large size of the state and number of trails, this book reflects just those from the central point of the state east. We drew a line down the middle of the state and covered trails of the eastern half. A second book is in progress for the western side of the state.

Please note: Except for trails in development stages and portions of the State Gamelands, or unless otherwise stated, I have visited and ridden at each of the trails listed in the front index of this book. Sometimes I had to bike a trail to make sure the trails and parking were suitable before bringing the horses. Even still, I have not covered every inch of trail or branch of trail at each of these places. That would be very difficult and time consuming to do as the trails are always changing, are extensive, and many are expanding as this goes into print. Nor does this book include every trail system in the eastern half of Pennsylvania. This is just a selection of diverse trail systems. It is my intention to give readers a reference point for trails in eastern Pennsylvania, a variety of choices (instead of riding that "same old trail"), and to provide information about the trails as I or we experienced them. It is my hope that this book will help trail riders learn about new trails and share some of the great trails Pennsylvania has to offer. And most of all, it is my personal goal to support Pennsylvania equestrian trails so that Pennsylvania trails may continue to stay open to horseback riders and expand in the future. If a trail stays open or a new one is opened as a result of this book, all the research and work that went into this book will be a great success! Let's keep the list of Pennsylvania's trails growing, maintain good relations with our co-trail users, support our equine trail associations including the Pennsylvania Equine Council (PEC), and make Pennsylvania a top trail destination.

**Enjoy, Share, and Preserve.**
*Carolyn B. Cook*

# About the Author

Carolyn Cook is originally from Long Island, New York. While living on Long Island, she acquired her first horse, Chipper. Chipper was a wonderful and bomb-proof trail horse, and inspired Carolyn to move to Pennsylvania where she could afford to own a home with property to keep Chipper on the grounds. With a love of the Pennsylvania countryside that was established in her youth, and a desire to discover more of Pennsylvania, Carolyn acquired a horse trailer and set out to explore Pennsylvania's equestrian trails.

Ultimately, while on a group trail ride, Carolyn met John Spotts from New Holland, Pennsylvania. With a common love of the outdoors, they soon began exploring new trail systems. Sadly, Chipper passed on. But his memory lived on as the trail rides continued. Carolyn and John soon found themselves with three horses, one as a spare. The herd was increasing and time spent on trails was extensive. So they headed out in search of a larger trailer with living quarters, to accommodate their evolving life style.

Trails from Maine to the Carolinas were being ridden and the list of states kept growing each year. While traveling, Carolyn was writing articles on some of these rides and getting much positive feedback. There were so many trails that equestrians were not aware of or did not have information on. After a very enjoyable trip throughout their home state of Pennsylvania in 2001, they decided to get to know Pennsylvania trails better. Along with an expression from many friends and fellow equestrians that more information on Pennsylvania trails was needed, this book became a reality.

vii

# Dedication and Thanks

First of all, thank you to all that have contributed to these trails to make them become a reality for everyone to enjoy. Thank you to our horses, Chipper, Tabasco, Bonanza ('Bo'), Moonshine, and Skip for safely carrying us through so many trail systems and making our adventures full of good memories. You have taught me so much and enriched my life. Thank you to John Spotts, my dear best friend, wonderful companion, and fun co-adventurer for so much during the time of my writing this book. Thank you for joining me in this endeavor and sharing your comments and guidance along the way. John is an excellent trail guide and has an amazing ability and sense of direction to keep us from getting lost. Together, we have made these the good old days.

And a major thank you to my parents, Barbara and Ed, for raising me with the love of exploring new places and instilling the respect and appreciation for the beauty and wildlife the outdoors has to offer.

A very special thank you to my editor and good friend, Connie Bloss, for her patience, support, and passion for this project. I would also like to thank all the wonderful folks that I have met along the way. The list of those that have been helpful, inspirational, volunteered their input, shared their knowledge, helped keep our horses healthy, watched our extra horse at last minute so we could cover a trail, shoed our horse at a moment's notice so we could cover that trail, gave training tips, and/or been wonderful, supportive friends has become long, but I would like to mention some of them: Sue Arnold, Dr. Balliet, Dr. Bateman, Matt Beaver, Gene Brandner, Terry Class, Pat Cook, Thomas Cook, Dominic Farole (Esq.), Jan Huffman, Brenda Imus, Pete Johnson, Dr. Jones, Dr. Landiak, Steve Luoni, Linda Mouton, Anne O'Dell, Teresa Proctor, Jane Przybyikiewicz, Rob Rosenberg, Garth and Kathy Rumsmoke, Dr. Robert H. Schuller, Ellie Snyder, Tina Spangler, Dr. Abbott-Thompson, Margaret Thompson, Christopher Walls and the Walls family, our local riding friends (Pat, Ray, Cheryl, Ray Jr., Monica, Dale, Katherine, Woody, Janet, and Al), and the folks at Willow Brook Farms whose clinics have helped me train my horses and myself for these adventures.

And thank you to all those individuals and groups who have worked so hard to open, develop, maintain, and preserve the equestrian trails. Thank you to the Pennsylvania Equine Council (courtesies: Bud, Gwen, Pete, Mary Lou, & Sandra), DCNR, the U.S. Army Corps of Engineers, the County, State, and National Parks, the State Forests, various private and public organizations, the Rails-to-Trails groups, the State Game Commission, and others who were so helpful and generous in their time in providing information. The kindness of everyone was truly a positive experience for me. And most of all, thank you God, for allowing me to enjoy the wonder of your world on horseback.

# What is the difference between State Forests, State Parks, National Parks, State Gamelands, etc.?

We have been asked many times, what is the difference between the types of areas and their effect on equestrians. Each category has their own set of rules and regulations, and even the same kind may differ depending on the region and other factors. It is also significant as to who oversees the land and the laws under which its use was created, as both will also affect what is permitted within and what types of facilities are available. The following is based on our own observations derived from our experiences, and also from information obtained upon inquiry with officials of the various trail systems. Further information, including contacts, is listed in the related chapters.

**State Parks**  Pennsylvania's state park system is one of our country's largest. DCNR, the Department of Conservation and Natural Resources, manage these parks. The purpose of State Parks has evolved over the years and, today, one of their key functions is to provide outdoor recreation for the general public in natural settings. They typically have accommodations including comfort stations, picnic areas, pavilions, water, paved parking, etc. Usually, the park's grounds are maintained and groomed. The State Parks have designated central recreational areas (i.e., picnic areas) where, generally, horses are not permitted. Often, they have more restrictions such as no alcohol, no pets (this may be changing; currently there are exceptions), and limitations as to where equestrians are allowed if they are permitted. Fees may be charged for camping (non-horse) in the State Parks. Usually, equestrian camping is not offered within the State Park. In general, trails are well defined. If horses are accepted, they may be directed to travel in the outlying or surrounding areas. Sometimes, equestrian trails in the State Park serve as links to other trails, and that is why they exist. Other state parks do have designated, extensive equestrian trail systems.

We have found Pennsylvania's State Parks to be great places to ride with many excellent, well maintained, and beautiful trail systems. But, State Parks are an area where equestrians need to be especially sensitive, aware, and considerate of other users, as the parks are more central and heavily used by a variety of visitors, many of which are unfamiliar and sometimes not in favor of horses. Please keep in mind that cleaning up in the parking lots or the scattering of manure in popular and well traveled areas will help keep these locales open to riders.

**State Forests**  State Forests are overseen by DCNR's Bureau of Forestry. Along with other purposes, these lands are intended to be left in mostly an undeveloped, primitive, and natural state. Also, importantly, one of the established purposes of the

State Forest is to provide outdoor recreation to the public in a manner that is consistent with the above goals. In keeping with "a natural state", the roads within the forest are often of a dirt or a gravel surface, and the trails are not as well defined. Generally, horseback riding is permitted throughout the State Forest's trails and roads, except for areas specifically prohibiting horses such as natural areas or designated hiking (only) trails.

The good news: we were informed that equestrians have 1.9 million acres of State Forest land open to horseback riding! Often, the Bureau and the local trail and equestrian groups perform the maintenance on the trails. So equestrians can have influence on and assist in the establishment or maintenance of these trails. Check first with the local Forest District Office as rules can differ among separate districts. Ask for information, guidelines, and restrictions, and then get out there and explore! Carriage drivers should check with the individual district office as to which State Forest roads permit and are suitable for carriage driving as some State Forest roads are of good grade and excellent surface. We have experienced Pennsylvania State Forests to be wonderful places to visit, with endless possibilities. This is a very good area for equestrians to be effective and make a positive difference. Ask the region office if volunteers are needed; help and support our State Forest trail systems!

In addition to trail riding, State Forests permit primitive and motorized camping. Primitive (non-motorized) equestrian and non-equestrian camping is allowed and is free. Permits are not required if not camping more than one night in one place. Motorized non-equestrian and equestrian camping is often allowed on the sides of the State Forest roads, pull-off areas, and sometimes at designated locations. However, established camping areas are often dispersed throughout the forest and are not concentrated. Motorized camping is also free, but a permit is required. Frequently, water is not available (so bring water). Comfort stations or restrooms are limited or nonexistent. Usually, there is a state park or two within the forest where facilities are accessible. Other special rules and limitations apply, and can be obtained from DCNR.

**US Army Corps of Engineers Trail Systems** The US Army Corps of Engineers also manage land that may be open to the public and horseback riders. They have numerous important functions, some of which include managing water resources, maintaining navigation areas, providing aid under national emergencies (including natural disasters), engineering shoreline protection, and other coastal projects. The permitted use of the land may vary in accordance with the intended purpose and function of the land. Blue Marsh Lake Trail System is an example of an excellent recreation area developed by the US Army Corps of Engineers, and is an extensive multiple purpose locale that welcomes a variety of users including horseback riders.

**National Parks** The National Park Service, US Department of the Interior oversees the National Parks. Some of our favorite riding destinations are Gettysburg National Military Park and Valley Forge National Historic Park, which are National Parks with historical significance. National Parks have their own rules and restrictions, and it is extremely important that riders adhere to these regulations. They may permit special camping events such as Gettysburg National Military Park does on occasion. Equestrian day use may be permitted in specified areas or on designated trails. Comfort facilities are available.

**County Parks** The local counties administer the County Parks. It is up to the individual county and location of the park as to whether equestrian day use or camping is permitted. Many County Parks are smaller or are located in congested areas, so equestrian use is not appropriate. Other County Parks, such as Green Lane, have both horseback riding and horse camping. Comfort facilities, recreational grounds, and picnic areas are usually available. While researching for this book, we noticed an increase in permitted equestrian use in County Parks and these County Parks had awesome trail systems. Do not overlook the County Parks! Equestrians, especially local riding groups, should support and stay active with the County Parks to help ensure that equestrians remain welcome and to retain a positive presence.

**Private Parks** A private park, such as the innovative and scenic Bucks County Horse Park, consists of owners and members who determine the use and purpose of the land. They establish their own objectives, rules, regulations, and permitted uses.

**Rail-Trails** Rail-trail lands can be owned or managed by rail-to-trail organizations, the county, the Pennsylvania Game Commission, and others. A rail-trail can travel through different land ownership, such as the O&W Rail-Trail which has one portion that has been acquired by the Rail-Trail Council of Northeastern Pennsylvania, and another section that is owned by private individuals. The rail-trail paths can also travel through the State Forests and State Parks, such as the Pennsylvania Grand Canyon Pine Creek Rail-Trail. Riders need to know who owns the rail-trail land and if they permit horseback riders.

Comfort facilities are not always available, but may be available at central locations or at historic attractions. The tendency seems to be the addition of restrooms or portajohns at various intervals along the trails.

The good, durable surface of the rail-trails has kept many of these trails open to horses and mountain bikes. After speaking to members of the Rail-to-Trail organizations who oversee many of the rail-trails, in general, their common intended purpose is to have these corridors open to non-motorized use such as hiking, biking, and horseback riding. Sometimes, only certain sections are or can be open to equestrians due to congested areas or paved surfaces. Many of the rail-trails, although operated by different groups, seem to adhere to this uniform usage for hiking, biking, and riding.

There has been an increase of rail-trail conversion in recent years, and much is still being defined. The trend currently seems to be that equestrians are being considered and permitted on many new rail-trails. The rail-trails offer some fantastic travels along the corridors of our nation's history; this is another area where equestrians should volunteer, join the organizations, and be actively involved in order to keep rail-trails open to them in the future.

**State Gamelands** Pennsylvania State Gamelands are administered by the Pennsylvania Game Commission. These lands have been designated for a specific purpose. Each gameland may differ as to its permitted use and the gamelands are currently in a period of transition. Check the Pennsylvania Game Commission rules and regulations prior to riding on State Gamelands. See the State Gamelands Trail Information chapter for additional detail, contacts, and information. The State Gamelands' settings are primitive and normally do not have comfort stations.

*A very special thanks to Matt Beaver and Brian Valencik for answering my questions and for providing their input.*

# The Pennsylvania Equine Council (PEC)

After the previous chapter on the differences between the various types of trail systems, it seems appropriate to follow with an explanation of the Pennsylvania Equine Council and its mission.  Based on the Council's dedication to the preservation and expansion of the equestrian trail systems in Pennsylvania, along with their many other contributions to equine interests, I believe this is a vital organization to support.  These folks are working with all types of trail systems for the future preservation and possible expansion of Pennsylvania's equestrian trails.  They take the time to be in the right places to represent our interests.  They have been making a difference but they need your help.  We need to join the Pennsylvania Equine Council, we need to support them, and we need to volunteer our time.  Much of the following was based on input from Bud Wills, of the State Trail Chair of the Pennsylvania Equine Council.  Bud and his wife, Gwen, along with other PEC officers and members, have worked tirelessly toward the promotion of trails in the state of Pennsylvania.  We trail riders owe our gratitude to folks like Bud and Gwen, who contributed so much to establish and maintain access to our equestrian trail systems.

Bud and Gwen state, and I absolutely agree, that "Pennsylvania is one of our most beautiful states to see from the back of a horse or mule." *(I will say "horse" going forward for simplicity's sake.)* Horseback riding in Pennsylvania allows riders to choose from a variety of terrains and scenery, whether it is riding hours into the depths of our State Forests or riding sandy flatlands.  Often these diverse landscapes are only hours away, and all in one state. Many folks wouldn't physically be able to see and enjoy all these sights that they can see on horseback. We had been fortunate; resources were abundant, and in many places we were used to being able to go to almost anywhere at anytime.  But times are changing. With the growing population and mounting land restrictions, many remaining trails have become more crowded and their use has increased significantly.  This has sometimes resulted in tension and controversy between the overseers of the land and the user groups, and also sometimes among the different user groups.  This is where equestrians need to adapt, be proactive, be considerate and cooperative, be on their best behavior, and positively strive to effect a favorable outcome.  We have to keep the doors open or we will lose our trails.  We need to do this through communication and action.

Bud and Gwen inform me that agriculture is still the largest industry and a leading economic indicator in the state of Pennsylvania, and studies support that the equine industry is becoming one of the prime drivers in agriculture's business. Horses consume or use great amounts of hay, grain, straw, and other agricultural products.  Bud and Gwen also shared with me that studies have shown that the equine industry has actually approached or possibly passed the dairy or beef industries in certain sectors. And this I know well: of all the equine disciplines, trail riding has become one of the fastest growing interests of the equine industry. I have found this clearly evidenced on a nationwide basis as more and more folks are taking to the roads to travel to their favorite equestrian destinations including horse camps and trail systems. (Just look at the increase in number of large, often very large, equestrian rigs on the highways!) Besides expensive horses and riding equipment, trail riders purchase large, pricey towing vehicles, extra fuel, added insurance, trailers, trailers with living quarters, special equipment, etc., all further stimulating the economy. Bottom line, the equine industry spends a lot of money and has a significant affect on our state's economy. People need to know this so that they appreciate what equestrians are contributing and doing for them. Equestrians need to be heard and they need to remind others of the importance that the equestrians hold for our state. Other groups, such as hikers and bikers, have been politically active and this has resulted in trails being kept open to them. Equestrians, possibly because of the additional personal time necessary to maintain the upkeep and training of their horses, and likely due to the diverse and numerous equestrian interests, have not, as one group, been as organized, active, or effective. If equestrians concentrate and structure their efforts, they can be more successful. Local groups and clubs are excellent and serve a very important purpose; but both individuals and those groups need to support another group, one group, who can focus and have more affect on the general good of the equine industry as a whole.

This is where the Pennsylvania Equine Council comes in. As a unified group, they can be more effective, efficient, and influential. I asked Bud and Gwen for a statement of the Council's mission. They stated: "In order for the equine community to continue to have access to public and other land (that) we have enjoyed in the past we must become organized, educated, and involved." "The Pennsylvania Equine Council was formed in 1988 and is the only state wide equine organization addressing issues that affect every equine owner regardless of what breed or discipline with which they are associated. The Council's purposes are: to promote and protect the common interest of all people involved with equines and to broaden the scope of understanding and knowledge in all areas of equine ownership and management, through education."

To help accomplish this, the PEC Trail Committee, in 2002, established a three-phase program to educate trail users, volunteers, agencies, and representatives on the following:
- Phase one is to provide education and assistance, and to coordinate efforts on trail design, engineering, construction, and maintenance.
- Phase two is a trail stewardship program offering training in the "best accepted practices" for trail design, engineering, construction, and maintenance. This includes the proper packing of materials and tools while performing the above.

- The third phase is an outreach program. This is targeted toward equine groups.

The Pennsylvania Equine Council also provides education on areas of interest such as "Barn and Trailer Safety", "Trail and Outdoor Ethics" including "Leave no Trace", and is working with the Pennsylvania Game Commission for a positive outcome on trail riding in the gamelands.

If you would like more information, including the Stewardship programs, or if you would like to join, or volunteer your time, you can reach the Pennsylvania Equine Council at 888-304-0281 or at the website: www.pennsylvaniaequinecouncil.com. Connect, unite, and invest in our future with the Pennsylvania Equine Council. This is one organization that I feel has the right approach and the resources to make a difference.

*Courtesy: The above extracts and quotes were obtained with the permission and consent of Bud and Gwen Wills of the Pennsylvania Equine Council. I would like to express a very special thank you to Bud and Gwen for their input.*

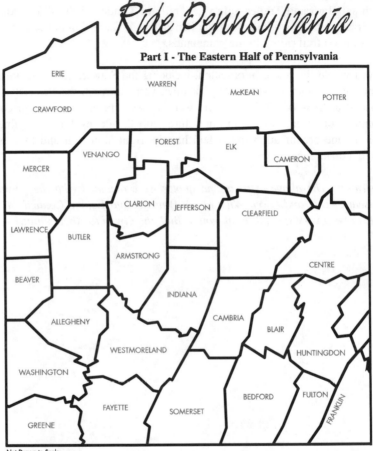

# Ride Pennsylvania

## Part I - The Eastern Half of Pennsylvania

Not Drawn to Scale

| | | |
|---|---|---|
| 1 | Green Lane Park | |
| 2 | Valley Forge National Historic Park & The Betzwood Rail-Trail | |
| 3 | Perkiomen Trail | |
| 4 | Evansburg State Park | |
| 5 | Wissahickon Trail System | |
| 6 | French Creek State Park | |
| 7 | Marsh Creek State Park | |
| 8 | Ridley Creek State Park | |
| 9 | Pennypack Park | |
| 10 | Tyler State Park | |
| 11 | White Clay Creek Preserve | |
| 12 | Blue Marsh Lake | |
| 13 | The Central Park Equestrian Trail System | |
| 13a | Chickies Rock Park | |
| 13b | Speedwell Forge County Park | |
| 13c | Lancaster Junction Recreation Trail | |
| 14 | Money Rocks | |
| 15 | The Conewago Recreation Trail | |
| 16 | Lebanon Valley Rail-Trail | |
| 17 | Lehigh Parkway | |
| 18 | Stony Creek Rail-Trail | |
| 19 | The Horse-Shoe Trail | |
| 20 | Bucks County Horse Park | |
| 21 | Nockamixon State Park | |
| 22 | Delaware Canal State Park | |
| 23 | Susquehannock Creek State Park | |
| 24 | Jacobsburg Environmental Education Center | |

# HORSE TRAILS

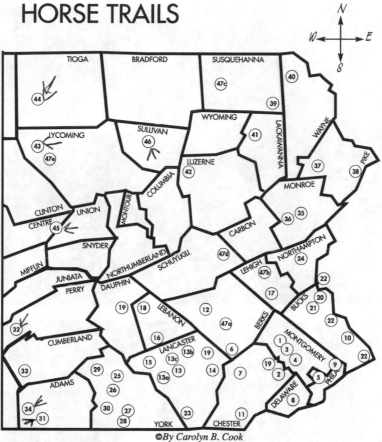

©By Carolyn B. Cook

25 Rocky Ridge County Park
26 William Kain County Park
27 Spring Valley County Park
28 Heritage Rail-Trail County Park
29 Gifford Pinchot State Park
30 Codorus State Park
31 Gettysburg National Military Park
32 Tuscarora State Forest & The Iron Horse Trail
33 Cumberland Valley Rail-Trail
34 Michaux State Forest
35 Big Pocono State Park & The Old Railroad Trail
36 Pohopoco Tract Recreation Area
37 Promised Land State Park
38 Conashaugh View Trail, Delaware Water Gap Equestrian Trail

39 D&H Rail-Trail
40 O&W Rail-Trail
41 Lackawanna State Park
42 Ricketts Glen State Park
43 The Tiadaghton State Forest & The Black Forest
44 Tioga State Forest, Home of The Grand Canyon of PA, & The Pine Creek Rail-Trail
45 Bald Eagle State Forest
46 Wyoming State Forest
47a The Thun Trail
47b The Slatedale Trail
47c Endless Mountain Trail
47d Owl Creek, Tamaqua
47e God's Country Shared Trail System

Connie Bloss, editor (top) and the author on her first horse, Chipper (bottom)

# 1. Green Lane Park
# Montgomery County Park

**Lasting Impression:**  A beautiful park offering almost everything: horse camping, scenic riding, easy terrain or challenging trails, and an expanding trail system!

**Location:**  Green Lane, northwest Montgomery County, southeast Pennsylvania

**Length:**  The park consists of 3,100 acres and includes Green Lane Reservoir, Deep Creek Lake, and Knight Lake.  The Red Trail is 10 miles, the Blue Trail is 6 miles, and the Orange Trail is 2 miles.  Riders can also trailer to the neighboring Perkiomen Trail where there are additional miles of riding.  (See the Perkiomen Trail chapter.)  Plans are for this trail system to connect to the Perkiomen Trail and ultimately to the Valley Forge Historical Park and other trail systems, resulting in miles and miles of continuous riding.

**Level of Difficulty:**  Red Trail-easy, Blue Trail-moderate to difficult, Orange Trail-easy to moderate ("moderate" due to rocky footing)

**Terrain:**  Easy, gentle rolling slopes with good footing on the Red Trail. Challenging, rocky, steeper terrain with ravines on the Blue Trail.  The Orange Trail is not as steep as the Blue Trail, but is rocky.  Horses should have shoes for the Blue Trail or the Orange Trail.  The trails vary from wooded to open fields.

**Horse Camping:**  Yes

**Non-horse Camping:**  Yes

**Maps and Info:**  Green Lane Reservoir Park, P.O. Box 249, Hill Road, Green Lane, PA 18054-0249, (215) 234-4863

**Activities:**  Boating, Boat Rentals, Fishing, Hiking, Picnicking, Biking, Horseback Riding Trails, Equestrian and Non-equestrian Camping, Sledding, and Ice Sports.  Hunting is prohibited.

**Fees for Trail Use:**  None

**Permits for Trail Use:**  None

**Fees for Camping:**  Yes

**Comfort Station:**  Yes, at the Red Trail (just past the parking lot, up on the left) and at the Blue Trail and the Orange Trail trailheads in the camping area (additional facilities are at the ranger station off of Hill Road)

## DIRECTIONS:

There are two lots where day-use riders can park.  One is the Red Trail on Knight Road and the other is the Blue Trail at the equestrian camping area on Hill Road. Both parking lots have plenty of room for big rigs.  The Knight Road lot is often used for group trail rides and can accommodate numerous rigs of all sizes.  There are plenty of turn-around and pull-through options.  With the open, adjoining field, there is ample room for overflow.

To reach the Red Trail on Knight Road, take the Northeast Extension (I-476) of the PA Turnpike to the Quakertown Exit #44, Route 663 south. Travel on 663 south for 5 miles until the town of Pennsburg and the intersection of Route 29. Make a left on Route 29 (heading south) and travel 3.3 miles to Knight Road. Make a right on Knight Road. (At the intersection of Route 29 and Knight Road there is a sign but it is partially blocked by a tree. The sign is visible as you get closer to the turn.) Proceed .2 miles west on Knight Road, parking is on the left.

To access the Blue Trail, Orange Trail, and equestrian camping area, travel on Route 29 south for a total of 4.5 miles from the intersection with Route 663. While proceeding on Route 29, you will pass the Knight Road turn and the dam spillway. Slow down, travel to the bottom of the hill, and make a right onto Hill Road. There is a sign at the turn. Note: this is a sharp turn and not recommended for large rigs (see below). Proceed .5 miles and the equestrian camping area and day-use lot for the Blue Trail and the Orange Trail are on the left off of Hill Road. There is a brown sign indicating equestrian camping and the Blue Trail.

To access the Blue Trail, Orange Trail, and equestrian camping area while hauling a large rig, do not turn onto Route 29. Instead, continue straight through Pennsburg. Proceed on Route 663 south for an additional 3.5 miles. (You will travel a total of 8.5 miles on Route 663 from the turnpike to the turn onto Hill Road.) Make a left onto Hill Road. Travel 3 miles on Hill Road. The equestrian area and the day parking for the Blue and the Orange Trails are on the right. There is a brown sign marking the entrance.

**THE TRAILS:**
John and I really like this trail system for a weekend get-away, and it just keeps getting better. Improvements are always being made and there is something for everyone. The Red Trail offers a diverse, relaxing ride with mostly wide trails, easy rolling hills, open grassy stretches, and woods to meander through. There are also hurdles for those who like to jump. Those preferring not to jump can ride around them. There is lots of wildlife; deer and turkey are abundant and can be seen throughout the park. The trails offer stunning views of Green Lane Reservoir.

The Red Trail is on both sides of Knight Road and some road crossing is required to ride all of the Red Trail. Caution should be exercised. Trails are marked, well used, and generally easy to follow; however, a map is helpful. The Red Trail connects with the Blue Trail at the Knight Road Bridge. From the bridge, the scene is just wonderful. The lake and the rolling countryside offer a must see view. The bridge is multi-user and has benches; it was recommended that we take a drive back to the bridge later in the evening for a great view of the sunset. (The bridge is quite a distance from camp, riding to see the sunset is not recommended as riders would be returning well after dark.) You can also watch the sunset from camp, as the equestrian campground is situated high, offering an excellent panoramic vista of the sunset.

The Blue Trail is accessed either from the Red Trail or from the equestrian campground lot. From the equestrian campground lot, cross over Hill Road and you will see signs to the trailhead. The Blue Trail follows the steeper banks of the western side of the reservoir. This side is challenging and not for beginners! The trail is wooded and varies from narrow widths to wide stretches. There are steep climbs and descents, and many ravines to cross. The footing is rocky but we found it passable. In the fall, leaf ground cover (when dry, avoid wet conditions) offers an extra cushion to the rocky feel of the trail. It should be noted that we have ridden this side of the trail many times and have taken groups of experienced riders with us and they have enjoyed it also. This trail offers superb views of the reservoir, shade in the warmer weather, and cover in the cold.

The Orange Trail can be accessed from the equestrian camping area (the Blue Trail lot). The trailhead is at the back of the camping area. The Orange Trail is a mostly wooded ride. There is some road crossing; it can be a little tricky to meet up with the trailhead so bring your map to stay on course. It is not steep, but it has lots of rocks, so only riders with shod horses may want to attempt it. Plans are for this trail to connect to the Perkiomen Trail, part of the rails-to-trails network to Valley Forge. The proposed Perkiomen Trail will add almost an additional 20 miles of trails using parts of the old Reading Railroad corridor. The Perkiomen is intended to be a link with other trails including Evansburg, the Schuylkill River Trail, and Valley Forge National Park.

**EQUESTRIAN CAMPGROUND:**
The equestrian campground is located .5 miles west of Route 29 on Hill Road. This is a nice, clean campground overlooking the reservoir. It is well thought out, situated high, and dry. Large rigs should have no problem as there is lots of room to maneuver, and there are pull-through sites. Check for a site that will accommodate your size rig. The camping area is in a large, grassy area with bordering woods. There are tie stalls for the horses in the open field area so you can keep an eye on your horses while camping. (Since our visit additional open tie rails near the camping areas have been added.) The tie stalls are covered and even have a heavy-duty plastic cover over the wood to keep the horses from chewing the wood. (We had not seen this before at other campgrounds and thought this was a smart idea.) Tying horses to trees is not allowed. Dogs are permitted but must be on a leash or under control. The equestrian camping area can be used for overflow from the non-equestrian camping areas. *This chapter was written when reservations were required; however, we were recently told that*

3

*there is now a new self-register honor system (first come, first served) in effect. Call (215) 234-4863 for more information.*

Equestrian camping is primitive; there are no electric or modern bathroom facilities, only a portajohn toilet. The good news is that equestrian campers can use the nearby Deep Creek facilities. The Deep Creek Camp area, which is part of the park, is just down the road from the equestrian camping area. Deep Creek has modern restrooms including showers. Water is available at the horseman's campground and water tanks can also be filled at the Deep Creek campground. Dumpsters are provided for campers.

At this writing, this campground is new and still testing many features and modifying as is considered necessary. Currently, there are not a lot of places to camp with one's horse in this vicinity. This is a positive step and the county is doing a great job.

Although the campground is in a choice setting, one disadvantage is that campers who prefer to ride the easy Red Trail need to trailer over to Knight Road. It can be accessed by horseback via the Blue Trail; however, to ride back and forth is a very full day's ride.

**HISTORICAL INFORMATION:**
Green Lane is a County Park. In 1958, construction of the dam was completed; the dam spanned 424 feet. Green Lane Reservoir's initial purpose was mainly to serve as a water supply. In 1983, the control of the reservoir and recreational easement rights was transferred from the Philadelphia Suburban Water Company to Montgomery County. Prior to this, in 1979, the Montgomery County Equine Council was established. The Equine Council directly contributed to the opening of the trails in Green Lane Park and nearby Nockamixon, Upper Perkiomen, and Evansburg Parks. In a cooperative effort, the Council has worked with government representatives, agricultural interests, conservation groups, and various types of trail users to establish these trails. Future plans include a trail system connecting Green Lane Park to Valley Forge National Park. The Green Lane Park (18 miles) will be the end site for the Perkiomen Trail (17+ miles) that will connect with the Schuylkill Valley Trail that connects Valley Forge National Park with the Fairmount Park System and center city Philadelphia (approximately 25 trail miles). That should be a long trail system!

There are many other public and private contributors to thank. These individuals, groups and agencies made important contributions, and spent countless hours to establish, maintain, and expand this extensive trail system and to create the equestrian horse camp. The dedicated efforts of the Montgomery County Equine Council including Annette Bishop, the local organizations, the

County officials and Park representatives especially Mike Marino and Frank Ball, deserve special mention.

**NEARBY AND SURROUNDING AREA VET SERVICES:**
- Quakertown Veterinary Clinic, Quakertown (215) 536-2726, (215) 536-6245
- Blauner, Vecchione, & Associates (24-hour emergency vet service), N. Wales (215) 699-4422

**NEARBY FARRIERS:**
- K. McCarty, Quakertown (215) 536-3372
- JR Rosenberger, Quakertown (215) 536-5256

Cheryl Groff, Katherine Mack, the author, and Pat and Ray Groff at Green Lane.

# 2. Valley Forge National Historic Park & The Betzwood Rail-Trail National Park Service

**Lasting Impression:** Ride where some of our nation's history has been beautifully preserved for all to see.

**Location:** Valley Forge, southeast Pennsylvania on the border of Chester County and Montgomery County

**Length:** There are almost 20 miles of trails at Valley Forge, plus the adjoining 120 mile Horse-Shoe Trail that begins at Valley Forge. In addition, there may be many more miles to ride, upon completion of the proposed Valley Forge trail extension to Green Lane Park.

**Level of Difficulty:** Mostly easy, however, horses and riders will need to be comfortable with multiple trail users, passing and/or crossing busy roads, new sights and sounds, and crossing rivers. (Rivers can be avoided but that will limit some of the riding available.)

**Terrain:** The surface varies, consisting of crushed stone, paved surfaces, grass, and dirt. The terrain within the main park area is gentle and diverse. The trails consist of flat stretches, rolling hills, open fields, wooded sections, and some park road crossings. The terrain is not rocky within the park. However, the west side of the Valley Creek, in the vicinity of The Horse-Shoe Trail, is rocky.

**Horse Camping:** No

**Non-horse Camping:** No

**Maps and Info:** US Department of the Interior, National Park Service, Valley Forge National Historic Park, P.O. Box 953, Valley Forge, PA 19482-0953, (610) 783-1077, website: www.nps.gov/vafo. Information can be obtained at the Visitor Center at the park entrance (610) 783-7503. There are at least two maps of the park. Both are helpful but ask for the "Valley Forge Trail Map" which reflects the equestrian trails and the location of The Horse-Shoe Trail trailhead.

**Activities:** Hiking, Picnicking, Biking, Horseback Riding Trails, Tours, and Group Education Programs. Hunting is not permitted. *(Always confirm with your destination source that hunting is not permitted, and that special herd-reduction hunts are not planned or do not apply.)*

**Fees for Trail Use:** None

**Permits for Trail Use:** None

**Comfort Station:** Yes, at the Visitor Center, Washington's Headquarters, and at various locations in the park

## DIRECTIONS:

From the north, take the Northeast Extension of the PA Turnpike (I-476) to the PA Turnpike (I-276) west. Take I-276 to Valley Forge Exit #326 (old Exit #24). If traveling from other directions, take the PA Turnpike (I-276) to the Valley Forge exit.

Get off at the Valley Forge exit and stay to the far right at the toll booths. After the toll booths, make the first right. That is North Gulph Road (Route 327). Follow the brown Valley Forge signs. Proceed 1.5 miles and see the Valley Forge Visitor Center on the left. Make a left (this is called Valley Forge Road). Continue past the Visitor Center. The park requests that visitors do not park or stop directly in front of the Visitor Center. The entrance to the park is in a busy area; obtaining a map prior to arrival will assist you as to where to proceed. With a map, you should not have trouble finding these places while hauling. If it gets confusing as to where to go upon entering the park, there are signs within and throughout the park. Even if you pass your destination, you can loop around and return. There are 2 places to park horse trailers in the main park area, each at different ends of the park. Both parking areas are labeled on the map with a red horseshoe indicating horse trailer parking. Horse trailers can park behind the Valley Forge Visitor Center or at Washington's Headquarters.

**Valley Forge Visitor Center Lot**- The Valley Forge Visitor Center lot is a large, gravel lot behind the Visitor Center at the back of the regular parking lot. (Just drive to the farthest corner of the lot and you should see the gravel lot. There is pull-through room and plenty of room for large rigs or groups of rigs.) There are three equestrian trailheads at this lot. One trail has an equestrian sign and is on the opposite side of the road from the lot; there is a park gate at the entrance. This starts through a wooded pine section, which is very shaded and picturesque. The other trailhead starts by following the fence line. Ride to the end of the lot toward the road. Do not cross the road, instead make a left (heading away from the Visitor Center) and ride outside, yet along the fence row in the back of the lot. The trail is well used so follow the hoof prints. This trail leads to what we call the "deer ambush area" that I write about below. There is also a dirt trail leading out from the other end of the parking area that you pass upon pulling into the lot. This leads to the trail that follows the river, not far from the railroad line. It has been a long time since we rode this section. A portion was closed for repair during our last visit so we have not ridden it in recent years. Riders, who prefer to avoid the busy park Route 23 crossing, can park at the Valley Forge Visitor Center lot and ride the southern side of the park. There are a lot of trails and fields to choose from.

**Washington's Headquarters Lot**- To reach Washington's Headquarters, which is known as "Stop #5" in the park, continue about 3 miles past the Visitor Center along Route 23. At Washington's Headquarters, follow the one-way road that heads in a loop behind the Headquarters. Pass the train station parking lot. Immediately after the train station lot, while starting up the incline, look on the right for the one-way entrance to the lot at the top of the hill. This is the equestrian lot. It is not marked; however, after our suggestion to put in a sign, the ranger said they would consider marking it for equestrians. Hopefully they will mark it, as it is easy to pass while pulling a rig. The parking area is a large, paved lot marked by long painted spaces. The trail markers near Washington's Headquarters have "no equestrian" signs. However, the opposite end of the lot, in the direction away from Washington's Headquarters, has equestrian signs marking the equestrian trailhead.

**The Horse-Shoe Trail**- Riders who want to ride The Horse-Shoe Trail can also park at Washington's Headquarters. The map is helpful in finding access to the Horse-Shoe Trail. From the lot, cross over Route 23 (we found Route 23 to be easier to cross if traveled a distance from the intersection of Route 252 and Route 23). We crossed toward the interior of the park with a good view of oncoming traffic on Route 23 (which seemed busier than Route 252), picked up the wooded trail, crossed Route 252 a few hundred feet south of the intersection with Route 23, and crossed the Valley Creek just north of the dam and small waterfalls. The trail picks up on the other side of the creek. The path is well worn making the trail easier to follow, and there are signs. The Horse-Shoe Trail has yellow blazes on the trees; multiple blazes indicate a change in the trail direction. Please note that riders are cautioned not to cross the bridge on Route 23 as it is heavily traveled and has a narrow shoulder. There are signs directing equestrians to cross through the Valley Creek just south of the bridge. The Route 23 crossing can be avoided by parking at the Visitor Center lot and riding the southern trails.

**Pawling and Walnut Hill Lots**-There are two additional horse trailer parking sites labeled on the map at the northwest end of the park off of Pawling Road and Walnut Hill, on the north side of the Schuylkill River. These are out of the main park area and have access to the Betzwood Rail-Trail. As we did not have time to ride these trails during our visit, we checked with one of the park's sheriffs to verify the parking and to inquire about the trails. He indicated the terrain is very similar to the trails we rode on. We hope to return in the near future to try these trails.

**THE TRAILS:**
This is an absolutely beautiful area to ride and visit. One would not imagine that this green, undeveloped section still exists in the middle of the surrounding congested areas. But there are lots of scenic trails and open space at Valley Forge, near the

historical sites and away from the main areas. Additionally, there are also many old historic stone homes in country settings within and surrounding the park to enjoy. Our most recent visit was on a warm Saturday on Easter weekend when the early buds were beginning to show. The park was not overly crowded and the ride was leisurely. Later in the spring, the park comes into bloom with its many ornamental flowering trees and fields of green. And there is much wildlife. On this visit, we saw a red fox, a hawk perched a short distance above us in a tree, and lots and lots of deer. I refer to the "deer ambush" above because we felt like we were on a safari with herds, and I mean herds, of deer just leaping out in front of us. We never experienced such a large volume of deer all around us. As we rode, they were lying in the woods or standing and staring at you. If you arrive early in the morning, you can enjoy the view of the many deer grazing in the fields. We want to return in the fall to see the bucks when their antlers are grown.

The trails loop around the park offering views of the many historic structures and monuments which are nicely preserved for all to enjoy. The grounds are very well maintained and the trail surfaces are easy to ride. The park rangers were very helpful and accommodating when asked about the location of the equestrian parking and trails. We were fortunate to encounter thoughtful drivers who stopped traffic on Route 23 to let us cross. (Note: Please do **not** count on this, as some drivers may not be familiar with horses or not willing to extend this courtesy.) Many of the trails are marked. It is not easy to get lost due to the numerous park attractions acting as reference points on the map. But it can be effortless to get off course, especially in the western end of the park, due to many intersections and road crossings. Use the map to pick up where the trails continue. Riders are permitted in most of the fields; path lanes are mowed for riders to follow. Be alert for approaching hikers and bicyclists as multi-users frequent many of the trails. Bikers are restricted to certain trails and are not permitted in the fields or wooded sections. For safety and/or preservation, horses are not permitted near monuments, historic structures, picnic areas, or points where the tour buses stop. The outlying fields and woodlands offer a more leisurely and solitary ride outside the core of this popular park.

Caution is recommended for riders in the open fields, as this is a popular destination for many other users of the park. Check to see if any special programs (that would attract large crowds or cause loud noises) are scheduled, as riders may prefer to visit on the park's quieter days and off peak periods. Also, as with any open fields, watch for holes. Groundhogs are part of the local wildlife.

The Valley Forge National Historic Park Trail Map from the Visitor Center clearly indicates where the roads, trails, historical attractions, adjoining Horse-Shoe Trail and trailhead (shown just west of Washington's Headquarters, near Route 23 and Route 252), and the proposed extension (which is in the northeast section of the park) are located. The map also reflects a Covered Bridge that can be visited in the southwest corner of the park by Yellow Springs Road near Route 252.

Riding northwest from the Visitor's Center or northeast from Washington's Headquarters will lead to a wooded trail overlooking the rail line, which runs east to west along the south side of the Schuylkill River. We rode a portion of this and we felt the line was a comfortable distance from the trail. However, please note, a section of the trail was closed during our visit and we are unable to comment on that portion. Years ago we rode this section of the trail on a weekend, and we do not recall a problem with the nearby rail system nor do we remember much weekend activity on the line. If equestrians prefer to avoid riding within hearing distance of the railroad, they can head south from the Visitor Center lot or south from Washington's Headquarters. The railroad is not far from the Washington's Headquarters site but there are trails that travel (south) away from the railroad. The railroad line is indicated on the map. There are many choices and alternative riding within the park.

Riders should note that in the southwest corner of the park, just after crossing Route 252, there is an area where visitors fly their remote-controlled planes. The trail passes behind this area. Our horses were okay with the planes, which did not travel over them, but the sound and sight may disturb some horses. Also, in the southern end of the park, the trail parallels a section of the PA Turnpike. Land and trees offer plenty of buffer between the trail and the turnpike, but the trail does come within hearing distance. If riders prefer a quieter route (heading in a clockwise direction on the map), they should proceed straight or north after crossing the Valley Creek in the south section vs. heading left or west. Again, there are lots of nice trails, and riders have many alternate trails to choose from.

Our favorite part of the trail is riding the outer borders of the fields. We just meandered around the park far away from pedestrian and auto traffic. The outlying fields offer wonderful panoramic views of the park. On a warm day we also enjoyed riding in the shade of the adjoining woods. My other favorite section of trail is the wide pine forest trail that can be reached by the Visitor Center parking lot. Riding around the gate at the trailhead, passing the small box canyon to the left, and continuing on the trail accesses this stretch. John liked the fields best, but he also liked the section just past the fence row by the Visitor Center lot, which had the highest concentration of deer.

The proposed extension, which would link Valley Forge with Green Lane County Park and other trails, is located in the northeast section of the park, north of the Schuylkill River.

This park has special, personal significance for me. When I was much younger, before I had my own horse and a trailer to travel to equestrian trails, I visited Valley Forge and was inspired to return and ride the park on horseback. The dream came true and I have ridden this special place many times.

## COURTESIES:
Thank you to George Kraft, with the park office, who was very helpful and answered many of my questions.

## HISTORICAL INFORMATION:
Valley Forge, which was named after an iron forge that once existed on Valley Creek, is most known for its role in the American Revolution. Events leading to the encampment were the result of the British's defeat of George Washington's army at Brandywine, and a standoff at Germantown ending in the British occupation of Philadelphia. With the British takeover of the capital of Philadelphia, the Patriot army was searching for a strategic location to position their forces. Valley Forge offered a view of the surrounding area, which enabled Washington's army to keep a watchful eye on approaching British in order to guard the interior of Pennsylvania, and yet was far enough from Philadelphia to discourage surprise attacks. This site is not a former battlefield but rather a tribute to the strong will, courage, and self-sacrifice of our Patriot forefathers.

Washington's weary, hungry, underclothed, and ill-equipped men arrived at Valley Forge on a cold winter day in 1777. Conditions were extreme that winter; food, shelter, and provisions were scarce. Washington tirelessly requested supplies from Congress but Congress was unable to provide help. During that winter of 1777/8, sickness and disease prevailed and as many as 2,000 men died that winter. Hundreds of horses also perished.

Eventually, conditions improved. A new drillmaster, Baron Friedrich von Steuben, successfully retrained the troops and instilled morale and confidence. Along with Washington's leadership, news of the French alliance, and the arrival of supplies and new forces, the surviving troops endured. Washington's troops pursued the British who were headed for New York, and defeated the British at the Battle of Monmouth, NJ.

Visitors can view a short film about the history of the park at the Visitor Center. The film is shown every half hour. A must see is the museum at the Visitor Center housing ammunition, tents, equipment, various personal artifacts from the Revolutionary War period including those of George Washington, and items found at Valley Forge. The Visitor Center provides information on the park and local attractions and nearby accommodations. Self-guided tours are also available.

11

## NEARBY AND SURROUNDING AREA VET SERVICES:

- Blauner, Vecchione, & Associates (24-hour emergency vet service), N. Wales (215) 699-4422
- Brandywine Veterinary Clinic, Coatesville (610) 383-1866
- Complete Equine Health Service, Coatesville (610) 466-0501
- New Bolton (24- hour emergency), Kennett Square (610) 444-5800

## NEARBY FARRIERS:

- J. Nolan, Perkiomenville (215) 990-9778
- R. Kass, Jr., Levittown (215) 943-8583
- R. Kass, Pipersville (215) 630-0390

# 3. Perkiomen Trail
# (Rail-to-Trail)

**Lasting Impression:**  A really nice trail in the making, with plans to be part of a major trail system!

**Location:**  The planned trail stretches from Green Lane Park in Montgomery County to Oaks in Upper Providence Township in eastern Pennsylvania. Eventually, this trail will connect via the Orange Trail at Green Lane Park. Plans are for this trail to also provide entrance to the Valley Forge riding area via the Schuylkill River Trail Extension. The total of the intended network of trails could equal 100+ miles of trails.

**Length:**  The northern section, which is currently open, is 5 miles of trails. A total of 18 miles of trails through the Perkiomen Valley from Oaks to Green Lane Park is expected to be completed in 2003.

**Level of Difficulty:**  We can only comment on the northern section to the beginning of the central section since that was the only portion completed and open at the time of our visit. The wide width and even surface of this rail-trail makes for very gentle and easy riding. Horses do need to cross some long bridges and roads to continue on the trail. We felt the bridges were a nice width, horse friendly, and very well constructed. We did wait for passing pedestrian and bike traffic to clear the bridge before crossing as a courtesy and as an added safety measure. The road crossings (of the northern section) are mostly back roads and were not heavily traveled during our visit. The trail is expected to eventually cross at Route 29, which is a busy intersection. Due to this consideration, details of the crossing are still in the planning stage.

**Terrain:**  The terrain is easy and consists of crushed stone, compacted gravel, dirt, wood chips, and is a flat surface.

**Horse Camping:**  Yes, at nearby Green Lane. Currently, the trails do not connect from camp but plans are for linked trails in the near future. See the Green Lane Chapter for more information on camping.

**Non-horse Camping:**  Yes, at nearby Green Lane

**Maps and Info:**  At this writing, Green Lane Park is the main contact for info at (215) 234-4528 or (215) 234-4863. For further info on the trails, write the Perkiomen Trail Coalition via e-mail: perkiomentrail@aol.com; or call the Central Perkiomen Valley Park at (610) 287-6970.

**Activities:**  Biking, Horseback Riding Trails, and Hiking

**Fees for Trail Use:**  None

**Permits for Trail Use:**  None

**Comfort Station:**  Yes, there is a portable toilet at the Harmon Road lot, which is near trail marker #13.5 (there will likely be more facilities upon the trail completion)

**DIRECTIONS:**

To access the northern most end of the Perkiomen Trail, take the Northeast Extension of PA Turnpike (I-476) to the Quakertown Exit #44, which is Route 663. Take Route 663 south, for 5 miles, to Pennsburg and Route 29. Make a left on Route 29 (now heading south), travel for 6 miles, and pass through the small town of Green Lane. It is easy to miss the turn so watch for it; the sign is slightly off Route 29 and hard to see until you have already made the turn. Make a sharp left onto Upper Ridge Road and an immediate right onto Crusher Road. Parking is on the right. About 6 to 8 horse trailers can fit in this gravel lot. The trail connects directly from the lot. There is a map on display at this lot and at other parking areas, and at various points along the trail. At this writing, there are two other lots at which equestrians are permitted to park. These are at Camp Rainbow and Harmon Roads that can be seen from the rail-trail. Some changes were being made at Camp Rainbow's lot, making it premature to comment on how much room there will be for horse trailers. The Harmon Road lot is not as large as the Crusher Road lot and has a playground and picnic area.

Plans are for the Green Lane camping area to access the Perkiomen Trail via the Orange Trail by crossing Route 29 just south of the town of Green Lane.

**THE TRAILS:**

The Perkiomen Trail is a newer trail and opened in the fall of 2001. At the time of our visit, a 5 mile section from the north end to the beginning of the central section was open and completed. The remaining sections were under construction. We rode this trail, a total of about 10 miles (to and from the temporary end point), on a very warm winter day (50+ degrees) in February. This trail was already getting lots of use and for good reason- this trail is very nice. A great job was done in restoring the path. The surface is even, wide, nicely drained, clean, well maintained, and well marked. There are signs for everything, including road crossings, river crossings, detours, and the trail itself. Even mileposts are planned to be placed every half mile. This is a well thought out trail!

The northern section of the Perkiomen Trail meanders along the picturesque Perkiomen Creek on the old Reading Railroad right-of-way. Most of the trail is wooded and winds around interesting historic homes that dot the landscape in a quaint, country setting that reflects a time of long ago. Other than the numerous trail users, the trail path feels far from the busy surrounding communities. However, horses will need to be comfortable with the many hikers, bikers, and dog walkers that frequent the path.

A word of caution: there is a high bridge crossing along the trail. There is plenty of clearance for horses to pass under, but cars make a loud rumbling noise as they pass overhead. Riders may be well advised to leave sufficient distance, listen for approaching vehicles, and wait until the vehicles have passed overhead before procceding under the bridge. Our horses had no problem going under the bridge, but when a truck hauling a horse trailer traveled over the bridge, creating a double rumble, they became very concerned. Even a nearby dog walker commented that his black Lab was startled by the sudden sound. Upon approaching the bridge, riders may hear the noise before seeing the bridge and may have an opportunity to prepare for how their horses will deal with it. We crossed under it twice and did not find this to be a major obstacle; we just thought some riders might appreciate the advance warning.

Riders should bring their own water. Although the corridor travels near the creek, we did not see places where horses were permitted to or could drink. Users of the trail are requested to stay on the trail, as many adjoining areas are private land. There are plenty of trail markings and fencing to provide guidance.

We found everyone we encountered to be extremely polite and considerate of the horses. If the trail sounds too active for some riders, they may want to consider trying it during an off-peak period. Our visit was on an unusually warm winter Sunday afternoon. An early morning, late day, or mid week off-peak ride may offer more solitary use. But we found the northern section of the Perkiomen Trail to be a don't miss trail. It's top quality, and the surrounding beauty makes it worthy of putting it on the "must do" list.

### HISTORICAL INFORMATION:
Thanks go to the many devoted and hardworking individuals, groups, county representatives, the Montgomery County Parks Department, the Montgomery County Commissioners and the Planning Commission, The Perkiomen Trail Coalition, and the Montgomery County Equine Council who have made this trail possible.

The northern section of this trail was opened in October 2001, and the complete trail is expected to be opened by the end of 2003. Three County Parks along the path will manage the trail. Subsequent to our visit, we checked out some of the lower sections of the trail, which were still in progress. Although this is developing into a wonderful multiple-use trail throughout its full length, we concluded that we favored the northern end of the trail for horseback riding (as described above) due to it traveling through more remote areas.

### NEARBY VET SERVICES:
- Quakertown Veterinary Clinic, Quakertown (215) 536-2726, (215) 536-6245
- Blauner, Vecchione, & Associates (24-hour emergency vet service), N. Wales (215) 699-4422

**NEARBY FARRIERS:**
- K. McCarty, Quakertown (215) 536-3372
- JR Rosenberger, Quakertown (215) 536-5256
- R. Kass, Jr., Levittown (215) 943-8583
- R. Kass, Pipersville (215) 630-0390

# 4. Evansburg State Park
# DCNR
### (Department of Conservation & Natural Resources)

**Lasting Impression:** A scenic reflection of the old Montgomery County countryside

**Location:** The park is 25 miles from the city of Philadelphia, between Norristown and Collegeville, in southcentral Montgomery County.

**Length:** Evansburg Park consists of 3,349 acres along the Skippack Creek. There is a designated 15 mile equestrian trail. Bicyclists have a separate designated trail system as they are prohibited on the horse trails in the park.

**Level of Difficulty:** We found the main equestrian trail predominantly easy. Some outlying trails branch off into more challenging sections. There are many crisscrossing trails and if you encounter a steep section, you may have wandered off the real trail. Usually, there are alternate paths to take.

**Terrain:** The terrain is mainly dirt with little or no rocks. There are lots of woods in a peaceful setting. The land is diverse and consists of flat terrain, some rolling hills, sections of open fields, river crossings, a few small wooden bridges, and back road crossings. Some lowland sections can remain muddy for a time after wet weather. (Those portions of the trail are nicer to visit after periods of dry weather.) However, there are also higher sections of the trail that quickly drain and dry.

**Horse Camping:** Not currently, though plans are for this park to be linked to the Green Lane to Valley Forge system. Camping is available at Green Lane (see Green Lane chapter).

**Non-horse Camping:** No

**Maps and Info:** DCNR, Evansburg State Park, 851 May Hall Road, Collegeville PA 19426-1202, (610) 489-3729, e-mail: evansburg@dcnr.state.pa.us, DCNR website: www.dcnr.state.pa.us. Call 888-PA-PARKS for general park info.

**Activities:** Fishing, Hiking, Biking, Picnicking, Horseback Riding Trails, Golf, Ballfields, Biking (in a separate designated area in the southern end of the park), and Hunting (during season)

**Fees for Trail Use:** None

**Permits for Trail Use:** None

**Comfort Station:** Yes, at the main park area

**DIRECTIONS:**
Take the Northeast Extension of PA Turnpike (I-476) to Exit #31 Lansdale. After the tolls, make a right onto Route 63 west. Go 3.5 miles on Route 63 west, then make a left onto Route 113 south/west. Travel on Route 113 for 6.5 miles. Make a left on Mill Road. Travel about 2.5 miles on Mill Road, which is very windy. Make a right on Skippack Creek Road; the lot is on the right.

An alternate from the above is to get off the Pennsylvania Turnpike, take Route 63 west for 3.5 miles, take Route 113 south/west for 7 miles, make a left on Route 29 south. Travel on Route 29 south for about 2 miles; make a left heading east on Business 422. Go a short distance; bear left onto Germantown Pike. Before the Eight Arch Bridge, make a left on Skippack Creek Road. The lot is on the left side. The parking area is nice, has tie rails, a supply of maps, and is large with ample room for large rigs or groups of rigs.

**THE TRAILS:**
Evansburg is a pretty park, with many canopied trails to offer a buffer from the wind or hot sun. The trails have various changing landscapes. If your horse has a problem with bikes, and you want a break from training him, this may be the trail for you, as bikes are not permitted on the equestrian trails. In addition, these trails have very little rocks, so the footing is mostly good. There are many places to water the horses along the trail.

The equestrian trails are well used and easy to follow. Using the map and the Skippack Creek as a point of reference, it should not be easy to get lost. However, by the ranger station on May Hall Road, the trail becomes a little bit confusing as to which way the arrow is pointing. Riders, do not go straight as that is a hiking trail. Instead, riders should head left down the back road a short distance and pick up the trail again. Between this stretch, there is a picnic area with tie rails and a water pump just off the road. The trail again meets with the back road briefly, and then heads back into the woods off to the right. The trails are well used and, with a little searching, it should be clear to see where the trail continues. There are post signs and silver round tree markers with arrows to assist riders.

Evansburg has lots of wildflowers in the spring and bright colors in the fall, making it a colorful ride. It is also a nice ride in the winter as the wooded sections offer shelter from the weather; however, hunting is permitted during certain months. In the winter, we prefer to visit on Sundays when hunting is not allowed.

Our favorite section of the trail is the stretch along the Skippack Creek called the "Mill Race" section. This portion of the trail winds around the Skippack Creek, where riders travel in the valley with views of the opposite side of the river and catch glimpses of striking stone cliffs and tall evergreens cascading over the water.

Although the surrounding area has grown at an intense pace in recent years, this park offers quiet, solitude, and natural beauty away from the busy atmosphere of many nearby communities. After a relaxing ride at Evansburg, we like to head into the charming nearby towns that offer a variety of restaurants to choose from. One of our favorites, The Back Porch, is in Skippack. There is an indoor and casual outdoor dining area where we can treat ourselves to a tasty lunch or early dinner after riding. We are able to park our 2-horse trailer in the corner of the lot behind the restaurant. (The restaurant has a very small parking area so drivers must be able to back their horse trailers.)

## HISTORICAL INFORMATION:

The Unami Indians of the Delaware Nation once inhabited this area. In the late 1600's, William Penn's purchases included the land to be known as Evansburg Park. By the early 1700's, the area's popularity was growing due to its close proximity to Philadelphia. The park became home to the German Mennonite farmers who first settled the area. The Skippack Creek provided power for their mills and industries. The remains of these eighteenth and nineteenth century mills and homes can be seen within the park. Visitors can learn about the park's history at the historical Friedt Visitor Center. The center itself is interesting as it was built in the early 1700's and was owned by the Mennonites for 190 years. Within, visitors can learn about the park's early settlers and their way of life.

The area remained mostly agricultural until the twentieth century. While touring the park, visit the Eight Arch (stone) Bridge on the Germantown Pike. Built in 1792, it is one of the oldest bridges in continuous heavy use in the nation.

In the 1930's the Tri-State Commission Regional Open Space Plan recognized this area as desirable for preservation. In the 1960's, through the actions of the Pennsylvania State Planning Board along with other state and local agencies, and under the "Project 70 Land Acquisition and Borrowing Act", funding was established. Development began in the 1970's and the park opened to the public in 1979. The park is currently run by the DCNR, Bureau of State Parks, Commonwealth of PA. In addition, efforts by dedicated local individuals and groups, including The Montgomery County Equine Council and The Evansburg Trail Committee, have made major contributions to the equestrian trail system.

## NEARBY AND SURROUNDING AREA STABLING:
- Red Buffalo Ranch (riding lessons, trail riding, and summer camp), adjacent to Evansburg Park (610) 489-9707
- Three Diamond Stable (boarding, and may be able to accommodate overnight stabling in an emergency, *Coggins required*), Collegeville (610) 489-0480

## NEARBY VET SERVICES:
- Quakertown Veterinary Clinic, Quakertown (215) 536-2726, (215) 536-6245
- Blauner, Vecchione, & Associates (24-hour emergency vet service), N. Wales (215) 699-4422

**NEARBY FARRIERS:**
- J. Nolan, Perkiomenville (215) 990-9778
- R. Kass, Jr., Levittown (215) 943-8583
- R. Kass, Pipersville (215) 630-0390

Photo: One of many old historic homes along the equestrian trail at Evansburg State Park

# 5. Wissahickon Trail System
# Fairmount Park Commission

**Lasting Impression:** A beautiful, extensive multi-use trail system near the city of Philadelphia. But don't be fooled; all of these trails are not an easy stroll in the park!
**Location:** Wissahickon is in southeast Pennsylvania, northwest of Center City, Philadelphia.
**Length:** We did not see an exact number of miles listed, however, unofficial estimates are about 14+ miles. The park is large with numerous trails and connecting networks. The southern section of the park travels toward the city, connects with the Schuylkill River Trail and is part of the planned large, interconnecting trail system linking some of eastern Pennsylvania's major parks and rail-trails.
**Level of Difficulty:** The trails vary greatly from easy to moderate to difficult. Some sections are steep and rocky, making the trail more challenging or difficult. Horses need to be comfortable with multiple users.
**Terrain:** The terrain is diverse, ranging from easy, flat, crushed stone surfaces, to dirt and rocky climbs through the woods.
**Horse Camping:** No
**Non-horse Camping:** No
**Maps and Info:** For park and permit information, call Fairmount Park Commission, Philadelphia (215) 685-0000 or (215) 685-0052, ranger station (215) 685-0144, or Friends of the Wissahickon (215) 247-0417.
**Activities:** Hiking, Horseback Riding Trails, and Biking. Call and check if special hunts are to take place during hunting season.
**Fees for Trail Use:** None
**Permits for Trail Use:** Permits are required for the upper trails and are checked. There is no charge. Call the above number to obtain a permit.
**Comfort Station:** Yes, by the Valley Green Inn and at other locations throughout the park as shown on the map

**DIRECTIONS:**
Get ready; this is a popular area and parking with a horse trailer can be challenging, but don't be discouraged. Although this was our toughest 'find a place to park' destination to date, this was very much worth it. Because we liked this trail system so much, we returned to Wissahickon without our rig and spent a few hours checking out where equestrians hauling a trailer could park, have adequate room to unload and turn around, and be reasonably assured that there will be sufficient availability upon arrival. Parking spaces on sunny, pleasant weekends are full as multitudes of hikers and mountain bikers are headed for these trails. (It should be noted that once on the upper trails of the park, the crowds seemed to disappear. It is

a large area and can support its many users.) We were told weekdays are the ideal time for parking as the lots are almost empty. If possible, you may also want to consider visiting these trails during the week; however, we were successful and did find a satisfactory location for weekend parking!

We drove to several parking areas following the "P" designation on the map. Most of the lots did not have sufficient room for a horse trailer. Many of the lots were either small or were long, but were narrow. If other cars are present, turning may be impossible or difficult. We did find one lot that looked like it would be suitable for horse trailer parking, **including on weekends**, and a few other lots that were possible options. To get to the Wissahickon Trail System and the lot that we preferred, take the PA Turnpike (I-276) to Norristown/Germantown Pike Exit #25 (old Exit #333). (The exit is just west of the PA I-476 interchange.) When getting off the ramp, follow the sign toward Plymouth Meeting. Go east on Germantown Pike. Travel east on Germantown Pike for 3 miles; make a right onto Church Street. Go .2 miles on Church Street and make a left onto Ridge Ave. Travel .8 miles on Ridge Ave. (will see a Friendly's Restaurant), and make a sharp left onto Northwestern Avenue. The road is a two-way road but is narrow. Travel .6 miles to the lot on the right. The lot is near the #2 Tree House- Andorra Natural Area (see "Places of Interest") on the Fairmount Park Commission Map. This is a small dirt lot, in a quiet, remote setting, and should be able to fit 2 to 3 standard 2- horse trailers if it is empty and with some maneuvering. The ability to back a trailer is necessary to exit this lot as it does not allow for pull-through room. The bridle trail is at the entrance to the lot and there are signs. Note that Northwestern Avenue does not continue after this lot, rather, the road is interrupted and continues on the other side of the park. (Due to the size of the park and the busy surrounding area, call for a map in advance and take a good look at the layout of the park before departing for this trail system.)

*In case the above lot is full or you choose to visit during the week, these might suffice as alternate lots in relation to their ability to accommodate small standard 2-horse bumper pull or gooseneck horse trailers:*
- *We checked out another parking area near marker #14 Pachella Field. This would be our second choice; we concluded this was tight but doable if not too crowded. Backing would be required. This might work quite well if you arrive early and park the trailer facing out in case of a game or event later in the day.*
- *On the opposite side of the park (see #1 Northwestern Stables on the map), on the "other" Northwestern Avenue, there is a parking area on the road in front of the Northwestern Stables. To reach the parking area next to location #1 on the map, do not turn on Church Street but continue on Germantown Pike, then make a right on Northwestern Avenue. The parking spaces are in front of the stables on the road and are paved and lined for*

*autos. We were told that riders do utilize this area to park, which leads directly to the trails behind the stable area. Do not park, block, or ride on the stable area property, as that is a private facility. This designated parking area along the road may be an alternative during the week but is likely not an option on weekends.*

- *We also traveled up to the parking lot near #23. This may work during the week when the lot is empty or early in the day on a weekend. This lot is long and narrow and backing is a necessity. Only small trailers should consider it. This lot is actually situated in a large area and, if expanded, could nicely accommodate equestrians with horse trailers.*

Since this is such a beautiful trail system, we kept persisting in our pursuit of a trailer friendly lot. Finally, we came upon the one by marker #2 which, on the Saturday that we visited, was empty and available. Hopefully, it will be when you visit this park too or maybe another lot will be expanded by that time.

## THE TRAILS:
We just really enjoyed this trail system! It is beautiful. Yes, it can be busy and yes, parking is tough on weekends. This is a popular place, but it is worth traveling to. We were told it is ideal and peaceful on weekdays, however, even on the weekends, we did not find much activity in the higher elevations of the Wissahickon Valley trails. The whole trail system travels around the Wissahickon Creek offering scenic overlooks of the creek and falls contrasted against the varied terrain of rocks and forests surrounding it. It is a large, stunning area and it is amazing that it has retained its splendor and natural state located so near a metropolitan area. Until recently, we were not aware of this trail system. (Thank you to Sue McCoy for putting us in touch with Lyndra Bills who, along with a really nice group of ladies, gave us a guided tour of this wonderful trail system. Lyndra was very helpful as she told us of the good parking area. Also, many thanks to Irv Lichtenstein who shared contact and permit information with us and, I have been told, has contributed much to this trail system.)

We mainly rode the western side of the Wissahickon Creek. There are additional trails on the east side, most of which we did not ride. Crossing over Mt. Airy Ave., we visited the eastern side for a short distance and returned back via Valley Green Road. Our ride began in the vicinity of Northwestern Avenue and the Andorra Natural Area. This area is in the northern section of the park and is a series of loops through the woodlands, meadows, and hillsides of the preserve. This natural area is a great place for bird watching as there are many species of birds and other wildlife to be seen. Bikes are not permitted in this area so it is a good area to relax horses before heading down to the busier areas. The trails are wide but not all of these trails are easy. There are climbs and more climbs! Horses need shoes and need to be fit to ride these upper trails. In addition, many

23

sections have lots of rocks. We did find these sections passable as the horses could pick their way through.

From the Andorra Natural Area, the trails follow and loop back to the Wissahickon Creek and Forbidden Drive. Forbidden Drive is a wide, level, gravel/stone dust surface, multi-use trail that parallels the border of the Wissahickon Creek. Forbidden Drive received its name from the time when automobiles were "forbidden" along its path in the 1920's. It is a nice, easy trail to ride and offers great views of the Wissahickon Creek and the surrounding greenery. However, at peak times, Forbidden Drive is where most of the other trail users trek and can be very busy. The mountain bikers do share many of the higher trails with the equestrians but we found most to be very trail savvy, polite, and considerate of the horses. In the lower areas near and including Forbidden Drive, users may not be as familiar with horses and may not know to act with caution, so riders will need to be even more alert on the main corridors. We chose to ride most of the upper trails through the woodlands on the west side rather than ride only Forbidden Drive. We still had many nice views of the valley below, but had the trails more to ourselves.

The trails wind to and from the Wissahickon Creek. There are old stone bridge crossings to reach the other side. These are quite old and picturesque against the backdrop of the creek and the thick woods. Many of the trails are clearly marked but there are some connecting trails that are not. Equestrians are requested to stay on the marked trails. It is not easy to get lost as the Wissahickon Creek and Forbidden Drive are a continuous point of reference. A map is still helpful, especially to locate various attractions along the way.

On our return loop we visited the Valley Green Inn. We had been out a few hours and were ready for some refreshments. What a pleasant surprise we had. Not only is this a lovely little spot where everybody seems to go (horses absolutely need to be comfortable with varied activity and curious onlookers), but there were tie rails in a lean-to where the horses could be tied! This is an excellent accommodation as it allows riders to secure their horses and use the restaurant and comfort facilities. There is also a take-out counter for quick food to go. However, we found that at least one lookout rider should remain with the horses and not leave them unattended. Children and adults come to see the horses and some bring themselves and bikes within close range. We saw one man leave his bike in the stall area with our horses (even though there was available room at the bike rack in a separate designated area); an opportunity for an injury if the horse got his foot stuck or if the man startles the horse. Riders need to be alert and proactive. If you are cautious and your horse is comfortable in such an environment, this is a really neat place to take a break and watch the diverse parade of visitors, various breeds of dogs (a definite dog show), and bicyclists go by.

After we visited the Valley Green Inn, we returned via the west side of the park. We were told that the opposite (east) side of the trail had some very steep and narrow, on the edge, sections. We choose, instead, to return via Forbidden Drive. Due to the wide width of Forbidden Drive, we were very comfortable, even with all the activity. There was room for everyone. While traveling along Forbidden Drive, look for a large stone watering trough with a spring running into it for the horses to drink from. As you travel down its path, you may see carriage horses as driving is permitted on Forbidden Drive. There is even a quaint covered bridge along the way. This park is awesome; I can't believe we haven't heard more about it. Certainly many others have, as it is obviously a popular destination.

Folks both near and far are very fortunate to have it preserved for all to enjoy. Bottom line; this trail is gorgeous. Visit and do bring a camera!

**HISTORICAL INFORMATION:**
The name Wissahickon came from the Lenni Lenape Indians and meant "catfish creek" or "yellow creek". In the late 1600's, many settlers came to the area and built mills along the creek. The area prospered and grew quickly. Roads and bridges were built. Many of these same stone bridges still stand today.

The Wissahickon location came into further popularity in the early 1800's, as its natural beauty attracted wealthy visitors as a vacation retreat. By the late 1800's into the 1900's, the park had become a popular recreation destination for hiking, picnicking, horseback riding, boating, and winter sports. This tradition continues today.

**THINGS WE LEARNED THIS RIDE:**
- Yes, big, beautiful parks near major metropolitan areas can be preserved, kept clean, and maintained for all to enjoy!
- This is a lovely area to visit. We returned without the horses and trailer to search for a suitable equestrian parking area. While driving from parking area to parking area, we found ourselves deviating from the park plan and touring the surrounding area. The majestic old stone homes that border the northeast section of the park are awesome. If you appreciate dramatic or interesting architecture, try to visit (without the horse trailer) and take in some of these wonderful surroundings. And of course, after an exhausting day of fun, take in a nice dinner at one of the many local dining establishments. On this visit, it seemed very appropriate to relax and dine at the historic Valley Green Inn, which is in the heart of the trail system that we enjoyed so much. If you choose to dine at the Valley Green Inn, ask to see the Inn's interesting booklet depicting the history of the Inn and the park.

**NEARBY STABLES WITH BOARDING FACILITIES:**
- Northwestern Stables (boarding stable located next to the park), (215) 242-8892. Thank you to Dick and the nice folks at Northwestern for the courtesies shown to us during our visit.
- Monastery Stables (boarding stable adjoining the park, *no transient stabling*), (215) 848-4088
- Other boarding stables also border the park.

**NEARBY EQUESTRIAN B&B:**
- Mill Creek Farm Bed & Breakfast (accommodations for horses, overnight stabling, and may be able to accommodate trailers with living quarters), Buckingham (215) 794-0776, e-mail: millcreekfarmbnb@aol.com

**NEARBY VET SERVICES:**
- Blauner, Vecchione, & Associates (24-hour emergency vet service), N. Wales (215) 699-4422

**NEARBY FARRIERS:**
- R. Kass, Jr., Levittown (215) 943-8583
- R. Kass, Pipersville (215) 630-0390

# 6. French Creek State Park
# DCNR
### (Department of Conservation & Natural Resources)

**Lasting Impression:** A trail system rich with local history and the opportunity to ride some of the Horse-Shoe Trail

**Location:** Elverson, Berks, and Chester Counties, southeast Pennsylvania

**Length:** French Creek State Park consists of over 7,300 acres. There are approximately 8 miles of equestrian trails within the park, which are on the Horse-Shoe Trail. There are additional miles of riding on the connecting Horse-Shoe Trail which is a 120+ mile trail system spanning from the Appalachian Trail at Fort Indian Town Gap (near Harrisburg) to Valley Forge National Historic Park, intersecting French Creek Park. Horseback riding is allowed on the Horse-Shoe Trail. (Please note that some sections of the Horse-Shoe Trail may not be suitable for horses due to populated areas and other factors. See the Horse-Shoe Trail Chapter for more information.)

**Level of Difficulty:** Within the park boundaries, the designated trail is mostly easy to moderate. However, some sections are more challenging due to rocks, but are navigable. *Certain areas that adjoin the park's trails (outside of the park) can be very difficult and possibly impassable.*

**Terrain:** Mostly woodlands, several very rocky sections, a few stretches with nice stone dust type footing ideal for gaiting or moving out, small stream crossings, trail (short) bridge crossings, and some park road crossings.

**Horse Camping:** No, however, at one time French Creek did have horse camping. John had camped there years ago and said it was nice, had access to the Horse-Shoe Trail, and offered seclusion from the non-equestrian camping areas. The designated horse camping area is still in existence, but not in use. Unfortunately, the equestrian camping area was closed in the early 1990's. Maybe with an expression of interest, equestrians can convince French Creek State Park to reestablish horse camping in this convenient park which has entry to the Horse-Shoe Trail. John also mentioned that there is an even more ideal location for horse camping which is away from the main park. He indicated the site at the former Six Penny picnic area is not in use. The Six Penny area already has a paved area, stream, is secluded, and has direct access to the Horse-Shoe Trail. Perhaps another future possibility exists with this site.

**Non-horse Camping:** Yes

**Maps and Info:** Maps can be obtained from the DCNR, French Creek State Park, 843 Park Road, Elverson, PA 19520-9523, (610) 582-9680. E-mail: frenchcreek@dcnr.state.pa.us, DCNR website: www.dcnr.state.pa.us. Call 1-888-PA-PARKS for general park info or for camping reservations.

**Activities:**    Boating, Boat Rentals, Fishing, Hiking, Biking, Picnicking, Swimming, Horseback Riding Trails, Hunting (in certain sections during season), Camping, X-C Skiing, and Disc (or Frisbee) Golf
**Fees for Trail Use:**  None
**Permits for Trail Use:**  None
**Comfort Station:**  Yes

**DIRECTIONS:**
French Creek is located southwest of Pottstown, PA.  Take Route 100 south from Pottstown.   Go 3.9 miles south of Pottstown until Route 100 intersects with Route 23.  Take Route 23 west.  On Route 23, go 6.9 miles.  Make a right onto Route 345 north. (At this writing, there is a car dealership at the corner of 345 north.)  Follow Route 345N. (This road winds; stay with Route 345N and follow the French Creek signs.)  Travel 2.4 miles on Route 345N to the park entrance. Make a left on South Park Entrance Road.  Proceed on the park road 1.1 miles to a stop sign.  Make a left at the stop sign.  A paved parking area is on the left. Horse trailers can park there.  This is the only lot where we were told riders are permitted to park.  This is not a large lot.  Only about five 2-horse trailers can fit or two 50' rigs can get in and out. (Note, if you went to the right at the stop sign, the ranger's station is a few hundred feet.  Maps can be obtained at the ranger's station.)  As you ride through the park you will see various other lots including one very sizable lot by the lake.  However, the ranger indicated that these are off limits to horse trailer parking.  He explained that the large parking area is too congested, so the park prefers to keep the horse trailer parking at the one small lot by the South Park Entrance Road.

The actual equestrian trailhead is a short distance down the road from the parking lot.  Head from the lot in the direction away from the ranger station (going left). With caution, ride on the side of the park road a few hundred feet.  There will be a trailhead with large rocks on the right; pass that.  Continue a short distance down the park road to where the trail begins on the right.  It is by another paved (but small) parking lot.  You will see the yellow blazes on the trees.  The yellow blaze marks the Horse-Shoe Trail and a double blaze indicates a change in direction.  Begin here and follow the yellow blazes.  We did not find the trails difficult to follow, but a map is recommended.

**THE TRAILS:**
French Creek State Park offers a nice, shaded trail in the heat of the summer and a colorful foliage ride in the fall.  Trails wind through mostly wooded areas.  A large variety of mature oak, maple, hickory, poplar, and beech trees now canopy the trails.  These species of trees replace the chestnut trees that were cleared during the area's 18th and 19th centuries' iron forge production period.  Lots of rhododendron and mountain laurel are also to be seen.  The trail has many rocky

sections, which is not uncommon on PA trails, however, there is usually dirt between the rocks, and the horses should be able to pick their way through. Shoes are recommended, as there are some rough sections. There are also several smooth stretches with a good surface that are excellent for a gait or faster pace. There are places along the trail to water your horse.

The trail leaves from the south entrance parking area, follows the yellow trail which makes a wide loop to Scotts Run Lake. The Lake is a nice area to stop for lunch, take some pictures, and enjoy the view. The trail then crosses behind the dam onto the Green Trail and over to Hopewell Lake, again offering a beautiful view. The trail passes the "Disc Golf" or "Frisbee Golf" area where participants throw a Frisbee to baskets and move up along a trail of baskets in the woods. The trail then continues on to the ranger station and back to the parking lot. Other than navigating around some rocks, this section of the trail is basically easy to ride. However, riders will need to cross the park roads at the end of the loop.

We noticed that rain had eroded certain stretches of trail since our earlier visits, leaving additional rocks exposed and making the trail more challenging than it had been in the past. However, the park has made improvements to a few sections, and covered the trail with a stone dust type of surface. Stone dust is a superior covering; continuation of this could result in the rocky sections being very minimal, which would offer a substantial improvement to the trails for all to enjoy.

French Creek State Park is rich with history. While riding the loop, remember to look for the ruins and old foundations of the homes that once occupied the park during the 18th and 19th centuries. And make sure you stop by nearby Hopewell Furnace to visit the historic village (fee) and to learn more about the local history. (The village is on the map and there are signs.) Note: my editor, Connie, informs me that equestrians have been permitted to ride through the village on horseback (no fee). Connie indicated that horseback riders are made to feel very welcome and that the rangers (even) gave their horses carrots on more than one occasion. How nice to hear of such a horse friendly place! Always, confirm in advance that horses are permitted and abide by posted restrictions. And to help us stay welcome in the future, riders should keep their horses at a walk and be especially considerate of other visitors.

## HISTORICAL INFORMATION:

French Creek State Park has an interesting past with many must see sites. The park is named after a nearby fort which was occupied by the French during the French and Indian war. The area woods were once used to produce charcoal fuel for the neighboring Hopewell Furnace. Wood cut from the forest would be burned in hearths to generate charcoal. The charcoal would then fuel the furnace operations. The French Creek waters provided the power to generate the necessary air needed to keep the furnaces incinerated. Hopewell Furnace is a National Historical Site open to the public. Visitors can learn from period costumed guides about the iron making that produced many useful items for early Americans, including ammunition for the Revolutionary War. There still remain traces of charcoal hearths and iron production throughout the park. The furnace was in production from 1771 until 1883.

The Federal Government first developed the park when the acquisition phase began in 1934. This area was designated to be developed as a recreation site, known as Recreation Demonstration Area. This undertaking provided jobs for the local communities. The Civilian Conservation Corps (CCC) and the Works Progress Administration (WPA) began construction of the park. There were two CCC camps established and they operated until the 1940's. In 1946, the Commonwealth of PA acquired the land and the area was designated as "French Creek State Park". Currently, the land is run by the DCNR, Bureau of State Parks, PA. The National Park Service manages the Hopewell Furnace National Historic site.

## NEARBY OR SURROUNDING AREA B&B:
- Living Spring Farm B&B (offers accommodations for horses), Adamstown (610) 775-8525, (888) 329-1275, website: www.livingspringfarm.com

## NEARBY OR SURROUNDING AREA VET SERVICES:
- H. Fortna, Ephrata (717) 733-1078
- Dr. Van Dyke, Churchtown (717) 445-7978

## NEARBY FARRIERS:
- Equine Management Service, St. Peters (610) 469-9332
- V. Mastrangelo, Elverson (610) 286-5560

# 7. Marsh Creek State Park
# DCNR
### (Department of Conservation & Natural Resources)

**Lasting Impression:** Rural beauty in close proximity to the city of Philadelphia
**Location:** Village of Eagle, Downingtown, northcentral Chester County
**Length:** 1,705 acres, about 5 to 6 miles of trail plus possible additional riding on connecting trails in the southeast section of the park.
**Level of Difficulty:** Easy
**Terrain:** Some flat, some rolling hills, open fields, wooded, and a railroad bed
**Horse Camping:** No
**Non-horse Camping:** Yes
**Maps and Info:** DCNR, (610)-458-5119, Marsh Creek State Park, 675 Park Road, Downingtown, PA 19335-1898, e-mail: marshcreeksp@state.pa.us, DCNR website: www.dcnr.state.pa.us. Call 1-888-PA-PARKS for general park info or for camping reservations. During our visit, there was a well stocked supply of maps near the equestrian trailhead by the boating area.
**Activities:** Boating, Boat Rentals, Fishing, Hiking, Picnicking, Swimming, Biking, Horseback Riding Trails, Hunting (during season), Camping, Sledding, and Ice Sports
**Fees for Trail Use:** None
**Permits for Trail Use:** None
**Comfort Station:** Yes, near the parking area

## DIRECTIONS:
Marsh Creek State Park trail system is located in the countryside surrounding Philadelphia, near Downingtown. From the north, take Route 100 south from Pottstown to the village of Eagle. In Eagle, make a sharp right onto Little Conestoga Road, then follow the directions below. From the south, take the PA Turnpike (I-276) to the Downingtown Exit #23. Take Route 100 north to the village of Eagle. In Eagle, make a left onto Little Conestoga Road.

Follow Little Conestoga Road for approximately 3.5 miles. The road winds. You will come to a T; Little Conestoga Road goes left. Stay on Little Conestoga Road. Pass over a bridge and dam. At Route 282, make a left. Take Route 282 east 1.5 miles to Lyndell Road. Make a left on Lyndell Road. Go to the top of the hill; the road curves around. You will see the park comfort station and the West Launch boating area to the left. Go left and down the hill toward the comfort station following the road to the boating area. Once at the bottom, bear left; follow a gravel road, which goes to the left or back of the comfort station. Horse trailer parking and the trailhead are at that lot. The lot is of medium size, offers pull-through spaces, and can fit several standard 2-

31

horse trailers. Although parking is limited, there are lots of open areas and adjoining fields for overflow or large rigs.

## THE TRAILS:
I first rode these trails while doing the research for this book. These trails were a wonderful surprise and well worth the trip. John and I found them relaxing and easy to ride in a beautiful setting overlooking Marsh Creek. We visited this park in the fall. Although there were hikers and bikers, the park did not feel crowded.

The equestrian trails lead directly out from the parking lot and are in varying loops in the western side of the park. They are intertwined and circle back so it should not be easy to get lost. The trails vary from wooded areas, to open fields, to old railroad grades. The trails are nicely maintained. Some areas were slightly rocky, but minimal, and we found the footing to be mostly good. There is a short stretch along the old railroad grade where the wooden ties have not been removed. Our horses had no problem walking over the ties but riders can also travel along the shoulder or to the side which has a more even surface. There are lots of open fields for canters and the finished sections of the railroad grades can be a fun stretch for gaited horse riders. With the creek running through the park, water can be found along the trail. We thought all the trails were very scenic but our favorite part was the section (to the right upon leaving the parking lot) that travels along the lake offering beautiful views of Marsh Creek.

The trails are historically interesting too. Look for the ruins of old stone buildings remaining from when this area and some of the surrounding areas were known for their iron forges. During the 19th century, the iron forges were a major producer of ammunition materials for the Civil War.

Please be reminded, although we found this park a joy to ride in the fall, hunting is permitted. We rode on a Sunday when hunting was not allowed.

## HISTORICAL INFORMATION:
Marsh Creek State Park was a joint effort of various government and county agencies to manage water resources in the Brandywine Creek Watershed. The land around the lake was acquired by the Department of Environmental Resources (now DCNR), to be used for recreation. The Commonwealth of Pennsylvania operates the recreational facilities.

## NEARBY OR SURROUNDING AREA B&B:
- Living Spring Farm B&B (offers accommodations for horses), Adamstown (610) 775-8525, (888) 329-1275, website: www.livingspringfarm.com

**NEARBY AND SURROUNDING AREA VET SERVICES:**
- Brandywine Veterinary Clinic, Coatesville (610) 383-1866
- Complete Equine Health Service, Coatesville (610) 466-0501
- New Bolton (24-hour emergency), Kennett Square (610) 444-5800

**NEARBY FARRIERS:**
- J. Nolan, Perkiomenville (215) 990-9778
- Chester County Farrier Assoc., Unionville (610) 347-2445

# 8. Ridley Creek State Park
# DCNR
### (Department of Conservation & Natural Resources)

**Lasting Impression:** A great get away near the city of Philadelphia with a far away feel. As bikes have a separate trail system, and are not permitted on most equestrian dirt trails, this trail can be attractive for riders with horses who are bike shy.

**Location:** The park is located southwest of Philadelphia, near Newtown Square in Delaware County, Pennsylvania.

**Length:** The park contains over 2,600 acres and includes about 5 miles of equestrian trails.

**Level of Difficulty:** The primary trails are mainly easy; some adjoining trails may be considered moderate due to ascending or descending terrain.

**Terrain:** The trail is mainly dirt, the beginning of the trail is a clay like surface, which can be muddy during or after wet weather. Further down the trail, there is crushed stone. There are very few rocks. Flat stretches, rolling hills, woodlands, and open fields comprise this trail system.

**Horse Camping:** No

**Non-horse Camping:** Organized group tenting

**Maps and Info:** Ridley Creek State Park, Sycamore Mills Road, Media, PA 19063-4398, (610) 892-3900, e-mail: ridleycreeksp@state.pa.us. Call 1-888-PA-PARKS for general park info or for camping reservations. Other local information can be obtained from the Brandywine Conference and Visitors Bureau at (800) 343-3983. During our visit, there was a well supplied stock of maps at the park office. However, maps can be obtained in advance. Also at the park office, near the bulletin board by the gardens, is a flyer detailing a 45 minute self-guided walking tour that describes the history of the Jeffords Estate. The Jeffords Estate is now part of Ridley Creek State Park and the park office currently occupies the former home of the Jeffords family. Hidden Valley Stable is located within the park and provides guided horse trail rides and horse boarding. The attractive stable is leased from the Bureau of Parks and can be contacted at (610) 892-7260.

**Activities:** Fishing, Hiking, Picnicking, Biking (on designated paved trails and roads only), Horseback Riding Trails, Guided Horse Rental Tours, Camping, Sledding, Hunting may be permitted during designated times (check with office prior to visit), and X-C Skiing

**Fees for Trail Use:** None

**Permits for Trail Use:** None

**Comfort Station:** Yes, there are flush toilets at the equestrian lot and there are flush toilets by the park office

**Other:** There are also drink machines near the park office.

**DIRECTIONS:**
Take Route 476 to Route 3 Upper Darby (Newtown Square) Exit #9. Get off of Route 476 and head west on Route 3. Travel 4.5 miles on Route 3 west, traveling through Newtown Square. Look for Providence Road; make a left onto Providence Road. Travel 1.4 miles on Providence Road; then make a right on Gradyville Road (will see the park sign). Go .4 miles on Gradyville Road and turn left; continue to stop sign. At the stop sign, make a left following signs to the stables. Take the second road on the left. At this turn, you will see a sign indicating stables and picnic grounds to the left. Just after left, make another left into the lots. Parking is behind the stable area. There are two lots; the second lot has a sign indicating equestrian parking. The small to medium sized paved lot is in a nice setting away from the main park area with the trails leading directly out the back of the lot. But the lot is long and somewhat narrow and drivers will need to be comfortable backing their rigs. About 4 to 5 standard 2-horse trailers can fit. There are picnic tables next to the equestrian parking and there are comfort stations nearby.

**THE TRAILS:**
The equestrian trails travel in loops in the northern end of the park. Riders can choose loops to shorten or lengthen their ride. The trails border the Ridley Creek and offer hours of relaxing rides along and around the creek. The main paths are mostly wide, gradual, easy to ride, and offer a variety of terrain and scenery. There are also side trails that may be more challenging and include a variation in terrain. The trails do have markers at the entry points and crossings but there appeared to be some gaps in markers so a map is helpful. We found the trails easy to follow, they are well used, and there are plenty of points of reference on the map to help riders stay on course.

Just a forewarning, shortly after setting out on the trail, riders will encounter a low clearance bridge which can be crossed over or under. This is a very busy road so judgment should be exercised before choosing to cross above. We chose to travel under the bridge and I dismounted, as my concern was a sudden loud overhead vehicle could cause my horse to rear not leaving any room for me. Leading my horse on the ground, I found plenty of clearance. (Although my horse is usually good, I still cautiously lead him in a way that, if he was to get suddenly startled at sudden overhead traffic, he would not run me over in the process. Bridges with loud, unexpected rumblings over head can make even the best-trained horses move very quickly and carelessly. The bridge had intervals when cars were not driving overhead and I timed my passage for that break in traffic.) This was the only impediment of this sort that we encountered, and we found it to be minor when approached with caution.

What a pleasant surprise these trails were! We went on a warm March day (a nice place to ride in the winter where the trees offer lots of buffer if there is wind). There were some hikers and riders, but the trails were quiet and felt far removed from the nearby busy city and suburban areas. Other than one section with a distant scenic view of the golf course on the opposite side of the river and the occasional view of neighboring buildings, the trails are mostly in a dense, wooded setting. There are very little sounds of nearby civilization. The trails offer a leisurely ride, winding around the Ridley Creek and passing interesting historic homes and old farmsteads along the way. Many of the trails are wide where you can ride side by side. And, there are places along the trail to water the horses.

We asked riders who boarded their horses at the park if the trails were always so pleasant and peaceful as when we visited them. They indicated that due to the trails being set away from the main park area, and that bikes had their own separate paths, the equestrian and hiking trails were usually as quiet as we had experienced. And this seemed to be supported by the abundant wildlife that can be seen along the trail. Along with other critters, we saw two large Blue Herons and a fox with a beautiful red coat.

In the northern end of the park, in the center of a small trail loop located at the crest of a hill tucked in the woods, is the Russell cemetery, which is enclosed by a waist high stone wall. In the early 1800's, this family built homes on Gradyville Road that are still standing today. The gravestones are dated between 1820 and 1861. There is a marker at the cemetery where Jesse Russell is buried. It is believed that Jesse Russell, who loved fox hunting, asked to be buried upright so he could hear the baying of the hounds!

Besides enjoying this trail in the late winter, we are looking forward to returning to this trail during other seasons. In the spring, the estate gardens and wild flowers are in bloom. During the summer, the woods offer a canopy from the hot weather; and in the fall, the woods are full of color due to the variety of trees and plant life.

## HISTORICAL INFORMATION:

Ridley Creek State Park has preserved a bit of history. Within the park, there is a restored 300 year old working farm called Colonial Pennsylvania Plantation, which portrays life before the American Revolution. For a fee, visitors can view livestock, food preparation and preservation, crop tending, and guides dressed in period garb depicting life in the 1700's.

In addition, within the park, there is a historic district with homes from an 18th century village (now) called Sycamore Mills. Still standing is the miller's house, mill workers' homes, the library, and other small homes. These are private homes and not open to the public.

Make sure you visit the park office, which is the former home of the Jeffords family. The mansion appears much like it did at the time the Jeffords lived in it. The stone home (circa early 1900's) is unusual in that it was built around an old stone farmhouse that was constructed in the 1700's. The park acquired the property in 1966 and established the park office in the home. As you walk into the park office, you can see the original stone colonial house that is the center of the mansion. The home and surrounding gardens are beautiful. During the spring, the Jeffords Estate grounds are a must see as the flowers blossom. The charm and tranquility of this section of the park feels like a step back in time.

The park, officially opened in 1972, is a result of the Project 70 and the Land and Water Conservation Fund purchases in the 1960's.

**NEARBY STABLES:**
- Gateway Stables (boarding, training, trail rides, and camps, *Coggins required*), Kennett Square (610) 444-9928, website: www.gateway.com

**NEARBY B&B:**
- Bed & Breakfast at Walnut Hill (with stabling nearby), Kennett Square (610) 444-3703

**NEARBY VET SERVICES:**
- New Bolton (24-hour emergency), Kennett Square (610) 444-5800
- Complete Equine Health Service, Coatesville (610) 466-0501
- Brandywine Veterinary Clinic, Coatesville (610) 383-1866
- Unionville Equine Center, Oxford (610) 932-6800

**NEARBY FARRIER:**
- Chester County Farrier Assoc., Unionville (610) 347-2445

# 9. Pennypack Park
# Fairmount Park Commission

**Lasting Impression:**  Lots and lots of nice, easy woodland riding just minutes from Center City, Philadelphia

**Location:**  Pennypack Park is located in southeastern Pennsylvania and is situated in the northeastern corner of the city of Philadelphia.  The park stretches from the Delaware River to Pine Road in northeast Philadelphia.

**Length:**  The park totals almost 1,600 acres and includes about 15 miles of equestrian trails.

**Level of Difficulty:**  Mostly easy, but horses need to be comfortable with multi-users, and with crossing over and under bridges.  *(We rode the central and northern sections of this trail system.  The southern tip of Pennypack travels near busy areas and roads so we avoided that section with horses.)*

**Terrain:**  Overall gentle, gradual climbs, mostly dirt, some flat, some rolling hills, mostly in woodlands

**Horse Camping:**  No

**Non-horse Camping:**  No

**Maps and Info:**  Friends of Pennypack Park, e-mail: Pennypackpark@aol.com, www.balford.com/fopp, (215) 934-PARK.  The Fairmount Park Commission manages Pennypack Park.  A (free) trail user pass is required; to obtain the pass, contact the Fairmount Park Commission, Attn: Permits Office, PO Box 21601, Philadelphia, PA  19131-0901, (215) 685-0052.  Violation of trail rules can result in a $25 fine and loss of trail rights.

**Activities:**  Biking, Horseback Riding Trails, Hiking, Picnicking, and Fishing

**Fees for Trail Use:** None

**Permits for Trail Use:**  Yes, see maps and info above

**Comfort Station:**  Yes, see the map for locations

### DIRECTIONS:

Do obtain a map when sending for your trail pass.  The Fairmount Park Commission will likely send one with your pass, but make sure you do have one prior to visiting these trails.  The Pennypack Trail System, although we found it peaceful and unhurried within, is surrounded by busy communities and road systems.  While hauling, you need to have a good feel for where you are going, and the map helps.  The good news is that, with these directions and staying alert for the turns, it should be pretty easy to get to.

We looked at several parking areas and thought these next two were most suited to horse trailer parking.  One is at the northern end of the park on Verree Road, and one is just south of the center of the park off of Rhawn Street by the picnic area (by reference #27 on the Fairmount map). To reach both of these, take the PA Turnpike (I-276) to Exit #28 Route 1 south toward Philadelphia. Travel on Route 1/Roosevelt Blvd. south for almost 7 miles to Rhawn Street. Both lots can be accessed via Rhawn Street.

For the Verree northern lot, while on Route 1/Roosevelt Blvd., bear right on the multi-lane highway and follow signs to the Pennypack Circle. **You need to be on the local access roads to make a right on Rhawn.** At Rhawn, make the right. (If you didn't stay to the right and ended up in the center lanes, you can not make a right onto Rhawn, instead proceed to Borbeck, make a right, go one block to Bradford, make another right, then proceed to Rhawn and make a left.) Travel 2 miles on Rhawn Road to Verree. (If you are like us, about now you will be wondering where can one ride a horse around here.) At the light on Verree, make a right. Travel 1 mile and slow down. Proceed another .2 miles and turn into the lot just before the bridge. With trees on both sides of the entrance, it is not easy to see until you are upon it. Be careful turning in. The entrance is slightly elevated and then drops off; if your trailer travels very low, this may not be the lot for you. In regard to both getting there and getting in, this is not the place to bring a large trailer. We did okay with our 2-horse trailer with tack room, but we had to take it very easy as the hump at the entrance really tilts the horses back and then forward. If they do not have a manger, bar, or partition to brace themselves against (a stock trailer would not have sufficient support), this may not be the choice for you as the horses need to lean and balance for this one. Getting out can be tricky too because you have to climb and wait on the hill to assess the traffic. We surprisingly did okay and the traffic was not heavy. But the lot itself is functional, of medium size, with sufficient turn around space, assuming others are not blocking it. The lot is not as well maintained as the Rhawn Street picnic area lot, but it is dirt, wasn't too busy during our visit, and can fit two or three 2-horse trailers. The equestrian trail leads directly from the lot on the side of the entrance away from the creek (to the right upon entering the lot) and there is a sign. The dirt bridle path quickly moves away from the lot and the road, and enters the woods of the park.

To reach the central or southern end of the park, travel on Route 1/Roosevelt Blvd. as indicated above, but do not go toward the Pennypack Circle. Instead, travel 6 miles straight on Route 1/Roosevelt Blvd. and get in the left lane. Look for the left lane turn onto Rhawn Street. The left lane exit is just after the underpass. Make the left onto Rhawn. Travel .8 miles on Rhawn; the lot is on the right by the picnic area, and has an easy access, is a large loop lot in a multi-use area, and is paved. (Bring a manure fork to clean up upon unloading and loading.) This lot is more attractive than the Verree lot, but is more central and may be busier. The Verree lot is in a more remote location with less activity. This lot can hold a few or a small group of standard 2-horse trailers. The lot is not large enough for very large horse trailers. From this lot, the trails lead out in various directions. The trails we covered were from the Verree lot to this lot and back.

## THE TRAILS:

Well, we were not familiar with this one and even though the info is out there, I had a heck of a time finding it at first even with the benefit of the Internet. We had heard mention of the trail once or twice but did not know this was part of the Fairmount Park Commission's domain, where to get directions, maps, etc. So this one was completely new to us. Once we were in contact with the Friends of Pennypack, they were kind enough to send a map with all the parking areas and trails highlighted. This was very helpful and we appreciate the courtesy extended to us by the Friends of Pennypack, especially Sheila, in getting us familiar with the Park.

The Friends of Pennypack, the Fairmount Park Commission, and all the contributing individuals, groups, and agencies have done a nice job on these trails. We were hesitant to bring the horses to what we speculated to be a congested trail system. We were thinking of biking it on our initial visit to test it out. However, we had the wrong impression and were glad we brought the horses. We visited on a hot August Sunday and parked at the Verree lot. While tacking up we weren't sure we picked the best of days, but once we were in the canopy of trees the air quickly cooled off and the temperature was much more comfortable. The trail disappears into the woods quickly leaving the (sometimes) busy lot behind.

The Pennypack Trail System offers a leisurely ride through nice woodlands that meander and crisscross the Pennypack Creek. The woods in the spring, summer, and fall offer a good sound barrier from nearby civilization. This trail must be beautiful in the fall when the variety of species of trees each have their own shade of fall color. The horse trail travels parallel to, and offshoots loop around the separate 9 mile paved trail for hikers and bikers. One section of the equestrian trail, for a short distance, travels directly along side the paved bike path, but there are alternate trails to take and both sides of the stream can be ridden.

Most of the other trail users seem to use the paved path, however, we did encounter several bikers and hikers on the equestrian path. According to some of the mountain bike websites, many of the mountain bikers prefer the equestrian path. But most of the experienced bicyclists and other regular users of the trail that we encountered were very courteous, friendly, and pulled over upon seeing the horses. (It seemed that those who didn't extend us this consideration, looked like they didn't do much bike riding and appeared to be new to trails and to proper trail etiquette.) It is nice that many of the seasoned bicyclists have gotten used to horses and were proceeding cautiously and safely.

With the many loops and crossings, it is helpful to use the creek as a reference point and to refer to the map to help stay on course. Even though the trail is not complex, it can be a little tricky and you can get turned around while traveling over and under all the various bridges. Obtain a map ahead of time, as we did not see any maps along the trail. There were some signs but not many, and at some of the bridge crossings it became unclear where to continue the trail. Most of the path is wide with firm footing. Some stretches are narrow but the well used area that parallels the Pennypack Creek is mostly spacious. The paths travel through some very special well-preserved areas with enormous trees. Check out the size and height of some of the oak trees as you pass by! We had no idea such a nice natural area was in close proximity to Center City, and the trails were relaxing. We really didn't encounter a large volume of other users. It was only under some of the bridges, where the trails came together, that we had to proceed with caution due to many users converging on each other. But most of the bridges were large with good footing and lots of airiness, making crossing easier. This allowed us to move on quickly and resume the dirt trails. We were, however, glad to see that other horseback riders were also using the trails.

As you travel through the trails, look for deer. The deer have become accustomed to trail users and are usually quite close observing you as you pass by. As for water, there are many places to water the horses along the trail. However, it is probably best to bring water for the horses as the water quality may vary.

An interesting local attraction is the Pennypack Creek "fall-line". This is where the stream rushes over the final series of rapids and declines to a level near to that of the Delaware River. The fall-line can be seen from the Pennypack Bridge.

We enjoyed our visit to this trail system and it was a pleasant experience, one we plan to share with others. Pennypack Park is a good example of where a shared use concept can be very successful even in heavily populated areas.

## HISTORICAL INFORMATION:

Pennypack Park is part of the City of Philadelphia parks administered by the Fairmount Park Commission. The park has lots of history. Early dwellers were the Lenni Lenape (aka the Delaware Indians) who lived and hunted in the area. Numerous spear points and stone points have been found in these parts. Many of the Indian's trails later were used by the European settlers and eventually became major roadways, including Frankford Avenue. One of the Indian paths traveled over the "Falls of the Delaware" river crossing. Travelers would cross in and through the river. The crossing could be hazardous as horses would sometimes trip and riders would land in the water. After William Penn purchased the surrounding land from the Indians in the late 1600's, he petitioned for permission to build a bridge. This bridge, completed in 1697, still stands today and remains one of the oldest stone bridges in use in the United States.

In addition, many other historic structures can be seen in the park, including the Pennypack Baptist Church (circa 1688) and The Verree House on Verree Road. This house was raided by the British during the American Revolution. In the mid 1700's, stagecoach travel through the area began bringing more development and settlement to the region. The convenient waterways provided power to run the mills that were built along the river. By the mid to late 1800's, coal, transported by railroads, became the new source of fuel replacing the need to build the mills along the creek. The economic importance of the creek decreased, the mills were abandoned, and eventually demolished.

By 1905, land was being set aside for a park for future generations to enjoy. The park was established; but by the late 1900's the park had become in need of attention. In 1987, the Friends of Pennypack Park was formed with the goal of improving the park and being active on a continuous basis to assure its continued preservation and upkeep. Much of today's accommodations and enhancements are a result of the hard work of this dedicated group.

## THINGS WE LEARNED THIS RIDE:
- When you are not sure of the direction you are heading, don't forget to look to the nearby stream or creek and the direction of flow. If we are traveling with the stream and we want to be heading north, we are going the wrong way. (We usually are much better at this!)
- With good planning and commitment, cities can have wonderful wooded retreats for all to enjoy, right in the heart of the city.

## NEARBY EQUESTRIAN B&B:
- Mill Creek Farm Bed & Breakfast (accommodations for horses, overnight stabling, and may be able to accommodate trailers with living quarters), Buckingham (215) 794-0776, e-mail: millcreekfarmbnb@aol.com

## NEARBY VET SERVICES:
- Blauner, Vecchione, & Associates (24-hour emergency vet service), N. Wales (215) 699-4422

## NEARBY FARRIERS:
- R. Kass, Jr., Levittown (215) 943-8583
- R. Kass, Pipersville (215) 630-0390

# 10. Tyler State Park
# DCNR
### (Department of Conservation & Natural Resources)

**Lasting Impression:** A lovely, accommodating Bucks County Park with separate trail systems for equestrians and bicyclists

**Location:** Newtown, Bucks County, eastern Pennsylvania

**Length:** The park consists of over 1,700 acres. There are about 9 miles of equestrian trails.

**Level of Difficulty:** Easy

**Terrain:** Some flat, some rolling hills, woods, open fields. Surface is dirt, some rocks but navigable.

**Horse Camping:** Not at Tyler, but there is horse camping at nearby Green Lane Park (see the Green Lane chapter)

**Non-horse Camping:** No

**Maps and Info:** DCNR, Tyler State Park, 101 Swamp Road, Newtown, PA 18940-1151, (215) 968-2021, e-mail: tyler@dcnr.state.pa.us, DCNR website: www.dcnr.state.pa.us. Call 1-888-PA-PARKS for general park info. Maps are at the trailheads. Additional info can be obtained from the Bucks County Tourist Commission at (215) 345-4552 or (800) 836-BUCKS.

**Activities:** Boating, Boat Rentals, Fishing, Hiking, Biking, Picnicking, Horseback Riding Trails, Sledding, Ice Sports, X-C Skiing, and Disc Golf Course. At this writing, there is no hunting except for one day per year.

**Fees for Trail Use:** None

**Permits for Trail Use:** None

**Comfort Station:** Yes

**DIRECTIONS:**

The park office indicated horse trailer parking is permitted in three areas. Parking is in the large lot by the craft center. The second lot is on Route 332 by the Spring Garden Mill and the Fisherman's Parking Lot. The third is on the northern side of the park near the Schofield Ford Covered Bridge. The Schofield lot is a large lot with pull-through spaces, and is located in a remote section of the park. We usually park at this location.

To travel to the Schofield Ford Covered Bridge lot, take PA Turnpike (I-276) to the Trevose exit, which is Route 1. Take Route 1 north 3.5 miles to Route 413 north. Travel 5.3 miles on Route 413 north and you will come to an intersection. (You will see the park entrance on the left and Route 413 (Newtown By-Pass) turning to the right.) Do not turn; instead, continue straight through the intersection onto Swamp Road. Follow Swamp Road about 1.7 miles. You will pass

43

Bucks County Community College. Make a left to Schofield Ford Covered Bridge entrance at the crest of the hill. Follow the stone drive to a large parking area for horse trailers.

To the same lot, if traveling from north of the park, take Route 611 to Pipersville. At Pipersville, take Route 413 south 15.6 miles to Twining Bridge Road. Make a right on Twining Bridge Road. Travel one mile and look for Swamp Road. Make a left on Swamp Road. Go .1 mile and make a right into the entrance to the Schofield Ford Covered Bridge parking area.

The Craft Center lot and the Fisherman's and Spring Garden Mill lots are on the south side of the park off of PA 332. If traveling from the Route 1 location, take Route 413 north to the intersection of PA 332; head west (make a left) on PA 332. If traveling from the north or from the Schofield Ford Covered Bridge Lot, take Swamp Road traveling south/east to PA 332. Head west (make a right) on PA 332. Both lots are just off of PA 332 and are clearly indicated on the map.

## THE TRAILS:
We found this to be a really nice trail system. Our ride was very relaxing, scenic, and the trails were mostly easy to follow and well marked. The trails wind around the Neshaminy Creek presenting many places to water your horse along the way. At some points, it became unclear where horses are permitted to cross over the river. However, if the trail appears too steep or not very horse friendly, you can always backtrack or ask a passing rider. It may be that you ventured off the equestrian trail. The trails are well used by local riders; these folks usually can provide direction as to the correct route. Also, bring your map. In many areas, there are white markings on the trees or horseshoe forms on the top of short posts marking the equestrian trails to help riders stay on course.

The trails vary from open fields to wooded areas. There are some rocky areas but rocks are not extensive. The unique thing about this trail system is that bikes have a separate path, usually paved, that parallels the horse trails. This is an especially nice feature for those horses that just can't get used to bikes.

Dog enthusiasts should visit the pedestrian causeway area; it is like a dog show! Lots of dog lovers with all sorts of breeds congregate to let their dogs play in the water. This short stretch of trail (where hikers, bikers, riders, and dog walkers meet) requires riders to dismount, walk their horses, and exercise caution.

## HISTORICAL INFORMATION:
The park was once owned by the Tyler family who purchased the land in the early 1900's. They built a mansion that later was acquired by the Bucks County Community College. The Tyler's farm consisted of well bred Ayrshire dairy

cattle, sheep, pigs, and poultry. The farm also had a stable of elegant riding horses as Mrs. Tyler enjoyed riding. Mrs. Tyler created many of the park's trails.

Old stone buildings can be seen throughout the park. Some of these date back to the early 1700's and are typical of the rural area at that time. The date of 1775 can be seen on the house in the center of the park, just north of the pedestrian causeway by the bicycle trail. A must see is the Schofield Ford Covered Bridge, Bucks County's longest bridge, which was originally built in 1874. Unfortunately, it burned in 1991, but it was authentically rebuilt and again stands for everyone to enjoy thanks to the cooperative effort of concerned, local individuals and groups.

This park is a result of "Project 70", "Project 500", and the Pennsylvania "Land and Water Conservation and Reclamation Act". The park was opened in 1974 and is now run by DCNR, Bureau of State Parks, Pennsylvania.

**NEARBY STABLES:**
- Rainbow Ridge Farm Equestrian Center (boarding, overnight stabling, lessons, tack shop, summer camp, and shows), Pipersville (215) 766-9357
- Breakaway Farms (boarding, overnight stabling, and trailer parking), Pipersville (215) 766-3769
- Kantagree Farm Riding Academy (schooling, lessons, boarding, access to park trails, overnight stabling, and trailer parking), Newtown (215) 968-5181

**NEARBY B&B:**
- Mill Creek Farm Bed & Breakfast (accommodations for horses, overnight stabling, and may be able to accommodate trailers with living quarters), Buckingham (215) 794-0776, e-mail: millcreekfarmbnb@aol.com

**NEARBY AND SURROUNDING AREA VET SERVICES:**
- Blauner, Vecchione, & Associates (24-hour emergency vet service), N. Wales (215) 699-4422
- Quakertown Veterinary Clinic, Quakertown (215) 536-2726, (215) 536-6245

**NEARBY FARRIERS:**
- Bucks County Farrier Service, Pipersville (215) 766-0242
- R. Kass, Jr., Levittown (215) 943-8583
- R. Kass, Pipersville (215) 630-0390

# 11. White Clay Creek Preserve
# DCNR
### (Department of Conservation & Natural Resources)

**Lasting Impression:** Meander and enjoy this pretty trail where Pennsylvania, Maryland, and Delaware meet. This land was a gift from the DuPont family.

**Location:** White Clay Creek Preserve is located near Newark, Delaware in southern Chester County, Pennsylvania.

**Length:** The park consists of over 1,200 acres and contains 8 miles of horse trails.

**Level of Difficulty:** Easy

**Terrain:** The terrain is varied from flat to rolling hills, open fields and meadows, lots of grassy stretches, old railroad grades with dirt and some small stone surface covering, stream crossings, and dirt paths through the woods. The trails are not rocky. From Lot #3, a very short distance of back rural road riding and road crossing is required to reach the trails. The roads were hardly used during our visit. We found this a fun place for gaiting or for enjoying a nice canter at the border of the meadows and along the old railroad right-of-ways.

**Horse Camping:** Not at White Clay, however, there is camping with your horse and additional trail riding at nearby Fair Hill Natural Resources Management Area in Maryland. Fair Hill is also a result of the generosity of the DuPont family.

**Non-horse Camping:** No

**Maps and Info:** Info can be obtained from DCNR, White Clay Creek Preserve, P.O. Box 172, Landenberg, PA 19350-0172, (610) 274-2900, e-mail: whiteclay@dcnr.state.pa.us, DCNR website: www.dcnr.state.pa.us. Call 1-888-PA-PARKS for general park information. The park manager and staff were very helpful, giving detailed directions and making us feel welcome. Maps are at the park office. We did not see extra maps at the lot or trailheads so do call and have a map sent prior to your arrival in case the office is closed. Although the trails are not complex and they are often clearly marked, they can be tricky due to road connections and some lapses in markers. One park representative did say they would consider our recommendation to use markers at the river crossings so riders know where to proceed. For nearby Fair Hill Natural Resources Management Area (MD) trails and camping call (410) 398-1246.

**Activities:** Fishing, Hiking, Biking (on paved roads but not on most of the dirt and grass horse trails), Horseback Riding Trails, Hunting (during season), and X-C Skiing

**Fees for Trail Use:** None

**Permits for Trail Use:** None

**Comfort Station:** Yes, at the Meeting House near the park office

46

## DIRECTIONS:

If traveling from the PA Turnpike, take I-476 to Exit #4, which is the Springfield exit. Take Route 1 south, passing the Brandywine Battlefield and Longwood Gardens. Travel to the intersection at Route 41. If traveling from other areas, take Route 1 to the intersection at Route 41 and proceed as follows.

At the intersection of Route 1 and Route 41, take Route 41 south for 3 miles and make a right onto Newark Road. Take Newark Road south and, after a mile or so, look for Buttonwood Road. Make a right on Buttonwood. Go .25 miles, come to a 'T'; make a right at the stop sign, which is Broad Run Road. Go a short distance on Broad Run Road, cross the bridge. See the White Clay park sign on the right. The road forks; bear left, which is called London Tract Road. Do not go to the first lot on the left; instead continue. Go up a hill, down a hill, and then make a right on New Peltier (you will see a brown park sign on the left and a large old barn to the right). Immediately after turning, make another right into the lot behind the barn. This is where equestrians park. It is not a big lot but large trailers can pull in and back into their spaces. (A lot of bulky farm equipment once moved around this lot.) A few standard 2-horse trailers can fit. This did not appear to be a busy or crowded parking area. To get to the trail, make a left out of the lot, ride the short distance back to London Tract Road and you will see the equestrian signs. You can make a right or left on London Tract Road to pick up the trails.

There is another small lot. Instead of turning on New Peltier, continue on London Tract Road, cross the one lane bridge and make a left after the bridge (still on London Tract Road). Go about .75 miles to Sharpless Road. Make a left on Sharpless Road, pass the park office and see the lot. Access the trail behind this lot, cross the creek, and then you will see signs on the other side of the creek after you cross.

## THE TRAILS:

John and I found this trail to be beautiful, clean, quiet, serene, easy, and relaxing to ride. There are open fields to ride, old railroad grades to enjoy, or trails along the White Clay Creek to explore. There were no sounds or sights of any nearby busy roads, evidenced by much wildlife in the area. Along the river there are trees which show fresh evidence of the beavers that inhabit this area. (The only roads we saw were the back country roads.) As you ride, look for old homesteads along the trail. The trail passes the remains of interesting old structures along with many historic homes that are nicely preserved. Usually, a clue to a former homesite or farmstead is the ornamental trees or fruit trees, that still stand today, which were once planted around the structures.

There are many helpful signs along the trail and the trail is generally very well marked, but sometimes there seemed to be a gap in the markers, or we did not see them. We found we did need to refer to the map to determine where to cross the river (especially after we took the wrong route). Early in the trail system, behind Lot #2, riders need to cross the river and the trail continues on the opposite side. The trail loops around the White Clay Creek. Later, horses again cross the river to reach the return loop. Riders should cross before the remains of the old railroad crossing where the railroad once traveled across the river. The bridge is gone but the pillars still stand. Do not go past this spot as a branch of the trail changes into a narrow footpath that the fishermen and hikers use. This is actually a footpath that at first looks horse friendly, but as it approaches the river can become very narrow at sections. See more below as to what you find if you go past where you are supposed to be.

The horse trail is in the northern end of the preserve. This park spans Pennsylvania, Maryland, and Delaware, and you can ride from Pennsylvania to Delaware. While traveling around the park, markers are present indicating historical significance along the Mason-Dixon Line.

During our visit, we did not find the park crowded or the trails heavily used by riders or hikers. Bikes are permitted only on the paved roads and certain sections, but not on most of the equestrian and hiker paths.

After riding this trail, I thought I should start a new section 'what I learned not to do on the trail' or 'things we learned this ride'. John and I accidentally passed where we were supposed to cross the river. We were trying to carefully follow the signs but did not see one at the crossing so we just continued along the trail. When it forked, we proceeded down the trail along the river. We even asked a fisherman if we were on the right trail. He nicely told us that we must be, that he had seen other riders pass through there (I guess some other lost riders). The trail descended to a narrow dirt trail winding along the river. Now, what I learned: There was a small ravine crossing with some logs across. My horse became concerned and backed up. If something scares him, he will take a few steps back for a short distance. A habit that is not a problem for me on a large, wide trail but one that can be dangerous on a narrow, 'on the edge' trail. He backed up, only for the ground to give way, and his rear legs dropped off. Luckily he pulled himself together and we did not proceed down the hill to the river. Ah, the things trail riders can encounter. Needless to say, that was very scary. Lesson #1: Retrain him to spook in place when appropriate. Some trails have no back up or turn around space. And for safety, when there is no room for a horse to react on a trail, try not to go on that trail, either turn around or take an alternative. Sometimes I dismount, as my horse is more confident letting me test the way and following me past something that he is fearful of. (He's no fool.)

He leads well if I walk in front of him, making sure to leave plenty of safety distance if he tries to jump past the obstacle into my space.

We then approached a small wooden bridge with railings and no bypass. We hesitated as it was more narrow than most equestrian bridges, but it appeared solidly built, had plenty of room for the horses, had 2 or 3 very wide steps, and someone had just told us that this was the horse path. (A sense of humor, perhaps?) The bridge did not have sufficient turn around space, so once you started, you had to proceed, unless you wanted to back your horse down those steps, which did not look like a good choice. Lesson #2: I learned that when I approach a bridge that I am unsure of, or cannot see the access and exit of, to dismount, have someone hold my horse, and check both sides in advance before bringing my horse across. When we got to the other side, two horses closely following each other, there were many more steps (than the first side), and it was not as wide and not at all horse friendly. We were grateful for the borium on our horses' shoes to help keep them from slipping, because it can be easy for a horse to slip on wooden steps. Our one horse, after some convincing, did manage to walk down the steps as I prayed he didn't slip. Our other horse chose to skip the steps and take a leap off the wooden bridge. I again held my breath. They were fine but we now knew this could not be the horse trail. There were no signs indicating it was a pedestrian bridge. We were not going to cross back over that bridge, so we had to proceed down the trail and find a place to cross the river. We did share our story with one of the park staff indicating we carefully tried to follow the trail but then became uncertain where to continue. We asked that the park please put signs where equestrians should have crossed, by the old railroad crossing, and where they should not proceed. She was very receptive to our recommendation, indicated her concern, and offered to recommend it to the park manager.

Well that was my least favorite part of the trail. My favorite part of the trail was the beautiful, wide stretches along the river and riding the old railroad grade. I could just re-ride this trail again and again. Greenery and lots of wildlife, a wonderful trail.

A must see is the London Tract Baptist Meeting House, circa 1729. During our visit, this was open to tour and contained much information on the local history and wildlife, and offered special programs for all to enjoy. The Meeting House still contains the Elder Church Bench trimmed in red velvet. Outside is a cemetery with stones dating back to the early 1700's. And try to guess what the stone steps are at the center of the intersection of the roads in front of the Meeting House. They form an old mounting step for riders and carriages. Although it must have been commonplace in its time, this was the first of its kind that I had seen.

## HISTORICAL INFORMATION:
In the late 1600's, William Penn purchased land, which included the preserve, from Lenni Lenape Chief Kekelappen. The chief lived in Opasiskunk, which was a sizable

Indian village. Previous archeological research and site remnants once provided proof of these early inhabitants, however, years of flooding have erased any visible evidence.

There are old dwellings of early settlers from the 18th and 19th centuries still standing today. There is the Yeatman Mill House, believed to be the area's oldest home, which can be seen in the preserve. There is also the London Tract Baptist Meetinghouse, built in 1729, which can be viewed at London Tract and Sharpless Roads. Adjacent to the London Tract Baptist Meetinghouse is an interesting graveyard where many of the area's early residents were laid to rest. A man by the name of Dr. Eaton is buried in the cemetery; his stone home with double doors still stands and can be viewed across from the graveyard.

Other areas of interest include the tri-state marker where Maryland, Pennsylvania, and Delaware meet, along with the various historical markers that are throughout the preserve.

The preserve land was donated from the DuPont family in the early 1980's with the intent to conserve the plants, land, and wildlife in their natural form. Also, nearby (just over the Maryland border) there is the Fair Hill equestrian trails and acreage that was also formerly owned by the DuPont family. Fair Hill is a wonderful, large place to ride. Fox hunting was a favorite pastime of William DuPont, who built bridges, tunnels, and fences to keep the foxes and hounds from getting onto the nearby highways at the Fair Hill estate. Riders travel over these bridges and through these tunnels while riding at Fair Hill.

## NEARBY ATTRACTIONS:
- Brandywine Battlefield, Chadds Ford (610) 459-3342, website: www.thebrandywine.com
- Longwood Gardens (also a gift from the DuPont family), Kennett Square (610) 388-1000. Longwood Gardens is a horticultural wonder, and on my list of nearby must see places. It is a destination for all seasons, especially spring at Longwood and Christmas at Longwood with the light display and the rainbow of illuminated fountains. Contact (610) 388-1000, or their website at www.longwoodgardens.org.
- There are also lots of nearby restaurants and interesting old inns, many of which the above websites have links to.

## NEARBY:
- Fair Hill Natural Resources Management Area, MD. 5,500 acres and 70 miles of multi-use trails including equestrian trails (410) 398-1246. Stalls and campsites are available, so equestrians can camp and ride at Fair Hill and also trailer to nearby White Clay.

**NEARBY STABLES:**
- Gateway Stables (training, trail rides, camps, and boarding, *Coggins required*), Kennett Square (610) 444-9928, website: www.gateway.com
- Fair Hill Stables (trail rides, riding lessons, and summer camp), Fair Hill State Park, MD (410) 620-3883

**NEARBY B&B AND STABLES:**
- Tailwinds Farm (B&B and horse stabling near Fair Hill State Park), MD (410) 658-8187
- Bed & Breakfast at Walnut Hill (with stabling nearby), Kennett Square (610) 444-3703

**NEARBY AND SURROUNDING AREA VET SERVICES:**
- Brandywine Veterinary Clinic, Coatesville (610) 383-1866
- New Bolton (24-hour emergency), Kennett Square (610) 444-5800
- Complete Equine Health Service, Coatesville (610) 466-0501
- Unionville Equine Center, Oxford (610) 932-6800

**NEARBY FARRIERS:**
- E. Scheckner, Christiana (717) 529-6056
- Chester County Farrier Assoc., Unionville (610) 347-2445

# 12.  Blue Marsh Lake
# U.S. Army Corps of Engineers

**Lasting Impression:**  Blue Marsh has some great trails, lots of riding, and is a popular multi-use destination offering a variety of terrain and scenery.  This is one of our favorite late fall or winter destinations, as Blue Marsh has several high points with awesome views of Blue Marsh Lake and the surrounding countryside when the leaves are off the trees.

**Location:**  Blue Marsh Lake is situated northwest of Reading near the town of Bernville, Berks County.

**Length:**  Over 6,100 acres and about 30 miles of equestrian and multi-use trails

**Level of Difficulty:**  Mostly easy to moderate but there are some sections that are more challenging or difficult due to steep terrain, "on the edge" riding, or busy road and bridge crossings.

**Terrain:**  Varied terrain, including flat sections, uphill climbs, wooded areas, open fields, dirt and grass surfaces

**Horse Camping:**  No

**Non-horse Camping:**  No

**Maps and Info:**  Blue Marsh Lake, U.S. Army Corps of Engineers, 1268 Palisades Drive, Leesport, PA   19533, (610) 376- 6337.  The Stilling Basin parking lot did have a good stock of maps and there are places for maps at other locations, but it may be best to call ahead for a map as they could be depleted. The map is extremely helpful, reflecting the numbered posts that are placed every mile.  The map also helps to guide where to park, when it is necessary to cross a major bridge or road, and to assist in determining the length and direction of trail to ride on.  Riders can choose what they are comfortable with.  Some sections of the trail do require crossing bridges that are on busy roads.  If preferred, these can be avoided by choosing trails on the map that do not cross those bridges or by backtracking.

**Activities:**  Boating, Hiking, Picnicking, Swimming, Biking, Horseback Riding Trails, Hunting (during season), and X-C Skiing

**Fees for Trail Use:**  None

**Permits for Trail Use:**  None; except for organized group activities.   Organized groups should contact the office for more information.

**Comfort Station:**  Yes, including at the Stilling Basin and the (Old) Church Road lot (see the map)

**DIRECTIONS:**

There are a few parking lots that are recommended for trailer parking.  One is at the intersection of PA Route 183 and Church Road *(Old Church Road and Church Road seem to be the same road.  On the map it says Church Road, however, some of the signs say Old Church Road)*, one off of Church Road on Lake Road, another off of Brownsville Road (which becomes Rebers Bridge Road) on Justa Road, and one on Highland Road. Except for the Highland lot, these are marked with a "P" on the Blue Marsh Lake Trail System map.

To reach the Church Road lot, proceed as follows: From I-78, at Strausstown, take PA Route 183 south for 9 miles (after 4 miles on Route 183, come to a stop sign, make a left, continue on Route 183 south until you have traveled a total of 9 miles) to the intersection with Church Road. Make a right on Church Road. Parking is on the left and there is a sign that says Church Road parking area. The lot at first appears to be small but is a medium sized lot offering some pull-through and turn around room. It can hold several 2-horse trailers, assuming it is not crowded with other trail users. There are brown posts with arrows to mark the trails. The Church Road lot is one of our preferred lots for parking, as we feel this is the easiest and most accessible lot if parking room is available. We also feel it is the best lot for very large rigs.

Additional parking is further down Church Road. Proceed down Church Road for approximately .8 miles. Approach slowly as the turn is sudden. Make a left on Lake Road. Follow Lake Road to the end; parking is on the left side. This is a small to medium sized pull-through loop at the end of a dead end road. It looks smaller than it is and can actually hold several rigs. We would not suggest this lot for very large rigs, as it could be tight if other vehicles are already parked there. This is also one of our favored lots as it is in a remote setting, and allows about an extra hour of nice riding if traveling the north loop.

Another lot for parking is the Justa Road lot, which can be seen on the map. Pass the two above lots, continue on Church Road for a few miles. (Church Road travels into N. Heidelberg Road before making the left.) Make a left on Milestone Road. Travel on Milestone until it intersects with Brownsville Road; make or bear left. Proceed about 2 miles and begin to look for a sharp left which is Justa Road. Travel on Justa Road, which is a small, windy road, for about a mile. There is a pull-through lot on left. It is not large but several 2-horse trailers or a few bigger rigs can fit. It is in a nice country setting away from the main roads. (Note: After I visited this trail system, I was informed that the Justa Road lot, which is on State Gamelands, may be closed to equestrians in the future. Please check with the State Gamelands prior to choosing this lot.)

The Highland lot can be accessed by continuing on Brownsville Road past Justa Road. Make a sudden left onto Highland. Some of these lefts may be too sharp. If so, travel further down Brownsville Road, turn around, and approach from the other direction (on one turn, we needed to do that). Highland did have a street sign, but looked like the wrong road during our visit, as it was narrow and very bumpy. To access the Highland lot, travel .6 miles (feels like much more than .6 miles on this patchwork road). You will come to where you can continue straight or go right. There are signs saying "No Outlet", which we found confusing. At these signs, do NOT turn right. Continue straight; go up the hill on the narrow road. Just after the small hill, you will see a yellow gate and the parking lot on the right. It is a small sized lot that can fit a few 2-horse trailers.

This drive on Highland Road is interesting as it passes the historical Dry Road Farm and the old log cabins, which are common to the Blue Marsh area. Although we found the Highland lot sufficient for 2-horse standard rigs, due to the tight entrance and narrow road, we would not use this lot for large rigs.

## THE TRAILS:

The Blue Marsh equestrian and multi-use trails circle around Blue Marsh Lake. With the exclusion of the Nature Trails, horses are allowed on all trails at Blue Marsh Lake. Due to safety reasons, riders are cautioned to avoid or bypass foot bridges along the trail. Usually, riders can see a clear path around these bridges clueing riders where the bypass is. The park also warns that bridges may be slippery when wet.

Water is throughout the park, however, purity is not tested. Therefore, drinking from the streams or lake is not recommended. Bring your own; horses will likely need it due to the many climbs.

The setting of Blue Marsh is in a rural countryside with lots of rolling fields, old farmsteads, and historical homes nestled in pretty country settings. It is possible to ride the whole loop in one day, however, the full circle is a very long ride and horses need to be fit. Riders can ride sections of the trail or backtrack; riding both directions of the trail offers different perspectives of the scenery. We prefer to ride clockwise and climb the steeper sections (in this order: markers #15, #16, #17, #18, to #19) heading toward the ski area (by marker #18), cross the bridge, and return via the flat area paralleling Route 183. This allows the horses to cool down on their return ride, and we feel it is easier to ascend this section than to descend. To complete the full circle or loops of the trail, riders must cross busy roads and bridges. There is a large bridge crossing between milepost number #18 and #19 near the ski area. We chose to cross the bridge between markers #18 and #19 as that bridge links some really nice sections of the trail. Fortunately, the bridge has a very wide shoulder lane and we felt comfortable crossing. (In the winter, the ski area got our horses' attention as snow tubers were slowly moving uphill on these huge tubes via the lift that is parallel to the trail. They couldn't quite figure that out!)

There is an even busier crossing on Route 183 between mileposts #24 and #25 at Mt. Pleasant. Riders are directed not to take the trail up the small hill, but to travel a short section along the shoulder of the road on the north end of the bridge to avoid the metal guardrail where the trail previously passed. There are signs directing equestrians. I prefer to avoid this bridge crossing, as there is a lot of fast moving traffic. Even with the wide shoulder, care and judgment should be exercised before choosing to ride over this heavily traveled bridge. However, riding this link is not necessary to enjoy several hours of riding on the trails at Blue Marsh.

There are brown mileposts with white arrow markers along the way to guide users. The trails are very well marked and the markers correspond with the map. Trail markers can often be seen from the road, giving a point of reference as you approach the area. The trails vary from open areas to wooded stretches, from flat to hilly to steep climbs. Although the nature trails are for pedestrian use only, the equestrian trails offer many picturesque views, including that of the lake. These trails, especially the steep sections, are popular with mountain bikers. Riders need to stay alert for the approach of fast traveling bikes. Starting at the Stilling Basin and heading along in a clockwise direction, the south and west sections of the trail system are more hilly than the northern and eastern sections. However, there is a very challenging, lofty section between markers #17 and #18 at the northern most end of the park.

We like many sections of the Blue Marsh trail system. One of our favorites is the stretch from marker #18, near the ski area, to marker #16 due to the secluded, wooded trails and incredible views that can be fully appreciated when the foliage is off the trees. However, this is a steeper section of the trail system that, for a short distance, travels somewhat close to the edge, which may not suit riders who have a fear of heights. (There was one short section where I did move along quickly, not looking down.) But still, I found the panoramic vistas in this section too beautiful to miss.

Call ahead to check for special equestrian, biking, or other events which might affect trail usage. Maps can also be obtained at this time.

## HISTORICAL INFORMATION:
In the early 1950's, studies were made to resolve the problem of flooding in Pennsylvania that had resulted in the loss of lives and property. It was concluded that the building of dams was needed, in strategic areas along the arteries of the Delaware River, to control the waters and prevent destruction in the future. One of these dams was built at Blue Marsh Lake benefiting Pottstown, Conshohocken, Reading, and some Philadelphia areas which experienced flooding prior to the erection of the dam. In the 1970's, the U.S. Army Corps of Engineers developed Blue Marsh Lake for water regulation, quality control, a reservoir source, and for recreation. In 1979, the recreation areas were opened to the public.

I would like to express my gratitude to Ranger Roland Zitzman for thoughtfully sharing his input and information on Blue Marsh. Ranger Zitzman has a wealth of knowledge regarding the Blue Marsh trail system.

## NEARBY PLACES OF INTEREST:

Prior to the dam, The Gruber Wagon Works was located near Mt. Pleasant. Operating from 1882 until the 1950's, the Wagon Works built wagons and was unique in that it still stood undisturbed and in good condition. It was decided the large building should be saved and the U.S. Army Corps of Engineers relocated the structure a few miles from its original site. The Federal Government later donated the Wagon Works to Berks County.

## NEARBY STABLING, STAY-OVERS, AND CAMPING:

- Mountain Springs Campground (boarding, overnight stabling, and camping), Shartlesville (610) 488-7175
- Windy Ridge Farm (B&B, overnight stabling, feed, hay, and trailer parking, just off I-78), Bethel (717) 933-5888
- Blue Marsh Stables (boarding, overnight stabling, and possible trailer parking), Robesonia (610) 488-7245

## NEARBY VET SERVICES:

- A. Worell, Leesport (610) 916-6220
- Willow Creek Animal Hospital, Reading (610) 378-0192

## NEARBY AND SURROUNDING AREA FARRIERS:

- G. Geesaman, Vinemont (near Reinholds) (610) 678-3099
- J. Strunk, CF, Fredericksburg (717) 649-0806

# 13. The Central Park Equestrian Trail System Lancaster County Parks

**Lasting Impression:** A pleasant, leisurely ride in a beautifully landscaped park.

**Location:** The Central Park Equestrian Trail System is located in southeast Pennsylvania in Lancaster County.

**Length:** The Central Park County Park contains over 500 acres of land. There are about 6 miles of trails to ride. Although this is not a long trail system, we consider this to be well worth the trip for both its beauty and its convenient access to the city of Lancaster and other local attractions. This trail can be combined with a visit to nearby Susquehannock State Park.

**Level of Difficulty:** Easy, but horses need to be comfortable with other park activity

**Terrain:** The terrain is gentle and flat, some rolling hills

**Horse Camping:** No. We stayed at the nearby Foxfield Farm (see below) and trailered to this trail.

**Non-horse Camping:** Yes, tent camping (primitive)

**Maps and Info:** Lancaster County Department of Parks and Recreation, 1052 Rockford Road, Lancaster, PA 17602, (717) 295-3605, e-mail: rangers @co.lancaster.pa.us. Ask for the equestrian map that is in color; it is an easier map to follow and gives a clear layout of the park. Although the trailheads were stocked with other park information, we did not see any equestrian maps at the trailhead. Call in advance for a map to be mailed or stop by the park office to obtain one.

**Activities:** Biking, Horseback Riding Trails, Hiking, Picnicking, X-C Skiing, Athletic Fields, and Other Activities. Hunting is not permitted at The Central Park location but may be permitted on adjoining lands.

**Fees for Trail Use:** None

**Permits for Trail Use:** None, however, a permit may be required for the unloading of horse trailers in certain grassy areas. Check with the office prior to arrival. The folks at the office were very helpful, and sounded very enthusiastic about sharing information on their equestrian trails and receiving the feedback from trail users.

**Comfort Station:** Yes, there is a comfort station behind the ball fields and at other various locations within the park. Also, water is available. You can fill a container from the hydrants by the ball field, but it is quite a walk to the equestrian lot. It is easier to bring water for the horses.

**DIRECTIONS:**

Take Route 222 north from the town of Willow Street. See the signs to the golf course. Make a right on Golf Road. Go a short distance and see the ball fields to your left. The parking area is on the right, opposite the athletic fields, just past Exhibit Farm Road. There is a sign that says trail parking, along with marked pointing to the direction of the trail. The lot is a large, open, roomy lot with ample room to pull through, space for large rigs, or group of rigs.

There are a few trail loops heading out from the lot; all are marked. Behind the lot, in the direction away from Golf Road, is the Conestoga Trail System that travels down Exhibit Farm Road, around the farm fields, past large sections of native wildflowers, and over a wide, mowed path meandering along the Mill Creek. (Do not confuse this with the Mill Creek Trail and the Wildflower Trail on the other side of the Mill Creek; they are closed to horses. There are signs indicating where equestrians are and are not permitted.) The other trailheads are opposite the lot in the direction of the ball fields and are easy to find and follow, as there are markers at the beginning and throughout the trail network.

**THE TRAILS:**
There are several trail systems within Central Park. Each are marked with a different color blaze: Mill Creek- yellow, Kinglet Trail and Scout Trail- white, Conestoga Valley Association Trail- blue, Conestoga Trail System- orange, and the Oak Trail- red. The trails offer a leisurely ride through a variety of woodlands, open fields, streams, and park settings of manicured lawns, wildflowers, and wildlife. Owls often visit the Kinglet Trail and have frequently been seen at the onset of dusk. The map indicates the permitted trail use for each trail system. Horseback riding and biking are permitted on many of the trails but are prohibited in the Mill Creek Natural Area, on the Wildflower Trail, and in the Kiwanis area.

All we could say after visiting this park was WOW! What a groomed, clean, beautiful park. However, if your preference is a several hour wilderness ride, this may not be the trail for you. But, if you would like a delightful, leisurely, few hour trail ride through an attractive park, you should enjoy this one. Do visit on a horse that is acclimated to other activity, as this is a popular destination for many different types of park activity.

Lancaster County Park has done an excellent job of establishing something for everyone, and this accommodating park gives the visitor the feeling that the park took special care to make each user feel welcome. Certain sections of the park are so meticulously manicured and beautifully landscaped that it reminded us of our rides at the Biltmore Estate (Asheville, NC) and the Rockefeller State Park Preserve (Tarrytown, NY) trails. The paths are wide and mowed throughout. Sections pass garden plots planted by nearby Lancaster residents who maintain them. This park must be wonderful to see in the spring due to the many ornamental trees throughout the park. Many of these trees have been donated and have plaques indicating whom they are dedicated to or in memory of.

There are several stretches that travel along or within view of the park or nearby local roads. The trail is not on the shoulder per se, but rather travels along a wide, mowed grass stretch of a few lanes width. We visited on a Saturday in early September, and the park and roads were not busy. But due to the beauty of the park and the park offering something for everyone, it is likely that the park does get a lot of use.

The trails circle in various loops around the ball fields, tennis courts, the skate park, and other activity areas. Even though they were a distance from us, our horses couldn't figure what to make of the skateboards. Although, the horses didn't seem to mind them, they did hold their attention. Many paths have lines of trees or tall cedar plantings to offer a smart and scenic buffer between other user areas. Where there isn't a separation, the trail is usually wide in width with plenty of room. The area toward Mill Creek, behind the parking lot in the direction away from the road, offers a retreat from the rest of the park's activities. Since horses do need to be comfortable with multiple park activities, this section is a nice area to relax your horse beforehand and ascertain whether he is quiet and responsive before heading to the busier sections of the trail in the park's main area. Galloping is prohibited on the trails. For the safety and consideration of others, all horses should be kept under control at all times. All droppings in the parking area should be cleaned up.

The trail system behind the parking lot, the section of the Conestoga Trail system traveling along the Mill Creek tract and the adjoining natural flower meadows, was our favorite. We only encountered two bicyclists and, except for the multitudes of curious deer, had this section of the trail system totally to ourselves. It was so quiet and peaceful that a flock of ducks taking off from the river momentarily startled our horses. (If they could only spook in place like that more often!) We also enjoyed The City View trail that offers a great vista of Lancaster City. This park demonstrates how nice, green sections can successfully be established within close proximity to heavily populated urban areas.

Near the Conestoga Section of the Central Park trail system is the Rock Ford Plantation, former home of George Washington's Adjutant General, along with a covered bridge and an American Indian burial site. The Oak Trail was once a landfill but now has returned to a state of natural beauty.

From our first conversation with the ranger's office, to the clearly marked parking areas and trails, this trail system was a totally positive experience. Thanks to Misty Spotts for telling us about the equestrian trails in this park; we were not aware of them. And also thank you to Rachael Wagoner (see photo below), Eric Lukacs, and the other Lancaster County Park personnel for providing information and making us feel welcome.

## HISTORICAL INFORMATION:
Lancaster is known for its rolling countryside of Amish farms, but Lancaster also has many other attractions including its County Parks. To preserve natural areas, the county began acquiring park land in the 1960's. Various parcels were also

contributed by individuals as early as 1903. There is much history to be seen while visiting the parks. Central Park is where Robert Fulton tested the paddlewheel boat on the Conestoga River, and where an ancient Indian burial ground was discovered in 1979. The Environmental Center, in a restored 1800's bank barn, displays some of the artifacts found at this discovery, along with providing other area information. The Kiwanis area in Central Park includes a restored covered bridge for visitors to view.

The County administers eight parks consisting of over 2,000 acres. Six of these permit horseback riding but, at this writing, all do not have marked and mapped trails or equestrian parking. The parks that indicate riding is permitted are Speedwell Forge County Park, Conewago Recreation Trail, Central Park, Lancaster Junction Recreation Trail, Money Rocks County Park, and Chickies Rock Park. The Conewago Recreation Trail and the Money Rocks County Park are covered in other chapters. We did not visit the Speedwell Forge County Park, Chickies Rock, or the Lancaster Junction Trail. The Speedwell Forge County Park is supposed to be a good riding trail system, but there isn't an equestrian map or designated area for horse trailer parking. We were told, though, that there are locations where smaller rigs (2-horse trailers) could pull off and park. Chickies Rock and the Lancaster Junction Trail have shorter equestrian trail systems and are not covered in detail in this book. We were also informed that equestrian maps were not yet available for Chickies Rock. Expectations are that Chickies Rock, which has some very pretty sections, may eventually be linked with other trails resulting in a nice, long ride. This is a trail to watch. With the ongoing improvements and expansions of the Lancaster County Park trail systems, do inquire with the office for updates. Considering the excellent work done on the Central Park system and other Lancaster County Parks, it is likely that these other parks will also have positive developments and additional information available in the near future. This chapter covers the Central Park trail which was recommended due to its being a marked trail, having plenty of parking, and the availability of an equestrian map.

## NEARBY:
- Historic City of Lancaster (with a variety of historical structures, dining attractions, and other areas of interest)
- Pennsylvania Dutch Countryside and Amish farms
- Susquehannock State Park equestrian trails is a short driving distance
- Numerous other local attractions including shopping outlets, PA Dutch cooking, antiques, and Amish farm stands

## NEARBY AND SURROUNDING AREA STABLES:
- Foxfield Farm (feed, hay, overnight stabling, and trailer parking), Lancaster (717) 484-2250. We stayed at this location and found it convenient, clean, and accommodating along with meeting some nice, friendly folks.

- Windswept Stabling (feed, hay, overnight stabling, and trailer parking), Columbia (717) 684-3975. We did not have the opportunity to visit this stable, but based on phone conversations with the helpful people at Windswept, it seemed like a good place to stay while riding nearby trails.
- Wendell Jones Stable (boarding, lessons, and training), Lancaster (717) 872-5885

## NEARBY AND SURROUNDING AREA VET SERVICES:
- H. Fortna, Ephrata (717) 733-1078
- J. Edelson, Manheim (717) 665-7626
- Dr. Van Dyke, Churchtown (717) 445-7978

## NEARBY AND SURROUNDING AREA FARRIERS:
- E. Scheckner, Christiana (717) 529-6056
- G. Geesaman, Vinemont (near Reinholds) (610) 678-3099

# 14. Money Rocks
# Lancaster County Parks

**Lasting Impression:** Enjoy the great view high above the Lancaster County Countryside!

**Location:** Money Rocks is located in Narvon, southeast Pennsylvania near the eastern border of Lancaster County.

**Length:** Money Rocks is in the early development stage. The park consists of 300 acres but feels much larger due to the additional woodlands surrounding it. We did not find an official equestrian mileage estimate, probably due to it being a recently acquired County Park and to there being many trails within and adjoining the County Park. Our estimate of the trail system within Money Rocks is a few miles plus additional trails in the bordering areas. We rode about 4 hours and did not cover all the trails. Although Money Rocks County Park is not large, the adjoining areas combined provide up to several hours of riding. Within the park, horses are permitted in all areas except where posted otherwise or areas of soft soil vulnerable to erosion. Adjoining Money Rocks is the Narvon Rail-Trail, which is almost 5 miles in length. Portions of this rail-trail are already very nice with a good surface. But, as a whole, this rail-trail system is in the proposed state and is not yet a finished, official trail. (After the above was written, I learned an additional 450 acres has been acquired by the park!)

**Level of Difficulty:** Easy to difficult

**Terrain:** The terrain is varied, from easy flat wooded trails and railroad grades, to very rocky stretches, and some steep climbs. There are numerous trails throughout the mountainside. Of the ones we rode, we did find some very challenging trails but we did not find any that were impassable.

**Horse Camping:** No

**Non-horse Camping:** No

**Maps and Info:** Lancaster County Department of Parks and Recreation, 1052 Rockford Road, Lancaster, PA 17602, (717) 295-3605, e-mail: rangers @co.lancaster.pa.us. We did not see the equestrian maps at the trailhead, so request a map be mailed prior to visiting. A map is available, but it is not comprehensive nor does it cover the many loops of trails that have been developed over the years.

**Activities:** Biking, Hiking, and Horseback Riding Trails. Hunting is permitted at Money Rocks during season. Information can be obtained from the Lancaster County Parks office.

**Fees for Trail Use:** None

**Permits for Trail Use:** None

**Comfort Station:** No

## DIRECTIONS:

Take Route 322. Midway between Honey Brook and Blue Ball, on Route 322, look for Narvon Road. Take Narvon Road south for about a mile to the top of the Welsh Mountain. The lot is on the right side and there is a sign. The lot is a small to medium sized attractive lot, however, this lot fills up and may be difficult for equestrians to access or turn around. We arrived early on a sunny Sunday in October and, at first, had the lot to ourselves. We had our large living quarter rig and had barely enough room to turn around; but a few 2-horse trailers could fit. There is not enough room for groups or several rigs. In a short period of time, this lot completely filled up. Since there is no separate designated parking area for equestrians, equestrians may be blocked from maneuvering around the lot. Visit this lot early in the day or during off peak times in order to have sufficient space, and back in for easy exiting. There are tie areas that are for the local Amish buggies which horses can be tied to while tacking up.

## THE TRAILS:

The Lancaster County Parks has only managed Money Rocks for a short time, so improvements are still being made. The paved parking area is a recent addition. The Money Rocks land and overlook have been a long time favorite of locals. Visit on a Sunday, and you will see large groups of Amish and Mennonite boys, girls, and young couples walking the trails and taking in the view. Often, the couples pack picnic lunches for their Sunday outing. On the trail, we encountered many of these friendly folks. Residing near this trail system is my editor, Connie Bloss. Connie has been riding these trails for years on her favorite Tennessee Walking Horse, General. John is also (originally) from this area and, as a teenager, he used to lead trail rides from a nearby campground. As an adult, he has continued to enjoy and explore this mountainside. He was very happy to hear it is Lancaster County's intention to keep it open to equestrians.

The trails within Money Rocks County Park are wooded, dirt and rock trails. Except for the short entrance to the north trail to travel below the overlook, we found the trails to be generally wide. New Holland Water Authority, townships, and private interests own adjoining lands. We were told that, except for the private land and sections posted or indicating otherwise, equestrians can ride many of the adjoining trails. There are some natural lands that are both posted and fenced with a wire, and some are monitored for trespassers. Do not cross these.

Within this trail system, the terrain can vary from easy, to moderate, to rugged or difficult, depending on which trail you choose to ride. The northern trails, other than the old railroad path, are steeper. The southern section, accessed by traveling out from the lot and making a left at the fork, is not as steep. The southern section varies from easy, level paths of mostly dirt to some very rocky but passable sections. With a little scouting around, one can find nice, leisurely trails without a lot of rocks.

The trail heads out from the north end of the lot. There is a fork in the trail with a sign to the Money Rocks overlook and a sign for Cockscomb. To reach the overlook and to head north, follow the sign to the Money Rocks vista. As you travel in this direction, there will be a somewhat narrow trail veering off to the right. After visiting the overlook, this will be the trail to return to in order to access the north side of the mountain. To travel to the overlook, continue straight. You can ride to the base of the Money Rocks overlook, have a co-rider hold your horse, and walk to the top to enjoy a view of the valley below. The Money Rocks overlook is a must see with a wonderful vista of the surrounding Lancaster County countryside and farmlands. Do bring your camera. To continue on the north trail, backtrack the short distance to the side trail mentioned above, and follow the path, which travels below the Money Rocks cliffs. To return to the south loop, travel back to the sign at the fork, take the Cockscomb route, and follow that trail along the top and south side of the mountain.

The trail that travels down below the Money Rocks vista has a significant slope and some very rocky patches. But when taken slow, we found it navigable. There is dirt between the rocks for the horses to pick through but horses need to be shod and comfortable with rocky terrain. As you pass the overlook, note the rock wall below the vista. This is a scenic and striking contrast against the landscape. The trail continues down the north side of the Welsh Mountain along a ridge trail with great views of the valley below. This is not a narrow, little cattle path on the edge (I don't like those); rather the lane widens and is buffered by a growth of trees along the slope. From this section, there are many splits in the trail heading in different directions. Blue blazes mark sections of the County Park trail. Since some trails travel out of the park's borders and many branch off of the main route, the markers will not always be present. It is easy to venture off. From this side of the mountain, you can descend down to an old railroad grade, the Narvon Trail, which parallels the north side of the Welsh Mountain. The rail-trail is mostly a gentle terrain consisting of dirt, small stone, or resurfaced stone dust. During our ride, we rode sections of the rail-trail then returned to the top of the mountain via a steep trail to the left. This trail was the rockiest we had encountered. Before ascending this trail, you can see it is challenging. For this stretch, horses need to be fit and at ease with a rough and rugged terrain. Riders may prefer to look for one of the alternatives further down the rail-trail or possibly backtrack. If riders and their horses are acclimated to tough mountain terrain, they may not have a problem with this. We did find it similar to other mountain terrain that we have encountered, and found it passable. Once at the top of the mountain, this trail levels off and has less or little rocks. At the top of the mountain, there are numerous other trails heading out in all directions.

There are some really nice trails on the south side of the mountain, which are relaxing and leisurely. At the time of our visit, there were not a lot of markings, so it can be easy to travel in loops and become disoriented. There are paths everywhere. We meandered throughout the network of trails (sometimes in circles) and ultimately returned to the lot. If you have a GPS, bring it. There is one long stretch that parallels the south side of the ridge. Using that as a reference, the parking area can be accessed at its eastern end. While traveling on the south side of the Welsh Mountain, be sure to look for the ruins of old homesteads of the original settlers along the mountainside.

As you travel from trail to trail on the south side, the condition and maintenance of the trail can greatly differ depending on whether the trail is gated and if unauthorized users can have access. The Money Rocks County Park land does have wire gates across the entrance to the trail to prevent unauthorized users from accessing the trails, littering, etc. We learned what a positive difference the gates can make to preserve the natural environment of the trails.

While traveling along the trails, stay alert for four wheelers. They are not permitted within the County Park, but they do travel in adjoining lands and sometimes illegally within the park.

## HISTORICAL INFORMATION:
Money Rocks obtained its name from the legend that local farmers, during the Civil War and/or the Revolutionary War period, hid their money in the rocks to protect it from the town raids. The Money Rocks County Park includes the old Narvon Clay Mine. Many of the trails were formerly logging and mining roads. In the 1980's and 1990's, there was much speculation as to what would become of the land. Fortunately, Lancaster County Parks acquired the property and preserved the park for all to enjoy. Many thanks to Lancaster County Parks, the New Holland Water Authority, Ranger Rachael Wagoner who rode with us and personally showed us the trails, and to the maintenance crew of Steve Booth and associates.

## NEARBY:
- Historic City of Lancaster
- Pennsylvania Dutch countryside and Amish farms

## NEARBY VET SERVICES:
- H. Fortna, Ephrata (717) 733-1078
- Dr. Van Dyke, Churchtown (717) 445-7978

## NEARBY AND SURROUNDING AREA FARRIERS:
- Alvin Beiler, Kinzers (717) 354-2825, cell (717) 468-0275
- E. Scheckner, Christiana (717) 529-6056

# 15. The Conewago Recreation Trail
# Lancaster County Parks
# (Rail-to-Trail)

**Lasting Impression:** A nice, easy, enjoyable ride through the Pennsylvania Dutch Countryside of Lancaster County.

**Location:** The trail is in Lancaster County beginning on Route 230 just northwest of Elizabethtown. The trail travels from Lancaster County to Lebanon County.

**Length:** The Conewago Recreation Trail is 5 miles (one way) in length and currently is in the process of being connected with the Lebanon Valley Rail-Trail. When completed, the Conewago Recreation Trail and the connecting trail to the Lebanon Valley Rail-Trail will total 10 miles, plus the 5+ additional miles of riding on the Lebanon Valley Rail-Trail for a grand total of 15+ (30+ round trip) miles to ride.

**Level of Difficulty:** Easy

**Terrain:** The terrain is mainly cinder. The trail is flat, gentle, and travels through wooded and open stretches.

**Horse Camping:** No

**Non-horse Camping:** No

**Maps and Info:** The Lancaster County Department of Parks and Recreation manages the trail. Maps and info can be obtained at Lancaster County Department of Parks and Recreation, 1050 Rockford Road, Lancaster, PA 17602-4624, (717) 299-8215, e-mail: rangers@co.lancaster.pa.us. Details can also be obtained from the PA Rails-to-Trails Conservancy, (717) 238-1717, www.railtrails.org.

**Activities:** Hiking, Biking, Horseback Riding Trails, Snowmobiling, and X-C Skiing. Hunting is not listed as a trail use, but use caution as adjoining areas may have hunting during season.

**Fees for Trail Use:** None

**Permits for Trail Use:** None

**Comfort Station:** Yes, there is a portajohn at the trailhead

**DIRECTIONS:**

In the northwest section of Lancaster County is the Conewago Recreation Trail, which meets with the Lebanon Valley Rail-Trail. To reach this trail system, follow Route 283 to the Elizabethtown exit, take Route 743 south for about 1 mile and look for signs to Route 230. Make a right on Route 230; heading west on Route 230 for 1 to 2 miles. Parking is on the right across from the Conewago Industrial Park.

Or take Route 283 to the Toll House exit (Route 341). Get off the Toll House exit. Follow signs to Route 230 east (Elizabethtown). Travel 3 miles east on Route 230. The lot is on the left (next to a gas station opposite the industrial park). There is a sign that says "Conewago Recreation Trail" and a fenced lot. The lot was recently expanded and modifications were in process during our visit. The lot could fit about 2-3 large rigs or 4-5 standard 2-horse trailers, but other trail users also park at this lot and less room may be available. We took our 50'+ rig in on a Friday when it was not crowded. Although there were other vehicles in the lot, we did not have a problem getting in or getting out.

## THE TRAILS:

The Conewago Recreation Trail is a clearly marked, nicely maintained rail-trail offering a relaxing ride through the Pennsylvania Dutch countryside of Lancaster County. John and I visited this trail on a warm Friday in April when the spring greenery was just coming into bloom. There were a few cars in the lot and some hikers and bikers on the trail. Closer to the lot, the trail looks more heavily used. Further down the trail, we had it mostly to ourselves.

The trailhead is located across from an industrial park. Although the entire trail travels through rural farmland, the actual trailhead is near a busy road. However, there is distance between the road and the parking area. The parking area has a smart new split rail fence bordering the lot that adds a buffer from the road. Other than passing traffic, we found the lot to be quiet and sufficiently secluded. But, it is likely that this trail is well used on weekends and parking may be limited at that time. During our visit, the lot was being expanded and tie rails were being constructed. There were other markers in place indicating additional modifications to be made. We really liked these changes, and very much appreciated the effort Lancaster County and the rail-trail groups were making to accommodate equestrians and make them feel welcome.

The trail is a wide trail, often with grassy borders providing ample room to let other users pass. The trail is linear and flat traveling through old farms, attractive homesteads, rolling fields, meadows, and horse farms. Much of the trail is shaded. The surface is mostly cinder with some dirt and grass covering the cinder in sections. This is an ideal trail for older horses or unconditioned horses due to its gentle grade. There are no rocks on the trail so it is easy on horses' feet and the level terrain is ideal for gaiting or cantering. There is some water along the trail but we found the most accessible place for horses to drink was the river by the trailhead lot. Since there is not a lot of water along the route, bring water in case access becomes restricted or if the water sources are low or poor in quality.

The trail is canopied with bordering trees and woods offering shade in the warm weather. As you travel away from the lot, the trail becomes more rural. The

67

surrounding countryside is wonderful with lots of farms, green pastures, horses, and other interesting livestock to be seen. There are quite a few friendly llamas along the way and one farm had the largest assortment of colorful, attractive, and well groomed llamas that we have ever seen. They were adorable! The friendly, but very curious, herds ran to their fence line to check us out as we passed.

There are a few short, wide bridge crossings with concrete surfaces and railings, and some local road crossings. There is one large overhead bridge to cross under with lots of room to pass below. We did not find any of these to be an obstacle and the trail was very comfortable to ride.

There are half mile posts along the trail, and the path is a cinch to follow and gauge. Just go straight! At the time of our visit, only 5 to 6 miles were completed but plans are for the trail to link with the Lebanon Valley Rail-Trail which, with the link and the Lebanon Valley Rail-Trail system included, will result in a 15+ mile trail system. However, a round trip on just the Conewago portion offers 10 miles of riding; and this is a very nice trail, well worth traveling to. During our visit, we did check out the planned extension that looked rideable, until we encountered a bridge that was not yet completed and had to turn around. We really enjoyed this trail and look forward to returning to ride the Conewago section, plus the link between the Conewago and Lebanon rail-trails.

Our favorite part of the trail was the section that penetrated through the large rock. The rail-trail travels between rock walls about 2 stories high that surround this portion of the tract. We were amazed at the manual work required in the 1800's to cut this path. Just phenomenal! Also, along the trail are boulder fields that were quite interesting and offered a contrast in scenery. There is evidence of the trail's former use as there are a few piles of old railroad ties along the trail. Also, as you travel through the surrounding area, note the old buildings and bridges made of red stone. The red stone is native to this area.

### HISTORICAL INFORMATION:
The Conewago Recreation Trail path was originally the Cornwall and Lebanon Railroad corridor, which began almost a century of service commencing in the early 1880's. The railroad was constructed to transport iron ore and was competition for the nearby Cornwall Railroad. Ultimately, this rail line was linked with the Pennsylvania Railroad and offered passengers connections to locations throughout the United States. In the very early 1900's, passengers could travel from this remote location in Pennsylvania to New York City in just 7 hours. That was record time in those days of the horse and buggy!

Later, upon the arrival of the interstate highways, the railroad declined. Eventually, sections of the tract were no longer used and by the early 1970's, the last section was closed. The Conewago Recreation Trail was purchased by the Lancaster County Parks Department in the late 1970's. Just recently, efforts resulted in the linkage of the Conewago Recreation Trail and the Lebanon Valley Rail-Trail. Currently, the Lancaster County Department of Parks and Recreation oversees the Conewago Recreation Trail.

## NEARBY ATTRACTIONS:
- State Capital of Harrisburg
- Hershey Park
- Shopping outlets in Hershey and other nearby areas
- There are many diverse restaurants and quaint country inns to dine at in the surrounding area.

## NEARBY AND SURROUNDING AREA STABLES:
- Double D Stables (boarding, breeding, and overnight stabling), Elizabethtown (717) 367-2053, www.double-dstables.com
- Foxfield Farm (feed, hay, overnight stabling, and trailer parking), Lancaster (717) 484-2250
- Triple S Stables & Supplies (miniatures, boarding, and overnight stabling), Lebanon (717) 865-6712

## NEARBY VET SERVICES:
- J. Edelson, Manheim (717) 665-7626
- J. Henderson, Elizabethtown (717) 664-2122

## NEARBY OR SURROUNDING AREA FARRIER:
- G. Geesaman, Vinemont (near Reinholds) (610) 678-3099

# 16. Lebanon Valley Rail-Trail
# Lebanon Valley Rails-to-Trails, Inc.

**Lasting Impression:**  Easy, scenic, leisurely ride through attractive woodlands.

**Location:**  The Lebanon Valley Rail-Trail is in Lebanon County and is in various phases of completion.  When finished, the trail will link the City of Lebanon to the Lancaster County Line and the Conewago Recreation Trail, which travels to Elizabethtown.

**Length:**  At this writing, the completed part of the Lebanon Valley Rail-Trail is 5+ miles in length, 10+ miles round trip.  When completed, from the City of Lebanon (through and including the Conewago Recreation Trail) to Elizabethtown, the trail length is estimated to total 15 miles (possibly up to 19 miles) one way.  Additional trail riding is also available at the Horse-Shoe Trail that intersects with this trail about 2,000 feet south of Colebrook.

**Level of Difficulty:**  The trail is easy but horses need to be comfortable with passing bicyclists, hikers, and joggers.

**Terrain:**  Horses travel on wood chips or grass surface along the side of the rail-trail.  Riders are requested to stay on the wood chip or grass border to prevent erosion.  The center of the trail is cinder which hikers and bikers are permitted to use.  All of the surfaces are flat, gradual, easy, and travel through lots and lots of woods.  Most of the Lebanon Valley Rail-Trail is a ride in the shade; however, the connecting trail to the Conewago Recreation Trail has some open areas.

**Horse Camping:**  No

**Non-horse Camping:**  No

**Maps and Info:**  Lebanon Valley Rails-to-Trails oversees the trail.  Maps and information can be obtained from the Lebanon Valley Rails-to-Trails, Inc., P.O. Box 2043, Cleona, PA 17042.  Lebanon Valley Rails-to-Trails, Inc. is a non-profit organization.  Info also can be obtained from the PA Rails-to-Trails Conservancy, (717) 238-1717, www.railtrails.org.

**Activities:**  Hiking, Biking, Horseback Riding Trails, and X-C Skiing.  Hunting is not listed as a trail use, but use caution as many adjoining areas, including the State Gamelands, may permit hunting during season.

**Fees for Trail Use:**  None

**Permits for Trail Use:**  None

**Comfort Station:**  We did not see any comfort stations at the time of our visit.  It is possible that they may be added in the future due to ongoing improvements.

## DIRECTIONS:

The trailhead is in Colebrook on Route 117.  Take the PA Turnpike (I-76) to the Lancaster/Lebanon (Mt. Gretna) Exit #266 (old Exit #20).  Travel north on Route

72 to Route 117. Take Route 117 north for about 5 miles until Route 117 intersects with Route 241 (Colebrook Road). The trailhead is at the corner of the intersection of Route 117 and Route 241. The lot is a nice sized lot of gravel and dirt and is medium to large in size with turn around room. There is ample space for a few very large rigs or several standard 2-horse trailers. There is a trailhead sign at the lot and the trail is clearly marked. Maps are usually stocked at the trailhead along with other trail information. Maps are also posted along the trail route. If this lot is full, there are other smaller places to pull off and park off of Route 117 just down the road. Check for signs indicating parking is or is not permitted at these locations. Most of these parking areas had close access to the rail-trail.

## THE TRAILS:

During our visit, several miles of the trail were completed including the section from Colebrook to Cornwall. The central parking lot at Colebrook Road offered a glimpse of what the trail was like before and after the conversion to a multiple-use trail. One side of the road had a single narrow path through the woods and fields. The completed side, much to the credit of the trail's creators, volunteers, and sponsors, is a beautiful, wide trail which should offer plenty of room for many users to pleasantly share and enjoy the trail. The trail itself has a central cinder path for non-equestrian users and wide shoulders of wood chips or grass for equestrians to utilize. This is a popular trail and well used. Riders who prefer more solitude, may prefer to visit on off peak times such as weekdays, warm winter days, late fall, or early spring. Users are requested to stay on the trail, so riders should bring water to provide to their horses before departure and upon return. During our visit, John and I met with a trail maintenance crew who enthusiastically shared their plans for the trail expansion. They were a cross representation of hikers, mountain bikers, and equestrians. The crew explained the reason that horses were not permitted on the cinder surface was due to concerns over erosion. Rather than exclude horses all together, the rails-to-trails sponsors and others went to great lengths and major expense to lay wood chips for equestrians to ride on, so that they too could enjoy this nice rail-trail.

The trail is beautiful, top quality, well marked, and meticulously maintained in a gorgeous setting. It is an easy to follow, easy to ride, gentle grade with lots of mile markers along the route. There are some road and bridge crossings, but we found none to be a drawback.

Between Cornwall and Mt. Gretna, there are many miles of woodland riding. We found it to be an excellent trail to just sit back and soak in the wonderful surroundings. The miles of forest offer shade in the summer, colorful foliage in the fall, and a weather buffer in the winter. As you ride down the trail, one can understand how once, a century ago, passengers delighted as they escaped the heat of the cities to travel through these cool, dense woods on their way to the resort communities of Mt. Gretna. What a wonderful path to travel along, now re-created for all to enjoy. We really enjoyed our visit to this great rail-trail and plan on returning often in the future.

## HISTORICAL INFORMATION:

The Lebanon Valley Rail-Trail was once the Cornwall-Lebanon Railroad built in the 1880's. During the late 1800's and early 1900's, the train was a popular means of travel for bringing tourists and vacationers to the Mt. Gretna resort destination. Eventually, sections of the tract were no longer used and, in the early 1970's, the last section was closed. In 1999, Lebanon Valley Rails-to-Trails, Inc. procured the land and began conversion to a multiple-use trail. The trail was formally dedicated in the fall of 2000.

Much credit for this trail system goes to Lebanon Valley Rails-to-Trails, Inc. They are a non-profit group of volunteers striving toward the goal of converting abandoned old railroad tracts to public, multi-use trails in the Lebanon area and to conserving a piece of railroad history. The supporters of the Lebanon Valley Rails-to-Trails group and the Lebanon Valley Rail-Trail itself consists of volunteers, county officials, corporate benefactors, the Commonwealth, and various local individuals, groups, and organizations. They have done phenomenal work in the establishment, transformation, enhancement, and maintenance of these trails. Many thanks go to all of these contributors. Users and supporters, who would like to show their appreciation and support, can offer their help via volunteer work or monetary contributions to the Lebanon Valley Rails-to-Trails group (see above) to help ensure the future preservation, success, and expansion of this trail system.

## NEARBY AND SURROUNDING AREA STABLES:

- Double D Stables (boarding, breeding, and overnight stabling), Elizabethtown (717) 367-2053, website: www.double-dstables.com
- Foxfield Farm (feed, hay, overnight stabling, and trailer parking), Lancaster (717) 484-2250
- Triple S Stables & Supplies, Lebanon (717) 865-6712

## NEARBY VET SERVICES:

- J. Edelson, Manheim (717) 665-7626
- J. Henderson, Elizabethtown (717) 664-2122

## NEARBY OR SURROUNDING AREA FARRIER:

- G. Geesaman, Vinemont (near Reinholds) (610) 678-3099

# 17. Lehigh Parkway
# Lehigh Valley Parks

**Lasting Impression:** Ride through a covered bridge and along a gorgeous, scenic greenway in Lehigh County.

**Location:** The park is in Lehigh County near Allentown.

**Length:** There are 999 acres and 8 miles of trails. Although this is not a very long trail, it is a very scenic trail and a nice trail for riders who prefer a shorter, easy ride.

**Level of Difficulty:** The trail is easy but horses need to be comfortable with multiple trail users.

**Terrain:** Some flat, some rolling hills, some wooded, some open areas. The surface is mostly stone dust and some paved sections.

**Horse Camping:** No

**Non-horse Camping:** No

**Maps and Info:** Lehigh Valley Park (610) 437-7616, City of Allentown Department of Parks (610) 437-7627 or (610) 437-7628

**Activities:** Hiking, Biking, Horseback Riding Trails, Fishing, Sledding, and Snowmobiling

**Fees for Trail Use:** None

**Permits for Trail Use:** None

**Comfort Station:** Yes, just down the trail near the police station and by the covered bridge

**DIRECTIONS:**
This trail is easy to get to and is just off of major roads. Take I-78 or Route 309 to Exit #55 (Lehigh Valley Hospital) Route 29, which is Cedar Crest Boulevard. Proceed south/west on Route 29, Cedar Crest Boulevard, for .2 miles. At the light, make a left on Fish Hatchery Road. Just after the turn, travel to the bottom of the hill. Trailer parking is in the gravel lot to the right. (Trailer parking is not permitted at the Indian Museum.) The trail starts on the opposite side of the road behind the Indian Museum, opposite the Boots & Saddle Riding Club stables. Horses will need to cross Fish Hatchery Road to meet the trailhead; riders should proceed with caution, as the road can be very busy at times.

**THE TRAILS:**
This trail is in a really pretty setting along the Little Lehigh River with a covered bridge, nature trails, grassy meadows, and the Lenni Lenape Indian Museum. On one side of the river the trail is mostly stone dust, and on the other side of the river there are some paved surfaces. The trail is in a loop around the Little Lehigh

River. The turn in the loop for the return trip is by the railroad tracks and the concrete bridge.

The trail starts out behind the Indian Museum and the Fish Hatchery area. It is very scenic and leisurely, however, there is one section that horses may have difficulty with. Soon after starting out, horses must pass under a large overpass. There is plenty of clearance but the large white arch and columns are huge and horses may need to get used to the appearance of this, as it can appear intimidating. Because the road overhead (Route I-78) is so high, we did not find a lot of overhead noise during our visit. Both sides of the river cross under this overpass. Although each side had a wide trail, we felt the opposite side of the trail (requiring crossing over the river before the bridge) was a bit more horse friendly as there was more visual space traveling under the arches.

There are 4 bridges to choose from that travel to the other side. Two of these are larger road bridges, one with a metal grate surface and one with a paved surface on a concrete foundation. These two bridges, although open to autos, were not heavily traveled during our visit. Closer to the trailhead there is a wooden surface bridge (more like what you see on equestrian trails) which is not open to autos. Additionally, there is the Bogart Covered Bridge, which is closed to autos but open to horses and pedestrians.

Local riders advised us that the trail could be busy with bikes and other users on the weekends during the warmer weather. When we visited on a very warm Saturday in late March, we saw very few bikes, but we did see lots of walkers and joggers. The riders said that during the week they usually have the trails mostly to themselves, even in the warmer weather.

**HISTORICAL INFORMATION:**
In the late 1800's, Rueben Troxell established the trout nursery. In 1909 General Trexler bought the property and, over the next years, expanded the hatchery to 28 ponds yielding 15 tons of trout per year. General Trexler died in the early 1930's. In the late 1940's, the City of Allentown acquired the property and subsequently rented it to sportsmen clubs. Now the Bureau of Parks and Watersheds, City of Allentown, operates the nursery.

Along the trail we met some equestrians and asked if horses were permitted on the paved path, or were they supposed to stay with the gravel surface. These riders informed us that horses were permitted on both the paved and gravel/stone dust terrain as the property, which includes the trail, had a deed clause specifying that equestrians must be permitted to ride the park. How nice!

## NEARBY AND SURROUNDING AREA STABLES:

- Boots & Saddle Riding Club, Inc. (stabling and boarding with direct access to the above trail system), Allentown  (610) 797-2922
- Timberland Acres (lessons and boarding), Walnutport (610) 767-2055, e-mail: elliesqh@yahoo.com
- Edgewood Valley Farms (rodeos, boarding, and possible emergency overnight stabling), Nazareth (610) 759-3340
- FD Koehler Stables Inc., F. Koehler Prop. (overnight stabling, tack shop, boarding, and lessons), Bethlehem (610) 865-0438, 865-5110, 865-0161

## NEARBY VET SERVICES:

- E. Balliet & Associates, Northampton (610) 262-3203
- Quakertown Veterinary Clinic, Quakertown (215) 536-2726, (215) 536-6245

## NEARBY FARRIERS:

- E. Brandner, Northampton (610) 502-0137
- K. Martin, Allentown (610) 791-2375
- D. Brewer (farrier and dentist), Nazareth (610) 759-3340
- B. Gannon, Kunkletown (610) 381-3213

# 18. Stony Creek Rail-Trail
# (aka Stony Valley Railroad Grade)
# Pennsylvania State Gamelands

**Lasting Impression:** Ride a remote, scenic rail-trail with a true wilderness feel.

**Location:** The trail is located mostly in Dauphin and Lebanon Counties, just northeast of Harrisburg, and runs from the Lebanon Reservoir to Ellendale Forge.

**Length:** The Stony Creek rail-trail travels through State Gamelands No. 211 which consists of over 40,000 acres of woodland. There are 22 miles (44 round trip) of trail to ride plus additional miles of riding on the adjoining Horse-Shoe Trail. (See the Horse-Shoe Trail chapter). At this writing, we confirmed with the Game Commission that this rail-trail is expected to remain open to horses subject to seasonal hunting restrictions. However, this is not yet final, so contact and confirm with the Game Commission for details prior to arrival.

**Level of Difficulty:** Easy

**Terrain:** Flat or gradual dirt and cinder trail with lots of shade

**Horse Camping:** No

**Non-horse Camping:** No

**Maps and Info:** For general trail info: Pennsylvania Game Commission, 2001 Elmerton Avenue, Harrisburg, PA 17110-9797, website: www.pgc.state.pa.us, (717) 787-9612. For a State Gameland #211 map, call (717) 783-7507 (small fee). For the PA Rails-to-Trails Conservancy, call (717) 238-1717, website: www.railtrails.org.

**Activities:** Hiking, Biking, Snowmobiling, Horseback Riding Trails (*designated trails only*), X-C Skiing, Fishing, Wheelchair Accessible, and Hunting (during season). Permitted uses may change; verify permitted uses before arrival.

Note: The area is heavily used for hunting and has multiple hunting seasons, including turkey in the spring. If visiting on a Sunday during hunting season, call the above number in advance and confirm that hunting is (still) not permitted on Sundays. The location is attractive for hunting, as there is extensive wildlife in the area including black bear and turkey.

**Fees for Trail Use:** None

**Permits for Trail Use:** None

**Comfort Station:** No

**DIRECTIONS:**
There are two parking lots where equestrians can park, an east and west lot:

East Lot- The east lot is the more remote, larger lot but also requires a very steep climb and a vehicle that can haul on an abrupt grade. The lot can be reached from two directions, but both travel up the mountain. To approach the east lot from the north side of the mountain range, take Route 325 west from Tower City for 1 mile. Make a left on Gold Mine Road. Follow Gold Mine Road 3.9 miles to the parking area. This is a windy, steep approach! There are parking areas on both sides of the road, but the right side has a larger lot. The trailheads are at the back of this lot and on the opposite side of the road.

To approach this same lot from the south side of the mountain range, take I-81 to the Route 72 Lebanon Exit #90 (town of Lickdale). Follow signs to Route 72 north. Take Route 72 north for 3 miles to Route 443. At the junction with Route 443, continue straight on Route 443 east for two miles. Begin to look for the left onto Gold Mine Road. Be careful not to miss it as it is at an odd angle veering to the left. There is a yellow "T" sign on the opposite side of the road indicating the road intersection. Make a left on Gold Mine Road (north). Travel about 2.5 miles on Gold Mine Road. This approach has a windy intense steep climb also! Do not attempt it if you do not have a heavy-duty hauling vehicle. Just after crossing the crest of the mountain and beginning the descent, watch for the State Gameland sign. Make a left at the State Gameland sign to the parking lot. The lot is large with a stone chip, dirt, and grass surface. If you can get them up there, there is plenty of room for groups of rigs. Although long, the lot is somewhat narrow requiring the backing of rigs to maneuver and turn around. We visited this lot with a 2-horse trailer that has an extended tack room and we had no problem. But we would prefer not to bring a very large trailer (i.e., a trailer with living quarters) as there is not enough space to turn around unless we wanted to back in. (Anyway, the climb is too steep for most vehicles with big trailers.) The Stony Creek Rail-Trail heads out from the back of the lot and travels 17 miles to the west lot. On the opposite side of the road, there are a few miles of riding along the rail-trail. Check first with the gameland to ascertain if this entire rail-trail is still open to horses.

West Lot- This lot does not require a steep climb and would be the better choice for rigs that cannot handle such grades. To reach the west lot, take I-81 to Route 322 west. Take Route 322 west to Dauphin and the Route 225 exit. Stay on Route 225 north; at the second right turn onto Elizabeth Avenue (by a bank). Travel about a half-mile, the road bears left. After the road bears left, make a right onto Denison Drive. Take Denison Drive to a stop sign. Make a left on Stony Creek Road. Take Stony Creek Road for about 4 miles and continue to the parking loop as indicated below.

An alternate access to the west lot is from I-81, take Route 322 west to Dauphin. In Dauphin take Route 225, travel one block on Route 225, make a right, follow signs to Stony Creek. This is Stony Creek Road. Travel a few miles to the parking loop at the entrance to the rail-trail.

The parking loop is a small to medium pull-through paved loop with a dirt shoulder and can accommodate several 2-horse trailers or a few large rigs. However, this lot is too small for very large trailers such as those with living quarters. Horse trailers should park here as the next 2 to 3 miles of dirt road after the loop parking lot is bumpy, too narrow for hauling, and does not have a lot that can accommodate horse trailers. Note: there is a parking area at the end of the dirt road which bikers and hikers can use, however, there is **not** sufficient space for trailers to turn around. From the equestrian parking area at the paved loop, there is about 2 miles of riding on the dirt railroad bed (which doubles as a back access road) before coming to the actual trailhead. This road was not used heavily during our visit and vehicles had to travel slowly due to its rugged dirt surface. The dirt road actually is part of the old rail-trail system; the designated trail is just a continuation of this. There is a trailhead marker by the back dirt lot. The ride is straight and easy to follow. Park at the west end to reach the Horse-Shoe Trail, which connects with the west end of the Stony Creek Rail-Trail.

**THE TRAILS:**
What a nice surprise this trail was! We came across this rail-trail while doing the research for this book. Our first visit to this trail was in mid April. Each end of the trail had a very different feel. The east lot is high in altitude, feels very remote and far from civilization (bring some friends to ride with), and the surrounding forest, view, and quiet are awesome. Lots of evergreens and assorted other varieties of tall trees shade the trail. Looking down the east end trailhead, the trees form an interesting arch over the trail. We kept thinking there was a tunnel ahead due to the canopy forming a tunnel-like appearance. The trail surface is wide, easy, gradual, and covered with cinder. The off-trail areas of the east end have boulders everywhere. The rail-trail, itself, is not rocky. However, had it not been for the smooth rail-trail built through this terrain, this section would not be passable due to the large rock formations. Riding out from the opposite direction of the east lot leads to a large lake in a beautiful setting which reminded us of places we have visited out west.

The west lot has an easier access and is closer to surrounding communities. We were told that the west lot gets more multi-user activity. This appeared to be so during our visit, as there were more users at the west trail. Even so, the west lot did not have a crowded feel because the trail quickly moved away from the access area. However, our visit was not during peak usage. As parking at the west end is limited, the west end may be more ideal on off peak periods. The east end has lots of parking and may be a better choice to visit when the west end is more crowded.

The west end is a beautiful section to ride and visit. The terrain of the west trail is wide and gradual. There is cinder, (some) chipped stone, and dirt covering it. Like the east end, the west end has a cover of foliage shading most of the trail and travels through dense forests with a wilderness feel. Additional riding is available just off the entrance to the west end as the rail-trail intersects with the end of the Horse-Shoe Trail. The Horse-Shoe Trail's terrain can differ greatly from the rail-trail, as the surface can be very rocky and rough in sections, and not gradual like the rail-trail. We did not ride the portion of the Horse-Shoe Trail near Stony Creek, but we were told that section is of good terrain.

During our visit, there had been recent rains and there were many places to water the horses along the way. Due to season and weather changes, or if adjoining areas become or are off-limits to horses, bring water just in case. Do keep your eye out for bikes as quite a few cyclists were enjoying the trails during our visit to the west end.

One word of caution: We were told that sometimes there is military training out of Fort Indiantown Gap which is on the other side of the mountain. Call the state gameland office to check if any special helicopter and ground training is planned to take place near the rail-trail. The military has a few special practices per year, in the vicinity of the rail-trail, which are scheduled ahead of time. We were also informed that, without notice, fighter military aircraft could fly overhead at any moment. This could be very sudden and loud causing a horse to spook. This does not transpire often, but could occur. We did not encounter any of this during our visits; however, we have personally experienced this riding at other locations not in this area nor covered in this book. In these days and times, this may not be as unusual an experience as it once was in Pennsylvania or other states.

Note: You can share this beautiful rail-trail with family or friends, who do not or are unable to ride, bike, or hike. Each fall, there is a drive-through where visitors can drive the trail in their vehicle. Call the numbers listed above for dates and times. Non-motorized users of the trail will want to check in advance for the date of this event and may prefer to visit at a different time. We attended the fall drive and it was very enjoyable. The Pennsylvania Game Commission provides a Self-Guided Tour handout at the beginning of the drive. This flyer is very informative and describes the history of the area and points of interest along the way. Do make sure you obtain and read the handout before departing as it makes the trip much more meaningful.

## HISTORICAL INFORMATION:
In the 1700's, the Moravian missionaries arrived with the intention of converting the local Indians, and called this area St. Anthony's Wilderness. Later in the early 1800's, coal was discovered in the area and nearby communities developed. In the mid 1800's, railroads were constructed to carry the coal to the canal towpaths. This line was affiliated with the Schuylkill & Susquehanna. The railroad also transported passengers to Cold Spring as the reputed healing ability of the mineral water attracted visitors far and wide. The surrounding forests were stripped for lumber.

By the 1940's, mining and lumbering resources were exhausted and those operations ceased. In 1945, the Pennsylvania Game Commission acquired the land and transformed it to a rail-trail. Stony Creek was a forerunner, one of the first such conversions in its time. The trail is now enjoyed by many users and doubles as a Pennslyvania Game Commission service road (unpaved) since the trail travels through State Gamelands No. 211. The Horse-Shoe Trail and the Appalachian Trail meet with this trail.

**THINGS WE LEARNED THIS RIDE:**
- Do not let horses get in the habit of freely eating or grabbing leaves along the trail. As often there is temptation directly in front of a horse's face, we learned to be consistent in the enforcement of no eating unless we cue them that they can. We are not always successful, but we do try to signal them that they can graze the grass during a break (*assuming there is no chance that the grass is sprayed or treated*). Even a very small amount of rhododendron can be toxic to their system. We were advised by a vet to keep both electrolyte paste and banamine paste or shots in the saddle bag as both can help in the treatment of colic, and possibly save a horse's life. (This worked for our friend's horse but may not work for your horse. First, prior to leaving for the trail, check with your vet to see what he or she recommends to use on your horse in case of an emergency.) Our personal thanks to Dr. Renee Nodine for her time, advice, and aid as our friend's pretty, black Morgan-Walker recovered very nicely.

**NEARBY STABLES AND STAY-OVERS:**
- Holley Hill Stables (hay, straw, and boarding, *no overnight stabling except in case of emergency*), just off I-81, Harrisburg (717) 469-0126. We are very appreciative to these nice folks for helping us find a nearby vet while we were traveling in this area.
- Windy Ridge Farm (B&B, overnight stabling, feed, hay, and trailer parking), just off I-78, Bethel (717) 933-5888
- Morrissey's Frosty Acres (overnight stabling and layovers), just off I-81 near Penn National, Grantville (717) 469-2255 or 469-7211

**NEARBY VET SERVICES:**
- Rockwillow Ave. Animal Clinic, Harrisburg (717) 545-5803

**NEARBY OR SURROUNDING AREA FARRIER:**
- J. Strunk, CF, Fredericksburg (717) 649-0806

# 19. The Horse-Shoe Trail

**Lasting Impression:** Over 120 miles of trail!

**Location:** The Horse-Shoe Trail is located in southeastern Pennsylvania and is a 120+ mile trail which connects from north of Hershey, near the Appalachian Trail on Stony Mountain, to the Valley Forge area. The trail travels through Chester, Berks, Lancaster, Lebanon, and Dauphin counties. Horses are permitted on the trail.

**Length:** 120+ miles

**Level of Difficulty:** This is a long trail which varies from easy, to moderate, to difficult. Along with nice, easy sections, there are also many rocky, rugged portions and steep climbs. Caution note: At certain trail locations, there are numerous obstacles to cross due to busy road connections and other crossings.

**Terrain:** The terrain varies greatly. There are lots of rocks; horses need to have shoes. Borium can be helpful.

**Horse Camping:** No

**Non-horse Camping:** No

**Maps and Info:** The Horse-Shoe Trail Club, 509 Cheltena Ave., Jenkintown, PA 19046; The Horse-Shoe Trail Club, P.O. Box 182, Birchrunville, PA 19421-0182; the Guide to the Horse-Shoe Trail book which is published by the Horse-Shoe Trail Club and can be obtained (fee) at the Valley Forge Park Visitor Center on Route 23 near US-422, Franklin Maps in King of Prussia (800) 356-8676, or by contacting the club. The club's website is www.n99.com/hst/index.

**Activities:** Hiking, Horseback Riding Trails, Biking, and Hunting

The trail passes through areas including State Gamelands that may have hunting during season. At this writing, the portions of the Horse-Shoe Trail that travel through State Gamelands are expected to remain open to equestrians. *However, confirm with the Pennsylvania Game Commission, prior to arrival, that horses are still permitted on those portions of the Horse-Shoe Trail.*

**Fees for Trail Use:** None

**Permits for Trail Use:** None

**Comfort Station:** There are comfort stations at French Creek State Park and Valley Forge National Historic Park.

## DIRECTIONS:

The southeast portion of the trail can be accessed at Valley Forge National Historic Park and at French Creek Park. The beginning of the Horse-Shoe Trail is located by Valley Forge. The trail starts near the junction of Route 252 and Route 23. Trailer parking is at Washington's Headquarters "Stop #5" in the park, which is close to the trailhead. See the Valley Forge and French Creek chapters for directions to their parking areas. The northwest end of the trail can be accessed via the west end of the Stony Creek Rail-Trail. See that chapter for directions to the west end lot.

**THE TRAILS:**
Certificates have been given to riders upon completion of this entire trail! The trail is marked with yellow paint blazes. Side trails leading to interesting points are indicated by white blazes. Double blazes reflect a change in direction. John and I have ridden sections of this large trail system but not the whole system. The terrain is very diverse and ranges from easy footing to extremely challenging sections. There is plenty of wooded riding and some sections have streams to water your horse.

Periodically, clubs sponsor rides which cover the whole trail in several days. For such a long trail system, there are many advantages to traveling with a group who has previously ridden the complete trail and is familiar with the trail, obstacles, major road crossings, etc. Usually, these group trail rides are listed in the coming events section of local equestrian publications prior to the event. But, if you are interested in riding this whole trail on your own, a word of caution: Sections of this trail travel directly through major congested areas (i.e., in the area of Hershey, PA) and along busy roads. It is important to check the course out in advance. There are too many varying factors to briefly describe in this book. It is very helpful, prior to departure, to contact the Horse-Shoe Trail Club and order the latest guide book. Check to see if any sections of the trail are rerouted or closed, and if there are any new concerns equestrians should have. We found the Guide to the Horse-Shoe Trail very detailed and useful in determining which sections we wanted to ride.

Riders who want to experience some (but not the whole course) of the Horse-Shoe Trail might want to combine riding the trail with a visit to the adjoining trails at Valley Forge, the Lebanon Valley Rail-Trail, the Stony Creek Rail-Trail, or French Creek (which is mostly on the Horse-Shoe Trail).

**HISTORICAL INFORMATION:**
Sections of this trail have been used since the 1700's, at one time connecting some of the old iron forges and furnaces that were common in the area. The Horse-Shoe Trail later evolved into today's trail as a result of the preservation work of various groups and individuals since the 1930's. The continuous trail is also a reality due to the generosity of many private and public landowners that have allowed the trail to cross over their land. Currently, the Horse-Shoe Trail Club members maintain the trail.

**CLUBS:**
There are various clubs that have ridden the trail in its entirety. These can be contacted to join one of their planned rides or for information. The Paper Horse publication out of Mifflin, PA, (717) 436-8893, is an excellent source of

information for these rides. The Circle T Trail Riders, 1090 K-ville Road, Stevens, PA 17578, (717) 738-1414, has been a frequent sponsor of the Horse-Shoe Trail rides. (Their annual ride is usually posted on various equine sites and can be found via a web search or in The Paper Horse and various other PA publications.)

## NEARBY STABLES:
- Mountain Springs Campground (boarding, overnight stabling, camping, and rodeo events), Shartlesville (610) 488-7175
- Holley Hill Stables (hay, straw, and boarding, *no overnight stabling except in case of emergency*), just off I-81, Harrisburg (717) 469-0126
- Foxfield Farm (feed, hay, overnight stabling, and trailer parking), Lancaster (717) 484-2250
- Morrissey's Frosty Acres (overnight stabling and layovers), just off I-81 near Penn National, Grantville (717) 469-2255 or 469-7211
- Centaur Farm (*emergency only overnight stabling*), Grantville (717) 865-5501

## NEARBY B&B:
- Living Spring Farm B&B (offers accommodations for horses), Adamstown (610) 775-8525, (888) 329-1275, website: www.livingspringfarm.com

## NEARBY AND SURROUNDING AREA VET SERVICES:
- H. Fortna, Ephrata (717) 733-1078
- Blauner, Vecchione, & Associates (24-hour emergency vet service), N. Wales (215) 699-4422
- New Bolton Center, Kennett Square (610) 444-5800
- J. Edelson, Manheim (717) 665-7626
- J. Henderson, Elizabethtown (717) 664-2122
- Rockwillow Ave. Animal Clinic, Harrisburg (717) 545-5803
- A. Worell, Leesport (610) 916-6220
- Willow Creek Animal Hospital, Reading (610) 378-0192

## NEARBY AND SURROUNDING AREA FARRIERS:
- Equine Management Service, St. Peters (610) 469-9332
- V. Mastrangelo, Elverson (610) 286-5560
- G. Geesaman, Vinemont (near Reinholds) (610) 678-3099
- J. Strunk, CF, Fredericksburg (717) 649-0806

# 20. Bucks County Horse Park

**Lasting Impression:**  An attractive park appealing to a variety of equestrian interests, operated by a private, non-profit club welcoming the public to join and enjoy.

**Location:**  The park is located on Route 611, between the towns of Ferndale and Revere in Bucks County, eastern Pennsylvania.

**Length:**  The park sits on 700+ acres and the total trail length (not counting overlaps) is approximately 25 miles.  There is the Blue Trail, which is 12 miles, that is used for competitive trail rides; the Red Trail, which has 7 miles, suitable for carriage driving; and the Yellow Trail, which has 8 miles of trails and has been utilized for Hunter Paces.

**Level of Difficulty:**  Easy

**Terrain:**  Some flat, some rolling hills, some wooded, some open fields

**Horse Camping:**  No  At certain times and during special show activities, overnight boarding or trailer parking may be available.  Check with the office prior to arrival.

**Non-horse Camping:**  No

**Maps and Info:**  Bucks County Horse Park is managed by a private, non-profit equestrian club open to the public to join.  The club does have a maximum number of riding members.  Maps and information can be obtained at the Bucks County Horse Park, 8934 Easton Road, Revere, PA 18953, (610) 847-8597, or the park's website: www.buckscountyhorsepark.com.

**Activities:**  Hiking, Biking, Horseback Riding Trails, and Equestrian Competitive Events and Show Grounds.  Hunting is not permitted.  *A place to ride during hunting season!  However, do check with the office prior to arrival to verify that no changes have transpired, and exercise extreme caution as adjoining lands may permit hunting.*

**Fees for Trail Use:**  Yes; there is a yearly membership fee that can be found on their website.  One day passes may also be available for a fee.

**Permits for Trail Use:**  A release form must be signed prior to using the park which makes the signer a member of the Bucks County Horse Park for the day.  The form can be obtained from the website also.  As a result of signing this form, the signer agrees to abide by the park's rules.

**Comfort Station:**  Yes

**DIRECTIONS:**

Take 611 south from Easton toward the village of Revere.  Pass Ferndale, and then one half mile before the village of Revere you will see the Bucks County Horse Park on the right.  There is plenty of parking, and ample room for large rigs and big groups.

## THE TRAILS:
Bucks County is in a lovely setting, with trails zigzagging over a variety of terrain, past streams, open fields, and wooded stretches. Equestrians of diverse backgrounds should enjoy this park. There are a variety of jumps including water, fences, brush, and logs for those preferring cross country eventing and jumping. There are carriage courses for carriage drivers to negotiate. Endurance riders also come to this park to condition their horses. For spectators who enjoy watching equestrian competition, there are many assorted shows and events including Polo. And for folks like myself, there is lots of pretty scenery to trail ride while soaking up the view.

Nearby attractions include many popular sites. Bucks County is home to arts, crafts, theater, antiques shopping, charming restaurants, museums, and many historic homes and sites. If you travel in the area, don't miss Bucks County's covered bridges. Call 1-800-836-BUCKS for more information.

## NEARBY AND SURROUNDING AREA STABLES AND B&Bs:
- Breakaway Farms (boarding, overnight stabling, and trailer parking), Pipersville (215) 766-3769
- Mill Creek Farm Bed & Breakfast (accommodations for horses, overnight stabling, and may be able to accommodate trailers with living quarters), Buckingham (215) 794-0776, e-mail: millcreekfarmbnb@aol.com
- Rainbow Ridge Farm Equestrian Center (boarding, overnight stabling, lessons, tack shop, summer camp, and shows), Pipersville (215) 766-9357

## NEARBY VET SERVICES:
- Quakertown Veterinary Clinic, Quakertown (215) 536-2726, (215) 536-6245

## NEARBY FARRIERS:
- Bucks County Farrier Service, Pipersville (215) 766-0242
- K. McCarty, Quakertown (215) 536-3372
- JR Rosenberger, Quakertown (215) 536-5256
- R. Kass, Jr., Levittown (215) 943-8583
- R. Kass, Pipersville (215) 630-0390

# 21. Nockamixon State Park
# DCNR
### (Department of Conservation & Natural Resources)

**Lasting Impression:** Enjoy a beautiful, scenic ride with a choice of trails.
**Location:** Between Quakertown and Doylestown, northern Bucks County, eastern Pennsylvania
**Length:** The park consists of almost 5,300 acres; the lake is about eight miles long with 20 miles of equestrian trails adjoining it.
**Level of Difficulty:** The trails are mostly easy with only a few sections that may be considered to be moderate or challenging. There are two separate trail systems; each on different sides of the lake and each are distinct. One trail is accessed via PA 563 on the west side (considered to be the "north" side but this is a little bit confusing because of the angle of the lake), and one is accessed via Ridge Road on the east ("south") side. When referring to the different trails, I will refer to one side as the PA 563 side and the other side as the Ridge Road side. The Ridge Road side has hours of long, flat, and easy wooded trails and open stretches to ride. We found these paths ideal for gaiting or cantering. As you travel between Kellers Church Road and Mink Road, the trail becomes a bit more rigorous due to hills and ravine crossings. The PA 563 side is mainly easy with diverse wooded trails, rolling hills, and a few short, rocky stretches, which are passable.
**Terrain:** These trails have a little bit of everything. The terrain is high, dry, low, sometimes wet, flat, hilly, open, wooded, soft ground, and rocky ground.
**Horse Camping:** No, but you can camp at nearby Green Lane and trailer to this park (see the Green Lane chapter)
**Non-horse Camping:** There are rental cabins in the park.
**Maps and Info:** DCNR, Nockamixon State Park, 1542 Mountain View Drive, Quakertown, PA 18951-5732, (215) 529-7300, www.dcnr.state.pa.us, e-mail: nockamixon.sp@al.dcnr.state.pa.us. Call 1-888-PA-PARKS for general info or cabin rental.
**Activities:** Fishing, Boating, Boat Rentals, Swimming, Hiking, Biking (limited), Picnicking, Horseback Riding Trails, Hunting (some sections during season), Ice Skating, X-C Skiing, Sledding, Cabin Rentals, and Nearby Trail Rides at Haycock Stables (fee) (215) 257-6271
**Fees for Trail Use:** None
**Permits for Trail Use:** None
**Comfort Station:** We did not find any comfort stations at the trailheads during our visit, however, there are comfort stations in the main area of the park.

**DIRECTIONS:**

The park is 5 miles east of Quakertown and 9 miles west of Doylestown. Take the Northeast Extension of the PA Turnpike (I-476) to the Quakertown Exit #44, heading east toward Quakertown on Route 663 north. (Or, instead of the PA Turnpike, take Interstate 78, to Route 309 south; take Route 309 to the Route 663/313 intersection.) At the Route 309 and Route 663 intersection, Route 663 becomes Route 313. Take Route 313 east and continue to either trail as indicated below.

To access the Ridge Road side of the trail: Take Route 313 east from the Route 309 & Route 663/313 intersection for 5.9 miles to Ridge Road. You will pass the main park entrance that is located on Route 563 and travel over the lake. To reach the equestrian trailhead and parking, make a left on Ridge Road. There are four trailhead parking lots that access the equestrian trail. As you travel on Ridge Road you will see the roads which lead to parking in this order: Elephant Road, Stover Mill Road, Kellers Church Road, and Mink Road. While on Ridge Road, make a left onto any of these four and the trailhead is a short distance down the road. Equestrian trailheads are marked at each of these locations. Most lots are not very large but can accommodate a few 2-horse or 3-horse trailers. The Mink Road lot is the largest lot, can accommodate larger rigs such as those with living quarters, and provides turn around space. When John and I recently visited this parking area, the Mink Road lot had a long, bumpy entrance but was navigable when taken slow. (We have not ridden from the Mink Road location in many years, however, we recall that the trails were more challenging or difficult in the vicinity of the Mink Road location.)

To access the PA Route 563 side of the trail: Take Route 313 east from the Route 309 intersection for 4.7 miles to Route 563. Make a left on Route 563 heading north. There are two parking lots. Neither lot had an equestrian sign at the entrance so proceed slowly. The first lot is about 2 miles on Route 563. After approximately 2 miles, make a right, which is Old Bethlehem Road. At the fork, bear right and proceed down the road; the lot is on the right. It is a very small lot, requires backing, and can only accommodate a few 2-horse trailer rigs. The second and roomier lot is 3.3 miles on Route 563 (from the Route 313 turnoff). There was no name on this road at the entrance, but there is a Fishing Pier sign. Make a right by the Fishing Pier sign and go down the road passing the brown Lake Nockamixon and equestrian trailhead signs. Parking is on the right. This is a nice, big lot with lots of room for drivers who prefer a pull-through option. There is room for large horse trailers, and many (our estimate 20+) standard 2-horse trailer rigs could fit in here if a group ride is planned. Call ahead in advance for a map, which clearly shows the parking lot locations and adjoining trails. We did not see maps at the equestrian trailheads.

## THE TRAILS:

The equestrian trails on the Ridge Road side of the lake connect in loops from the Elephant Road parking lot to the Mink Road parking lot. The trails are well used and easy to follow, as they parallel the lake which offers a continuous point of reference. When departing from the Elephant Road lot, the trails wind in and out of wooded areas, open spaces, and are mostly flat or slightly hilly. They continue this way past the Kellers Church Road lot. These provide an easy ride. There are areas to access the lake, enjoy the beautiful view, and water your horses. (As with any trail, prior to use, equestrians should check to see if watering the horses is permitted and to ascertain if the quality of the water is adequate.) Continuing toward the Mink Road lot and the dam, the trails become a bit more challenging due to the ravines. Some sections of the trail can remain wet in the early spring and after a rainy period.

This is a nice trail system to enjoy on a cool, fall day while taking in the foliage. We visited this side of the trail in November, when the leaves were off the trees offering an even nicer view of the lake and the surrounding area. Wildlife is abundant. Deer, wild turkeys, and other wildlife can be seen. Sections of the trail are open to hunting during hunting season; at that time this area is well used. Check with the office for hunting dates. Normally, Sundays are closed to hunting; but confirm this ahead of time as well.

We found the PA Route 563 side of the trails to be a really pleasant ride. The trails are wooded except for the southern most portions. The trails offer a variety of scenery as the paths wind along the lakeside, through pine forests, out over a high open area overlooking the whole lake, past ruins of old homesteads and structures, through rocky stream crossings, and beside stone hedges lined with mature hardwoods and the beginning of young cedar forests. There are some sections that get close to the edge (caution do not pick up a footpath as often the footpath travels closer to where the trail drops off), but usually there is an alternate inland trail to take. We rode this side of Lake Nockamixon on a Sunday in mid December. A record warm winter, there had been no snow or extreme cold to date. Riding in about 35-40 degree, sunny weather with no wind was just awesome. Other than only a few visitors, we had the woods to ourselves. It was quiet, serene, and with the fallen leaves, we could take in wonderful views of the lake from all directions. We do caution, however, that riders stay on the designated trail. Due to the old homesteads and prior occupants, there are some remains and debris such as wire fencing in off-trail areas. These are difficult to see until you are upon them. Except for one fallen tree that pulled some fencing down close to the trail, we found the trail, itself, to be clear of such concerns. As for staying on course, there are signs and ribbons, but sometimes there are lapses in markers. However, with the map and the lake as reference, it should not be easy to get lost.

A don't miss section, our favorite part, is the ride on the PA 563 side of the lake in the southern most portion of the trail. This is just south of the first parking lot on the PA 563 side. Looking at the map, the trail goes around a peninsula or point and is on the opposite side of Three Mile Run. This portion of the trail offers a high, panoramic view of the lake. Superb scenery and a great picture opportunity! *Please note: in this section of the trail system, riders are advised to proceed cautiously as this is where the foot(only) vs. equestrian trails can get a bit confusing. Steer clear of footpaths that can be narrow and dangerous for horses.*

We found Nockamixon State Park to be a fun and interesting ride, and we really enjoyed and appreciated it. We look forward to re-visiting this park in the very near future.

## HISTORICAL INFORMATION:
The original dwellers of the area were the Lenni Lenape Indians. Nockamixon got its name from a Lenape Indian phrase meaning "place of soft soil". By the early 1700's, the settlers had arrived and cleared the land for farming. By the 1730's, the settlers were coming in great numbers and forced the Indians out.

In the late 1950's, Dr. Maurice Goddard, of the Department of Forests and Water, recommended the location be set aside for a park. Dr. Goddard had the vision and desire that every Pennsylvanian should be within 25 miles of a state park system. In the 1960's, land acquisition for the park began and the park's name was changed from Tohickon State Park (named after a stream feeding Lake Nockamixon) to Nockamixon State Park. Lake Nockamixon is a manmade lake and was planned to serve multiple purposes including providing a water resource, a water management tool, and a recreational area. To establish the park, 290 properties were condemned. Some of the remains of these properties can be seen throughout the park. By the 1970's, the nearly 120 foot dam was completed, the lake began filling, and the park was open to the public. The park is currently run by DCNR (formerly the DER).

For more interesting information on Nockamixon State Park's historical sites, call the park office at (215) 529-7300 for a free "Self-guiding Auto Tour" pamphlet, or stop by the park office.

The Nockamixon State Park equestrian trails are the result of the dedicated work of numerous individuals and local organizations, including the Nockamixon Trails Committee. The Nockamixon Trails Committee, a volunteer group of local horseback riders, designed and constructed the trails.

**NEARBY STABLES:**
- Haycock Riding Stables Inc. (public guided trail rides in Nockamixon State Park, boarding, and possible emergency overnight boarding available, *no transient boarding*), website: www.haycockstables.com, Perkasie (215) 257-6271
- Breakaway Farms (boarding, overnight stabling, and trailer parking), Pipersville (215) 766-3769
- Rainbow Ridge Farm Equestrian Center (boarding, overnight stabling, lessons, tack shop, summer camp, and shows), Pipersville (215) 766-9357

**NEARBY EQUESTRIAN B&B:**
- Mill Creek Farm Bed & Breakfast (accommodations for horses, overnight stabling, and may be able to accommodate trailers with living quarters), Buckingham (215) 794-0776, e-mail: millcreekfarmbnb@aol.com

**NEARBY VET SERVICES:**
- Quakertown Veterinary Clinic, Quakertown (215) 536-2726, (215) 536-6245

**NEARBY FARRIERS:**
- JR Rosenberger, Quakertown (215) 536-5256
- Bucks County Farrier Service, Pipersville (215) 766-0242
- R. Kass, Perkasie (215) 795-2600
- K. McCarty, Quakertown (215) 536-3372

# 22. Delaware Canal State Park
# DCNR
### (Department of Conservation & Natural Resources)

**Lasting Impression:** Ride the Delaware Canal, the only complete, unbroken canal in existence from the 19th century canal towpath period.

**Location:** The Delaware Canal is located in eastern Pennsylvania near the New Jersey border, and spans 60 miles from Easton to Bristol. There is talk of plans for this trail to extend to Wilkes-Barre.

**Length:** The Delaware Canal State Park is 60 miles in length. The whole trail is open to horses, however, certain areas may be difficult to cross or present hazards. Due to ongoing improvements, changes, and construction, it is recommended to check with the ranger station before arrival and obtain a DCNR map.

**Level of Difficulty:** The surface is very well maintained, gradual, and easy, but there are obstacles for horses. Numerous bridges cross the canal, which horses must cross over (some long, slightly narrow, but many with guard rails for safety) or cross under (some low clearance) to continue along the trail. Note: see the trail description below.

**Terrain:** The terrain is mostly flat and of dirt or cinder material, with gradual changes in elevation.

**Horse Camping:** No

**Non-horse Camping:** No

**Maps and Info:** DCNR, Delaware Canal State Park, 11 Lodi Hill Road, Upper Black Eddy, PA 18972, (610) 982-5560, e-mail: delawarecanalsp@state.pa.us. Call 1-888-PA-PARKS for general park info. Maps were at the ranger stations and at various intervals including at the comfort stations. However, maps can be obtained in advance at the above DCNR number. For information regarding mule-drawn boat rides, call (215) 862-0758.

**Activities:** Canoeing, Hiking, Biking, and Horseback Riding Trails

**Fees for Trail Use:** None

**Permits for Trail Use:** None

**Comfort Station:** Yes, at various intervals and as marked on the map

**DIRECTIONS:**
The canal path runs along Route 32 and Route 611, beside the Delaware River on the Pennsylvania and New Jersey border. The canal path can be accessed along these two routes. There are numerous parking lots adjacent to the trail, but most are too small for horse rigs. Although everyone tried to be very helpful during calls to the ranger station, and seemed to welcome horseback riders, they could not tell me where horseback riders were permitted to park horse trailers. I was told the Virginia Forest Recreation Area and the Raubsville lot do not permit

horse trailers, but no one could tell of a suitable lot for equestrians with trailers. We observed a larger lot (not mentioned as being closed to trailers) where Routes 611 and 212 meet near Riegelsville, and it is accessed by crossing a bridge. But, just south of this lot is a low clearance bridge which riders may find difficult to pass under. Rather, we observed equestrians using the Tinicum County Park lot, which is part of the Bucks County Department of Parks and Recreation (215) 757-0571. We called their office to obtain and confirm permission and they generously stated that horseback riders could park in their lot for day rides (no overnight), even though Tinicum County Park does not have horseback riding trails. As a condition, they did request that riders travel directly to the Canal Path and not ride around Tinicum County Park. Their lot offers plenty of space for large rigs and a pull-through area. This park can be seen on the DCNR Delaware Canal State Park map between Frenchtown and Smithtown, about 7 to 8 miles north of New Hope, and is located on the west side of Route 32. In this area, the canal is inland from the lot and riders must ride a short distance west to the back of the park (away from Route 32) to reach it.

## THE TRAILS:

The Delaware Canal State Park towpath offers lots of beautiful views of the Delaware River, surrounding historic communities, and old covered bridges along its route. The trail is unique and the views are diverse. There are warm, sunny open stretches, canopied wooded sections, and cool cliff shaded tracts. The trail passes many picturesque 17th, 18th, and 19th century homes and farms. There are lots and lots of restaurants, antique dealers, and curiosity shops at various intervals along the canal path. It is an interesting trail, but also one that is a popular path and well traveled by dog walkers, hikers, and bikers.

In certain sections, the highway is within close (hearing) distance and, although the canal is in between the trail and the highway, the ride will likely be more enjoyable if your horse has no problem with the sound of passing motor traffic, including motorcycles. However, there are also lots of quiet and tranquil sections where the path winds away from the road. We first rode this trail on bikes to assess which sections were the most horse friendly, due to nearby populated areas, and to evaluate trail obstacles. The main concern was the numerous bridges with low clearance. Often there is only about 7 feet of clearance, which most average sized horses can get under if they do not have a fear of crossing under low bridges. But riders need to dismount and should be alert for cars crossing the bridge above. Waiting to walk the horse under the bridge until the car passes overhead is likely a safer choice as the sound can cause the horse to spook, rear, or lift his head. Sometimes horses can go around the bridge, but other times there are no other options. Although we were told horses were permitted along the entire canal path, there are a few bridges (5' to 6') that would be difficult or impossible for horses to cross under (such as at Raubsville and Monroe). The only way to cross would be in the canal water or on private property. Since neither is a desirable alternative, these sections may have to be avoided unless or until changes are made. (Riders are not permitted to go through the canal and horses may sink due to the soft bottom.) One bridge crossing appeared to have been elevated, so perhaps some of the very low bridges will also be raised higher in the future. I was told there were no current plans for bridge changes due to the prohibitive cost, unless a bridge needs replacement. Maybe as the trails lengthen and expand with coming plans, that will be reconsidered. In certain sections, horses also need to be willing to cross over long, wooden bridges that pass over aqueducts and waterways to continue down the trail. Some of these crossings can be quite long.

In spite of these challenges, this is a beautiful, interesting, and special place to visit. Our experience was that the most horse friendly (accessible) section and our favorite stretch was to ride from Tinicum County Park north to Monroe and south to the Point Pleasant area. Traveling from Monroe to Point Pleasant and back would be about 15 to 16 miles of continuous riding. (To travel south of this section, from Point Pleasant onto the Virginia Forest Recreation Area parking lot, the trail remains at least one lane in width but has an abrupt drop to the Delaware River side of the trail not allowing much room if a horse should spook. Some riders may feel uncomfortable without the usual buffer of trees or land along the trail in that section.)

Before visiting this area, consider taking a smaller horse trailer if you have a choice. Traveling with a large horse trailer could be difficult. Route 32 and Route 611 to the north are narrow roads, and are best traveled with smaller rigs such as 2-horse trailers.

## NEARBY:

One of the nearby popular attractions is historic New Hope which offers numerous antique and specialty shops, along with an assortment of dining establishments. New Hope is a tight and congested area for horse rigs. The lots near the Mule Boat Concession just below New Hope on New Street, if space permits, could accommodate parking a small 2-horse trailer for a quick visit to New Hope. However, due to the crowds, congestion, and narrow corners, this area is not recommended for parking or riding out of. If you desire to stop at this lot to visit New Hope, approach it from the south end as the northern approach has too many sharp turns for trailers. Tinicum County Park is more suitable as it is north of town in a country setting, and more accessible for rigs.

## HISTORICAL INFORMATION:

The Delaware Canal State Park is both a registered National Historic Landmark and a National Heritage Hiking Trail. The canal is one of a kind in that it remains the only unbroken, complete canal in existence from that era. In the 1800's, the

Delaware Canal served as a convenient and inexpensive channel to move coal to Philadelphia, New York, and other markets. Teams of mules, walking on the towpath, would pull canal barges full of cargo along the canal. During this time, the canal was also used for fishing and canoeing. When the canal was closed to commercial activity, it was used only for recreational purposes. In the 1940's, the canal became a State Park and visitors would hike, picnic, and canoe in the park.

A point of interest along the trail can be seen in Easton where there is the "Fish Passageway" for shad fish that migrate from the Delaware River to spawning grounds in the Lehigh River. Visitors can view the passageway through a window. In addition, the Delaware Canal State Park includes two natural areas: River Islands and Nockamixon Cliffs. These were determined to be "natural" and protected areas due to either rare species of wildlife or unusual environmental factors. The Nockamixon Cliffs offer a sharp contrast to the landscape as they rise 300 feet above the Delaware River. The River Islands offer sanctuary for migrating birds and waterfowl. The Visitor Center in New Hope provides a history of the canal and the surrounding area. During season, visitors can experience life along the towpath by traveling in mule-drawn canal boats along the original canal path.

## NEARBY STABLES:
- Rainbow Ridge Farm Equestrian Center (boarding, overnight stabling, lessons, tack shop, summer camp, and shows), Pipersville (215) 766-9357

## NEARBY EQUESTRIAN B&Bs:
- Mill Creek Farm Bed & Breakfast (accommodations for horses, overnight stabling, and may be able to accommodate trailers with living quarters), Buckingham (215) 794-0776, e-mail: millcreekfarmbnb@aol.com
- Fairfield Paso Finos (guesthouse, boarding, and overnight stabling), New Hope area (215) 794-3616

## NEARBY VET SERVICES:
- Quakertown Veterinary Clinic, Quakertown (215) 536-2726, (215) 536-6245

## NEARBY FARRIERS:
- R. Kass, Sr., Perkasie (215) 795-2600
- JR Rosenberger, Quakertown (215) 536-5256
- K. McCarty, Quakertown (215) 536-3372
- Bucks County Farrier Service, Pipersville (215) 766-0242
- R. Kass, Pipersville (215) 630-0390
- R. Kass, Jr., Levittown (215) 943-8583

# 23. Susquehannock Creek State Park
# DCNR
### (Department of Conservation & Natural Resources)

**Lasting Impression:** Enjoy great panoramic views overlooking the Susquehanna River where eagles soar.

**Location:** The park is located in southern Lancaster County and adjoins the Susquehanna River.

**Length:** The park consists of 234 acres. Sources claim between 6 and 10 miles to ride, plus there are possible adjoining lands to ride. We were told of an additional 17 miles of trails that directly connect in the northern section of the park, along with numerous other trails in the area. (Note: Some of the trails in the outlying northern section can be very steep and rocky; be careful when exploring and make sure you only travel on lands that permit equestrian riding. It is probably best to travel with riders who are familiar with the area.) The Valley Lea Riding Club is a local group who rides the area. We met some members along the trail and asked what trails were better to ride (see below).

**Level of Difficulty:** Easy to difficult. Initially, we thought the equestrian trails were mainly easy to moderate. However, in the northern section of the park we encountered difficult trails. The level of challenge can vary greatly.

**Terrain:** Most of the equestrian trails in the eastern and southern section of the park, including near Hawk Point and Wissler's Run, are wonderful, easy, wide, gradual dirt, logging type roads. There is some but not a lot of rock. However, the northern section near the Five Points Trail where it meets with the Rhododendron Trail by the Wissler Run River has some extreme terrain with large rocks. Certain sections can be impassable on horseback.

**Horse Camping:** No

**Non-horse Camping:** Organized Group Tenting is indicated on the State Park map.

**Maps and Info:** DCNR, Susquehannock Creek State Park, c/o Gifford Pinchot State Park, 2200 Rosstown Road, Lewisberry, PA 17339-9787, (717) 432-5011. The website is www.dcnr.state.pa.us. Call 1-888-PA-PARKS for general park info or for camping reservations. For other local information, call Pennsylvania Dutch Convention and Visitor's Bureau (800) 723-8824. Maps were stocked at the Landis lot trailhead.

**Activities:** Hiking, Group Tenting, Picnicking, Group Pavilions, Softball Fields, and Horseback Riding Trails. We were told that there is no hunting within the park. (However, confirm there are no special hunts prior to visiting the park during hunting seasons.) It is possible that neighboring lands have hunting.

**Fees for Trail Use:** None

**Permits for Trail Use:** None

**Comfort Station:** Yes (there is also a frost-free hydrant to provide water for the horses at the Landis lot)

## DIRECTIONS:

From the intersection of PA Route 272 and Route 372 (at the town of Buck), take Route 372 west for a short distance and make a left on Susquehannock Drive. Take Susquehannock Drive south for approximately 4.5 miles, following signs, to Park Road. (Susquehannock Drive winds through farm land.) See a large Susquehannock Park sign. Make a right at the sign onto the park road. Travel into the park. There is equestrian parking in a very large lot behind the Landis House, and there are tie rails toward the back of the lot. Or continue past the Landis House to the back of the park. There is equestrian parking in the grass area off the side of the road next to the tie rails. We liked this spot due to the shade it offered. This is a roomy parking area, however, there is a tight turn at the end of the park road. We were fine with our 2-horse rig, but could not get through that turn with a larger rig. Big rigs should park behind the Landis House, and enter and exit the park through this lot, and avoid proceeding further down the road.

## THE TRAILS:

We loved this pretty park. This park is so attractive that a wedding was being held in the picnic area during our visit. We traveled in a clockwise direction and the trail started off beautifully, offering a leisurely ride along the Chimney Trail into the Landis Trail. The wide trail is mostly dirt with some rock. The trail travels through tall, straight trees offering shade in the warmer weather. We would like to return to this trail in the fall, when the leaves are off the trees, to further enjoy the view along the trails as they approach the cliffs.

The park is situated on high ground overlooking the Susquehanna River. The cliffs of the park tower over the river by almost 400 feet, providing beautiful views of the surrounding area and the river. Bring your panoramic camera. The trails run in loops around the park and vary from wooded to open fields. The trails were quiet and we only met two pairs of horseback riders. Except as described below, we found most of the trails easy to follow and clearly marked.

Horses are not permitted on the Rhododendron Trail. The Rhododendron Trail is very rocky and is a steep trail, but in late June and early July it is worth hiking to see the rhododendron in bloom. Also, horses are not permitted at the actual overlook site. However, riders can tie their horses at the tie rails and walk to the view. The overlook is a must see during a visit to the park. A prime attraction, Hawk Point, provides a view of the Susquehanna River/Conowingo Reservoir. The reservoir, which is in both Maryland and Pennsylvania, offers power and cooling for the Peach Bottom nuclear reactors. The dam for the reservoir is on the Maryland side. Looking down from Hawk Point, one can see many islands.

We thought the equestrian trails might not offer access to the overlooks, which is often the case, but not at Susquehannock State Park! We were pleasantly surprised to find that the Landis Trail joins the Overlook Trail as it approaches Hawk Point. There, at the Hawk Point overlook, the park has tie rails where equestrians can dismount, secure their horses, and walk the short distance to enjoy the overlook. The initial intention was likely to accommodate the local Amish. However, what a smart idea to have tie rails near the vista for trail riders also. This is one idea we will recommend to other parks. Often, we have heard parks indicate a concern over complaints of horse droppings at the overlooks, resulting in equestrians not being permitted to have access to them. But that should not be a problem here as the park has the tie rails a close but comfortable distance so that all can share and enjoy the overlook. We were very appreciative of this and took in the view.

At the Hawk Point overlook, there were numerous bird watchers with high tech equipment to observe the eagles, hawks, osprey and various birds that reside off the cliffs and on the islands. One friendly group had their binoculars on tripods and shared their view with us so we could see a bald eagle off in the distance. The park also has binoculars (nominal fee) at these sites for the public to enjoy. We proceeded onto the Wissler's Run overlook. This section did not have a tie rail but the park may want to consider it for the reasons mentioned above. We dismounted and took turns enjoying this vista, which provided views of the nearby Muddy Run Power operations.

Upon departure from Wissler's Run, still heading in a clockwise direction, we proceeded along Fire Trail, Holly Trail, and Pine Tree Trail. Sometimes it is confusing where to proceed in this section of the park. We encountered some hikers who said the Rhododendron Trail is a must see when the trail is in bloom. Most of the Rhododendron Trail is for hiking only, as the trail can be steep and rocky and travels through "tunnels" of Rhododendron. As we connected into the Five Points Trail, the trail terrain changed dramatically from easy to challenging to difficult. We don't believe we took a wrong turn as we were following the signs, but we encountered a vertical, boulder type trail where we had to dismount so the horses could leap up it. Once we started up this trail, we could not turn around; safely descending this trail would have been almost impossible. Had we known, we would have avoided this section all together.

Especially in the above area, be alert for the "no horseback riding" signs. Besides the obvious reasons for following the rules, they are indicative of trails too steep, rocky, or dangerous, and not suited to horses. There are lots of other rough sections in these parts. If you prefer a more gentle terrain, avoid this portion and backtrack to the more gradual trails of the park. Those sections of the trail are too nice to miss. We checked with some local riders that frequent this trail to ascertain where these difficult or impossible trails were, so that we made sure we could warn people of them, especially because the rest of the park is such an easy surface to ride. They said that, basically, the only extreme equestrian trail section **within** the park is in the Five Points/Rhododendron Trail vicinity that we described above. (There are some additional challenging areas outside of the park.)

While riding, look for eagles soaring overhead. Mt. Johnson Island, which can be seen to the left of the Hawk Point lookout, is the world's first bald eagle sanctuary. Eagles have been nesting on this island and have also moved to other islands. In addition, hawks and osprey may be seen. Another overlook is Wissler's Run Overlook, which provides a view of the Norman Wood Bridge, the Susquehanna's rocky riverbed, and the Muddy Run hydroelectric plant.

## HISTORICAL INFORMATION:

The Susquehannock Creek State Park is an area rich with history, which recounts the tragic account of its once powerful native people. The river and park were named after the Susquehannock Indians who originally occupied the area. The Susquehannock Indians had only a single village at this site, but it was a significant location as it dominated the trade along the Chesapeake Bay and the Susquehanna River.

Between different Indian tribal groups, there were numerous conflicts to control the trade in this strategic area. In the early stages, those tribes having first access to European rifles won. Then the Susquehannocks also obtained European rifles. "Beaver Wars", which were wars over the control of the beaver pelt trade, ensued in the mid 1600's. The Susquehannocks prevailed over these years but suffered a large loss in 1675. European settlers began to interfere and Maryland invited the Susquehannocks to move to a new location and live in peace. That was short lived.

Those were times where settlers heard news of horrifying Indian attacks on the frontier. Their fear of similar attacks brought misunderstanding and aggression to the peaceful Susquehannock people. While the settlement was surrounded, five (well intended) chiefs traveling to negotiate were unjustly killed. Indians in the settlement escaped during the night, ultimately making their way back to their original village along the river. Betrayed and enraged from the murders of their chiefs, the Susquehannocks tormented the European settlers in return for their actions. In the late 1600's, the Susquehannock were again invited to move, this time to New York. Later, again, some returned to the original site. In the following years, Delaware and Shawnee refugees began to join them. But, by the early 1700's, European settlers forced the majority of the Indians to move permanently. Many settled in Ohio where they mixed with other tribes, thus losing their Susquehannock identity. The few who did not leave for Ohio, settled in Conestoga in Lancaster County and were later called "Conestogas".

In the 1760's, the Conestogas were protected under the commonwealth and, for a while, lived peacefully in Lancaster. However, an Indian uprising in the western part of the state agitated an anti-Indian vigilante group. They proceeded to murder six Conestoga Indians. The local government indicated shock and banned any further injustice. The Indians were gathered at a separate location in Lancaster for their safety. But this was in vain. Sadly, within two weeks, the group murdered those Indians as well. History indicates that two surviving Conestogas or Susquehannocks worked on a nearby Lancaster farm. They received government protection until their death, at which time they were buried at the farm.

In the very early 1800's, the river was being studied for steamboat feasibility. A product of this study was the survey map of the river, which the British destroyed in the War of 1812. The surveyors decided against steamboat navigation; instead canals were built along the river. But these were soon abandoned in favor of railroad transportation.

In close proximity to the park office, is another chapter in history. In 1850, James Buchannon Long constructed the Landis house. The house consists of stone, slate roof, and horsehair plaster. One of its residents, Jacob Schoff, aided the "Underground Railroad". The "Underground Railroad" was a network of anti-slavery supporters who assisted slaves to escape to the free States and Canada. Visitors can view the stone house from the outside. The home is named after a more recent owner whose name was Landis. The Commonwealth of PA obtained the building as part of the park purchase. There are ruins of old homesites to be seen from the trails in the park including that of Thomas Neel's, a revolutionary war veteran, which is along the Rhododendron Trail.

**NEARBY:**
- Pennsylvania Dutch countryside and Amish farms
- Lancaster County Park Central Park Equestrian trails (see that chapter)
- One of our favorite farm stands is near the Susquehannock State Park. During our visit, we particularly enjoyed the fresh baked goods and scrumptious barbecue chicken at the Amish farm stand (Saturdays only) at the intersection of Route 272 and Route 372 in Buck. Warning, if you are on a diet, their wonderful food is hard to resist. We ate delicious pecan sticky buns for breakfast on the way to a trail, bought some other goodies to go, and returned when the barbecue chicken was ready in the afternoon!

**NEARBY AND SURROUNDING AREA STABLES:**
- Foxfield Farm (feed, hay, overnight stabling, and trailer parking), Lancaster (717) 484-2250. We stayed at Foxfield and traveled to this trail.
- Windswept Stabling (feed, hay, overnight boarding, and trailer parking), Columbia (717) 684-3975

**NEARBY AND SURROUNDING AREA VET SERVICES:**
- New Bolton (24-hour emergency), Kennett Square (610) 444-5800
- Complete Equine Health Service, Coatesville (610) 466-0501
- Unionville Equine Center, Oxford (610) 932-6800
- Greenglen Equine Hospital, Glen Rock (717) 235-4312
- Brandywine Veterinary Clinic, Coatesville (610) 383-1866

**NEARBY FARRIER:**
- E. Scheckner, Christiana (717) 529-6056

# 24. Jacobsburg Environmental Education Center DCNR

### (Department of Conservation & Natural Resources)

**Lasting Impression:** This is a very well maintained and scenic trail system. One of our favorite day trips and that of many locals as well!

**Location:** Situated south of the Blue Mountains, Jacobsburg Environmental Education Center is in the northern Lehigh Valley region, in the town of Wind Gap, Northampton County in eastern Pennsylvania.

**Length:** The park sits on almost 1,200 acres and contains over 18 miles of equestrian and multiple-use trails.

**Level of Difficulty:** Mostly easy

**Terrain:** The terrain varies from wooded trails to open fields and flat railroad grades to rolling hills. Many of the trails' surfaces are excellently maintained with stone dust or cinder footing to prevent erosion and to improve the surface. There are a few narrow, wooded trails but they are navigable (watch for approaching bikes at the blind turns).

**Horse Camping:** No

**Non-horse Camping:** No

**Maps and Info:** Jacobsburg Environmental Educational Center, 835 Jacobsburg Road, Wind Gap, PA 18091, (610) 746-2801, e-mail: jacobsburgsp@state.pa.us. Jacobsburg is part of the Department of Conservation and Natural Resources, Bureau of State Parks, PA. Call 1-888-PA-PARKS for general park info. Relevant trail information is posted at the trailhead. Maps are usually available at the trailhead, but it is recommended to call in advance for a map in the event they are out. Maps are helpful, as the many loops can be confusing to some riders.

**Activities:** Fishing, Hiking, Picnicking, Biking, Horseback Riding Trails, Hunting (during season), and X-C Skiing

**Fees for Trail Use:** None

**Permits for Trail Use:** None

**Comfort Station:** Yes, at the trailhead in the parking area

## DIRECTIONS:

From the south, take Route 22 to Route 512 north (just east of Allentown). Take the Route 512 exit (one exit for 2 directions) to the end of the ramp, make a right heading north on Route 512 toward the town of Bath. Go through the town of Bath and proceed to the Moorestown intersection. From the light at the Moorestown intersection, continue north on Route 512 for 2.3 miles to another light at Bushkill Ctr. Road. Make a right on Bushkill Ctr. Road. If coming from the north, take Route 33 to Route 512 south. Proceed on Route 512 south for 3 miles to Bushkill Ctr. Road and make a left onto Bushkill Ctr. Road.

Go 1.3 miles on Bushkill Ctr. Road. Make a left on Belfast Road. Travel .6 miles on Belfast Road. Make a right into the gated lot on the right. At this writing, there is no equestrian trailhead sign, however, one is planned in the future. The current sign says "Road Closed" and "No Parking", however, we confirmed that this is where equestrian trailhead parking is permitted. The gate has a chain and it appears to be locked but is not. Undo the chain and enter; reconnect the chain after entering and leave the gate in a closed position. The gated entrance, at first glance, seems a little tight for big rigs but we got our larger rig (50') in without any trouble. The lot is very large and there is plenty of room for large rigs and groups. The trail proceeds out of the back of the lot, just past the restrooms.

## THE TRAILS:

John and I have always found Jacobsburg to be a wonderful place to ride. These trails are on our "best maintained trails" list. Low-lying areas are covered with stone dust; they are well kept even though multiple users utilize them heavily. We have used this park for training our trail horses, as there are many well built, solid wooden bridge crossings to introduce them to. (However, as with all trail systems, the bridges can weather quickly. Be cautious and alert for signs of weaknesses in bridges. Report any concerns to the management of the park, as they may not be aware of the current condition of an individual bridge unless it is reported.) There are some road and stream crossings, although bridges are replacing most stream crossings. The paths wind around the Bushkill Creek, with many places to water the horses along the way. The trails are varied and interesting. The trails travel over stone dust/cinder covered old railroad grades where a nice gait or canter can be enjoyed for long stretches. The trails wind through the woods, meander around Bushkill Creek, cross over open rolling fields, and twist around low-lying brush. There is much wildlife to be seen throughout the park.

The Jacobsburg trails also pass the Old Henry Homestead, home to the Henry family who made the Henry rifle. Note the tree-lined entrance to the home; one can just imagine fine carriages traveling down its path carrying visitors for the Henry family. Also note the neighboring historical homes. *At the homestead, the horse trail previously required crossing the steel bridge, which is on a busy road. However, now, riders can cross within the park on the new wooden bridge near the homestead. A significant improvement, look for this interior bridge as it is a much safer crossing than the steel bridge which is on a blind turn. We confirmed with the office that equestrians are permitted to cross this bridge.* Also to be seen are the foundations and ruins of the colonial village of Jacobsburg, which can be viewed throughout the trail system.

While proceeding through the park, be alert for bike riders. This park is popular with mountain bikers and caution should be exercised at all times. However, we have found most of the bike riders who regularly utilize this park to be some of the most considerate that we have encountered, and to be an excellent example of how bikers and horseback riders can cooperatively share trails. Many thanks to the Keystone Mountain Bike Association and the Keystone Trails Association who published a trail etiquette guide to educate mountain bikers, horseback riders, and other trail users on proper trail etiquette, cooperative shared trail usage, and conservation of our trails. There are additional mountain bike groups, such as the Valley Mountain Bikers, that we have met at Jacobsburg who are striving toward the same objective. The positive efforts of such groups are reflected at Jacobsburg and other trails that we have visited, where so many trail users pleasantly share the trails. More unified and collaborative effort between bikers, horseback riders, and other trail users will help keep our trails open and preserved for all of us to share and enjoy.

For those whose horses just can't get used to bikes or are still in the early stages of training, try a visit during the week on a non-holiday. This is a really nice place to ride, and worth making the time to experience and enjoy it.

**HISTORICAL INFORMATION:**
The Jacobsburg Environmental Education Center includes most of the Jacobsburg National Historic District. The Jacobsburg name originated from Jacob Hubler who established the community circa 1740. The Jacobsburg National Historic District embodies the Henry family homestead. The Henry family's small arms business played a significant part in our nation's history. In 1750, William Henry I founded the first Henry gun factory in Lancaster (Pennsylvania). Later, in 1778, William Henry II began a gun making operation in close proximity to Jacobsburg. In 1792, William Henry II purchased the Jacobsburg land from the Jacob Hubler estate. About the same time, William Henry II built another gun factory, this one at Jacobsburg. An iron-producing forge was later added to produce guns. In 1812, an even larger factory was constructed nearby to meet increasing government needs. The Henry Homestead was also built, which is still standing today. The home can be seen from the equestrian trail on Henry Road in the southeast section of the park. Until the latter 1800's, the Henry family continued to produce small arms. During two centuries, the Henry family were major providers of firearms for early America's wars and conflicts including the Revolutionary War, the Civil War, and disputes on the Western Frontier. The enduring success of the Henry rifle was due to its quality, precision, toughness, and reasonable cost.

In 1959, the Department of Forests and Waters acquired the land from the city of Easton. In 1969, Project 70 appropriations resulted in additional land acquisitions. In 1980, the Henry Homestead site was restored as a direct result of the efforts of the Jacobsburg Historical Society. Later, in 1985, The Jacobsburg Environmental Education Center was officially dedicated as an educational center to be operated by the Pennsylvania Department of Environmental Resources (later DCNR),

Bureau of State Parks. In 1989, the Jacobsburg Historic Society was fortunate to have the opportunity to also obtain the nearby John Joseph Henry House (circa 1832). Periodically, both the Henry Homestead house and the John Joseph Henry House are open to the public for viewing and for educational presentations, including gun exhibits. Information can be obtained at the Jacobsburg Environmental Education Center.

Thanks go to everyone who has contributed to this wonderful, multiple-use park. So many well thought out improvements have been made. Over the years, we have personally seen this already good park just keep getting more and more user friendly for all types of trail enthusiasts. DCNR, various Jacobsburg trail volunteers and organizations, the Lehigh Valley Horse Council, the local mountain biker groups, and others have gone to great lengths to make the park what it is today. In addition, the Jacobsburg Historic Society has helped preserve a part of our nation's history so beautifully for all to see.

## NEARBY AND SURROUNDING AREA STABLES:
- Timberland Acres (lessons and boarding), Walnutport (610) 767-2055, e-mail: elliesqh@yahoo.com
- Edgewood Valley Farms (rodeos, boarding, and possible emergency overnight stabling), Nazareth (610) 759-3340
- FD Koehler Stables Inc., F. Koehler Prop. (overnight stabling, tack shop, boarding, and lessons), Bethlehem (610) 865-0438, 865-5110, 865-0161

## NEARBY VET SERVICES:
- E. Balliet & Associates, Northampton (610) 262-3203
- L. Wessel, E. Bangor (610) 588-9467

## NEARBY FARRIERS:
- E. Brandner, Northampton (610) 502-0137
- K. Martin, Allentown (610) 791-2375
- D. Brewer (farrier and dentist), Nazareth (610) 759-3340
- B. Gannon, Kunkletown (610) 381-3213

# 25. Rocky Ridge County Park
# York County Parks

**Lasting Impression:** A nice York County Park to ride with great overlooks!
**Location:** Rocky Ridge County Park is located near the city of York in Hallam, southcentral Pennsylvania.
**Length:** The park contains 750 acres and 12 miles of equestrian trails.
**Level of Difficulty:** The trails we rode were mostly easy to moderate. However, one section on Trail #3 was very difficult due to a steep, vertical angle. *(Regarding Trail #3, there are better alternates to take. We did note that maintenance is usually done on these trails, and some of the trails that become severely eroded were either improved or closed and substitutes were established. If this occurs with these types of trails, steepness or poor footing may not be a factor to consider, and the trails would be basically easy to moderate.)*
**Terrain:** The trails are a variety of flat terrain, gradual climbs, steep ascents and descents, lots of woods, nice, easy stone dust covered surfaces on a few sections, and rocky surfaces on many portions of the trail. Some stretches are very rocky but most had enough dirt surrounding the rocks for the horses to pick through. We did not find the rocks to be a major obstacle, however, horses need to be shod.
**Horse Camping:** No. (We camped in Gettysburg and traveled to this trail. See the Gettysburg chapter for more information.)
**Non-horse Camping:** No
**Maps and Info:** Call ahead as the trail may be closed if wet conditions exist. York County Parks, 400 Mundis Race Road, York, PA 17402-9721, (717) 840-7440, website: http://www.york-county.org. As it seemed with all the York County Parks, the trail maps were well stocked at the main areas and at some of the trailheads.
**Activities:** Hiking, Picnicking, Biking, Horseback Riding Trails, Hunting (during season), and X-C Skiing
**Fees for Trail Use:** None
**Permits for Trail Use:** None
**Comfort Station:** Yes

**DIRECTIONS:**
Take Route 30 from the east end of York to Mt. Zion Road/Route 24. (See the small Rocky Ridge County Park sign. Go north on Mt. Zion Road/Route 24 for 1 mile and slow down looking for Deininger Road, which is opposite the cemetery (you will see another Rocky Ridge County Park sign). Make a right, at the crest of the hill, onto Deininger Road. Follow Deininger Road to the park. Take the main road into the park. Do not take the first lot to the left, rather, bear right toward the Oak Timbers Picnic area. Continue all the way on the park road until the

road dead ends. You will know you are in the right spot if you are in the lot under the high power lines. The lot is huge, the largest we have parked at. Equestrian parking is located to the far right by the tie rails and the brown sign "equestrian unloading zone". There is room for all sized rigs. Trailhead #1 is by the unloading sign and is marked. Note some horses or riders will not feel comfortable unloading with the sound of the power lines above. If this is an issue, the lot is large enough to avoid parking directly underneath the lines.

## THE TRAILS:

The trails are multiple-use, offer scenic views of the Susquehanna Valley, and meander in and out of open fields and wooded sections. There are two observation decks and scenic overlooks. Departing from the lot, there is a power line, but most of the trails soon move away from this and enter the woodlands.

We really liked these trails and found them very enjoyable. We discovered another nice York County Park to ride! We rode Trails #1 to #2, #9 to #3 (see below), to #8, returning to #1; traveled via #4 to #1 and picked up another section of #8. We then rode Trail #6 to #5. Based on the name Rocky Ridge, we expected extremely rocky trails, but the trails were only slightly rocky. A few sections do have stretches with a higher concentration of rocks, but our horses had no problem picking through. Shoes are helpful, at least on the front. A stone dust type of gravel was laid on Trail #1, offering a wonderful, easy surface. The fitness trail also had fine stone or gravel added to it, resulting in an excellent surface. The trails are usually wide and should offer lots of room for multi-users to pass one another. Most trails were gradual except for the portion of Trail #3 coming off of Trail #9. During our visit, this was extremely steep with much weather erosion. In addition, with the run of hot dry weather, the surface was packed hard like cement resulting in poor footing. Do not take this trail if it is still in this described condition. This is best avoided until improvements are made; an alternate would be to bypass via Trail #8 and avoid Trail #3. We found that York County Parks do a great job of maintaining their parks and trails, so it is likely that this trail will be improved or rerouted in the future. The southern section of Trail #5 has a steep portion but the park laid railroad ties, which greatly enhanced the trail and prevented further erosion due to weather conditions. The railroad ties also provided a series of wide steps making it easier for the horses to travel its course. If the same improvements are made to Trail #3 with railroad ties or logs laid on the steep section to halt further decline, and some stone dust is added to restore traction, Trail #3 could be greatly improved and be usable.

Bring water for the horses. We rode the east section of the trail system, returned to the lot for water, and then rode the west section. Please note that during rain or "muddy conditions", the trails may be closed. Call in advance. Absolutely avoid the area near power lines during any wet weather.

We look forward to returning to this trail system, along with the other fine York County Parks. The variety or diversity of the York trails is immense, offering something for everyone.

**HISTORICAL INFORMATION:**
One of the first York County Park purchases, the county purchased this park in 1968. The park sits on a rocky hilltop near Hallam and provides two scenic observation decks. One is located at the southern end of the park and gives a view of the York Valley, and the second is located at the northern end of the park and provides views of the Susquehanna Valley.

**ADDITIONAL INFORMATION:**
- York County Chamber of Commerce, website: www.yorkonline.org, (717) 848-4000
- York County Visitor Bureau, website: www.yorkpa.org, (888)-858-YORK

**NEARBY AND SURROUNDING AREA STABLES:**
- Windswept Stables (boarding, lessons, overnight stabling, and trailer parking), Columbia (717) 684-3975
- Westfield Farm LLC (boarding, training, lessons, and possible emergency overnight stabling with Coggins and shot documentation), Dillsburg (717) 432-2828

**NEARBY VET SERVICES:**
- Greenglen Equine Hospital, Glen Rock (717) 235-4312
- Nandi Veterinary Associates, New Freedom (717) 235-3798

**NEARBY FARRIERS:**
- G. Lepley, York (717) 767-2433
- M. Wharton, York (717) 938-4323

# 26. William Kain County Park
# York County Parks

**Lasting Impression:** This ride has lots of changing scenery and offers an enjoyable ride around Lake Redman and Lake Williams. Ride high on the breast of the Lake Redman dam!

**Location:** William Kain County Park is located just south of the city of York in York County.

**Length:** The park contains over 1,600 acres and 10+ miles of equestrian trails.

**Level of Difficulty:** The trail varies greatly, from easy to moderate to difficult. We rode sections #2, #3, #4, #1, and a portion of #7. We found #2, #3, and #4 to be easy, leisurely, and mostly wide trails of good footing with very little rocks. Trail #1 varied from easy to difficult due to steep sections. The section of Trail #7, west of I-83 off of Trail #1, leads to and dead ends at a very small tunnel that horses can not physically pass through. We did not ride Trail #7 east of I-83, but we were told that the rest of Trail #7 was of a rough surface.

**Terrain:** Lots of rolling, gradual hills of firm dirt and grass terrain through open stretches and woodlands overlooking the lakes on Trails #2, #3, and #4. Other trails are steep, requiring switchbacks, such as Trail #1.

**Horse Camping:** No. (We camped in Gettysburg and trailered over to this park. See the Gettysburg chapter for more info.)

**Non-horse Camping:** Not within the park

**Maps and Info:** Call ahead as the trail may be closed if wet conditions exist. York County Parks, 400 Mundis Race Road, York, PA 17402-9721, (717) 840-7440, website: http://www.york-county.org. Maps were stocked at the parking areas during our visit.

**Activities:** Boating, Boat Rentals, Fishing, Hiking, Picnicking, Biking, Horseback Riding Trails, Hunting (during season), Sledding, X-C Skiing, and Radio Controlled Airplanes (off South Pleasant Ave.)

**Fees for Trail Use:** None

**Permits for Trail Use:** None

**Comfort Station:** Yes

**DIRECTIONS:**

Take I-83 to Exit #14 (Leader Heights Road). Take Route 182 west to South George Street. At the light at South George Street, make a left. Take South George Street for 1.8 miles, traveling through the town of Jacobus. Slow down and look for Church Street as it comes up quickly. Make a left on Church Street. Equestrian parking is at the Lake Redman parking lot which is on Church Street. Go down the hill and see the sign for the parking area. It is situated at the edge of Lake Redman in an open area. Within the lot, parking for horse trailers is on the left on the gravel surface. There is plenty of room for large rigs and groups of rigs. The parking area is a spacious, open loop so rigs can pull through. The trailhead is behind the concert stage and there is also another trailhead at the other end of the lot, which leads to trails east of I-83. We visited the trails west of I-83. (There is another lot at Lake Williams on Water Street, but trailers are not permitted due to the road being too narrow and windy.)

**THE TRAILS:**
The park surrounds two lakes, offering a diverse and captivating ride. This trail system was a very pleasant surprise as the scenery was stunning, the park was very well maintained, and there are some really nice trails and wonderful riding. The views along the lakes are absolutely beautiful. We rode on a Tuesday in mid September and it was quiet and we had the trails to ourselves. I am sure that this will differ greatly on the weekends, but either way we found this very worth the trip and just a really great ride. There was lots of wildlife, including multitudes of rabbits, deer, and birds including waterfowl. This is a good place for bird watching as there is an abundance and variety of colorful birds in the brush along the trail, and sleek herons in the shallows of the lake and also flying overhead. In the spring and fall, this trail system must be even more beautiful with the assortment of flowers and colors including honeysuckle and rhododendron. In the summer, on a hot day, riders may prefer to ride earlier in the day due to the sunny, open stretches.

The difficulty of the trail fluctuates. It is mostly easy on Trails #2, #3, and #4, which are wide, grassy paths or dirt stretches and, at the most, offer gradual climbs. (Although, watch for trails that are not marked that lead to the edge or ledge of the river; these may be foot paths, not horse paths, and not suitable for horses. Usually, there is a sign indicating where the horse trail continues.) Although Trail #2 is a nice pretty stretch, riders must cross a long car bridge of narrow width. We visited on a Tuesday and there was not a problem with heavy traffic, but there will likely be more activity on weekends or during peak season. If riders prefer to avoid this bridge, there is still plenty of riding on the south side of the bridge. To reach Trail #1 on the west side of I-83 and in order to ride the breast of the dam, riders need to cross South George Street. This is a very busy main road (even during the week). We did find, however, that there was lots of good visibility and wide shoulders by the bridge and dam. Keep in mind that riders and horses will need to be comfortable with passing motor traffic. After crossing the road, the trail travels to the top of the breast of the dam, which is a high, scenic, gorgeous ride. One side is a manicured lawn and the other side is a panoramic view of Lake Redman. For those who, like myself, aren't crazy about riding along high areas that abruptly drop off, I found that this one wasn't as bad as it looked or sounded. The path is very wide on the top and well designed. I felt comfortable riding across.

The dam accesses the Trail #1 loop. We prefer to ride clockwise so that the steep portion of the trail is ascended vs. descended. Once past the steep portion of switchbacks, the trail becomes wide and much easier. Riders then return over the dam and need to cross back over South George Street. Equestrians can either backtrack over the same crossing and re-ride the significant distance of Trails #2, #4, and #3 to return to the lot, or take the direct, shorter route by traveling on the side of South George Street to connect back with Trail #3 to the lot. We did not find walking over the bridge on the side of the road to be a problem, as there was a very wide shoulder. Rather, we found it more challenging trying to get back onto Trail #3 just after the bridge. On the left side of the road, traveling away from the dam and after the bridge, there is a brief but very vertical climb back to Trail #3. This connecting section is likely even more difficult to descend. The path appeared to be a shortcut made by frequent users of the trail to avoid riding the long stretch along the busy road to connect back to the trail system. If modifications could be made to the trail (such as a switchback), this would greatly help link up access to the dam with the rest of the trail and improve safety. We weren't crazy about this link as it was, but wanted to cover most of the trail during our visit so we took it. To avoid the leap up the side of the hill, riders would have to head further down South George Street to pick up where Trail #3 crosses to #4. That is a long ride down South George Street and the shoulder isn't as wide as it is on the stretch near the dam area. That is also a lot of busy road riding which we would not feel comfortable doing due to safety concerns. This section of the trail system is a personal judgment call of the rider, based on each individual rider's preference and ability of their horses to deal with the adjacent busy road. Also, if riders choose, they can keep the ride simple and just ride the relaxing lengthy loops of Trails #3 and #4, and avoid both the road and bridge crossings and any steeper terrain. However, choosing this will exclude some very picturesque portions of the trail system.

The trails are clearly marked but have a different system of marking than what we are used to. Some trails number from intersection to intersection, which correspond to the map and are a favorite method of ours as it allows for easy location identification. Others number a stretch, and the next stretch will be a different number. This park numbered the loops instead of the intersections or individual trails. So intersections with three different branches may have the same number because they are part of one loop. John, who is the more directionally gifted of the two of us, found this confusing. Ironically, I didn't. But either way, it is easy to get around with the lakes and map as a reference.

Since the lakes are public water sources, bring water for the horses to provide upon departure and return. In addition, there are brooks along the trail, but these may be dried out due to weather.

110

# *Ride Pennsylvania* Horse Trails

*E*arly spring camping at Tuscarora State Forest (top) and
summer camping at Wyoming State Forest (bottom)

# *Ride Pennsylvania* Horse Trails

*Garth* Rumsmoke enjoying the mountain laurel at Tiadaghton State Forest (top) &
John viewing the rhododendron at Promised Land State Park (bottom)

# *Ride Pennsylvania* Horse Trails

Wyoming State Forest (top and bottom)

# *Ride Pennsylvania* Horse Trails

*W*yoming State Forest (top) and Spring Valley County Park (bottom)

# *Ride Pennsylvania* Horse Trails

Wyoming State Forest Trails (top and bottom)

# Ride Pennsylvania Horse Trails

Covered bridge, Lehigh Parkway (courtesy of Barbara Cook)

# *Ride Pennsylvania* Horse Trails

Monument (top) and battlefield (bottom) at Gettysburg National Military Park

# Ride Pennsylvania Horse Trails

Bald Eagle State Forest (top and bottom)

# *Ride Pennsylvania* Horse Trails

Tuscarora State Forest (top and bottom)

# *Ride Pennsylvania* Horse Trails

The rail-trail cut through walls of rock on the Conewago Recreation Trail (top)
and the ruins of old homesteads along the White Clay Creek Trail (bottom)

# *Ride Pennsylvania* Horse Trails

Green Lane Park equestrian campground (top) and scenic view from the
equestrian campground (bottom)

# Ride Pennsylvania Horse Trails

Tioga State Forest (top and bottom)

# *Ride Pennsylvania* Horse Trails

Ricketts Glen State Park (top and bottom)

# *Ride Pennsylvania* Horse Trails

Lyndra Bills showing us the trails at Wissahickon Trail System (top) and the view along the path at Pennypack Park (bottom)

# *Ride Pennsylvania* Horse Trails

Bridge (top) and path (bottom) along the Delaware Canal State Park towpath

# Ride Pennsylvania Horse Trails

The entrance to the Pine Creek Rail-Trail (top) and the Pennsylvania Grand Canyon (bottom)

Our thanks to the park rangers and staff who made us feel very welcome, both during phone conversations and upon our arrival. All were very friendly, professional, and accommodating. We look forward to returning to this park in the near future, re-riding our favorite trails, and exploring the rest of the trail system.

## HISTORICAL INFORMATION:
William Kain County Park was established in the 1970's. The park derived its name from and credits its creation to William Kain, former Chairman of The York Water Company, who created the idea of a cooperative arrangement and lease between The York Water Company and the County of York. This is an interesting arrangement and has proved to be a successful concept. We are grateful to the creators and contributors of this trail system, as it is a true pleasure to ride.

## THINGS WE LEARNED THIS RIDE:
- We were reminded how diverse in level of difficulty one trail system can be and not to conclude too quickly that it is all together "easy". As it is, it can be difficult to give a rating to a trail due to different riders' expectations, perspectives, experience, and ability. Had we not crossed over to Trail #1 and #7, we would have generalized and concluded this trail system to be 'easy'. Depending on what section of trail we rode, we could walk away with a totally different impression of this trail system. To accurately describe or thoroughly rate a trail system, every branch and length of trail needs to be covered. However, the reality of time, weather, or other circumstances does not always permit this. So going forward, where possible, we will try to be (even) more specific as to what portion of the trails we rode.

## ADDITIONAL INFORMATION:
- York County Chamber of Commerce, website: www.yorkonline.org, (717) 848-4000
- York County Visitor Bureau, website: www.yorkpa.org, (888)-858-YORK

## NEARBY AND SURROUNDING AREA STABLES:
- Windswept Stables (boarding, lessons, overnight stabling, and trailer parking), Columbia (717) 684-3975
- Westfield Farm LLC (boarding, training, lessons, and possible emergency overnight stabling with Coggins and shot documentation), Dillsburg (717) 432-2828
- Artillery Ridge Camping Resort & National Riding Stable (overnight camping with hookups and stabling), Gettysburg (717) 334-1288
- Hickory Hollow Farm (trail rides, overnight stabling, and boarding), Gettysburg (717) 334-0349

111

**NEARBY VET SERVICES:**
- Greenglen Equine Hospital, Glen Rock (717) 235-4312
- Nandi Veterinary Associates, New Freedom (717) 235-3798

**NEARBY FARRIERS:**
- G. Lepley, York (717) 767-2433
- M. Wharton, York (717) 938-4323

Photo: Trail crossing Lake Redman Dam

# 27. Spring Valley County Park
# York County Parks

**Lasting Impression:** Wow! This is a park with a designated "animal activity" area, including equestrian show rings and fenced dog-training grounds.

**Location:** Spring Valley County Park is located south of the city of York in Shrewsbury, North Hopewell and Springfield Townships in southcentral Pennsylvania.

**Length:** The park contains 868 acres and 12+ miles of trail and road riding (many of the roads are dirt or gravel) within the park, of which, 5+ miles are trail riding. There are more miles of adjoining trails.

**Level of Difficulty:** Moderate due to climbs, some sections easy

**Terrain:** The park is made up of fields and wooded riding. The surface is mostly dirt or grass. There are some rocks but not a lot. The river area and Trail #3 have a greater concentration of rocks but are passable.

**Horse Camping:** No. (As with the other York County Parks, we camped at Gettysburg and trailered to this location.)

**Non-horse Camping:** No

**Maps and Info:** Call ahead as the trail may be closed if wet conditions exist. York County Parks, 400 Mundis Race Road, York, PA 17402-9721, (717) 840-7440, website: http://www.york-county.org. Horse show rings and dog-training rings are also available for rental. Maps are stocked at the entrance to the park.

**Activities:** Fishing, Hiking, Picnicking, Biking, Horseback Riding Trails, Hunting (during season), Sledding, and X-C Skiing

**Fees for Trail Use:** None

**Permits for Trail Use:** None

**Comfort Station:** Yes

**DIRECTIONS:**
Take I-83 to the Glen Rock Exit #8. Get off Glen Rock exit, bear right; at stop sign, make a left, go under I-83, traveling east on Route 216. Go 100 yards, see a road to the right, turn onto Potosi Road. Take Potosi Road for about 2 miles to Crest Road. The show grounds and training area can be accessed off of Crest Road. To access the trail parking area, continue straight past Crest Road and take the first road to the right. This is an uphill turn and is called Line Road. (Note that there seems to be a lot of Line Roads within the park and that can be confusing. Use the map as a point of reference.) Go right on Line Road, the lot is on the right just after the house. This is a big gravel lot with plenty of room to turn around. The trails lead directly out from the back of the parking area or across from the lot where the stage is. On Potosi Road, if you cross the creek, you have passed the turn and can travel to the next lot. There will be a T and

another "Line Road". Make a left, the lot is .25 miles down on the left. This is also a large lot.

## THE TRAILS:

I really enjoyed these trails and found them to be another pleasant York County surprise. This is a nice place to meander and offers a variety of terrain and scenery. The trails are nicely groomed (as we found the rest of the York County Parks), the trailheads well marked, the paths offer jumps for hunter/jumpers, and the picturesque trails meander along rolling farmland, and crisscross the Codorus Creek.

The trails vary from cut paths through fields, to wide woodland trails, to narrower trails winding throughout the forest. Although the trailheads are clearly marked, once on the trail it can be confusing due to many interweaving trails. But there are lots of points of reference and it should not be easy to get lost. The map is helpful. There are some short road crossings, but much of the park roads are gravel and not paved. We visited on a weekday so we could not comment on how busy it is during peak usage. It was very quiet during the week, although we did see other riders.

Riders should not expect a flat trail system. There are quite a bit of hills, but we did not find these to be difficult. The footing was good; and if you and your horses are comfortable with hills this should be no problem. Riders should be cautioned however, that often there are branches of the trails that deviate from the main trail system. Observe prior to entering the trail. If it looks steep, it may be. We encountered one such section on the east side of the Codorus Creek near Trail #3. We called it the 'Ridge Trail' because it was a really nice trail traveling along a wide ridge for some distance. At the end, a trail dropped off to the left. We did not take that trail, as it appeared to be a footpath or deviation from the equestrian trail. We instead took a trail to the right and soon we saw the trail markers again. A few times, within the interior of the trail system, it was unclear as to where the main trail continued. In the section near the 'Ridge Trail', we were able to hook up with the rest of the trail, which was a winding path that zigzagged through the forest, and return to the road and back to our parking area.

We thought some of the prettiest parts were along the Codorus Creek. There is plenty of water for the horses along this creek. It is a little rocky by the creek but it was navigable. During your visit, make sure you check out the show grounds and the neat, fenced-in area for dog training. The fields, where the rings are situated, offer a nice view of the surrounding countryside of rolling hills. There are numerous jumps throughout the park, making this an ideal destination for hunter/jumper/cross country enthusiasts. However, one thing we did observe is that bees like to nest in those wooden jumps, which often are situated in ideal, sunny locations. Prior to an event or trail ride, if it is peak bee season as it was during our visit, do inspect or exercise caution around these sites. Luckily, I did not directly follow John's horse and we only had a slight encounter. Depending on the pace, it's usually the second, third, and fourth horses that get hit heavily. (We have found the first horse on a trail ride encounters the snakes, bears, and other wildlife, and the rest of the horses encounter the ground bees.)

## HISTORICAL INFORMATION:
Spring Valley County Park was opened in the early 1970's. Old farm fields comprise Spring Valley Park. Many of the fields still have the stone walls that divided pastures and farmland. The park was established for recreational activities and includes an "animal activity" area. The facilities include rings for equestrian events and a dog training area.

## ADDITIONAL INFORMATION:
- York County Chamber of Commerce, website: www.yorkonline.org, (717) 848-4000
- York County Visitor Bureau, website: www.yorkpa.org, (888)-858-YORK

## NEARBY AND SURROUNDING AREA STABLES:
- Windswept Stables (boarding, lessons, overnight stabling, and trailer parking), Columbia (717) 684-3975
- Westfield Farm LLC (boarding, training, lessons, and possible emergency overnight stabling with Coggins and shot documentation), Dillsburg (717) 432-2828
- Artillery Ridge Camping Resort & National Riding Stable (overnight camping with hookups, trail rides, and stabling), Gettysburg (717) 334-1288
- Hickory Hollow Farm (trail rides, overnight stabling, and boarding), Gettysburg (717) 334-0349

## NEARBY VET SERVICES:
- Greenglen Equine Hospital, Glen Rock (717) 235-4312
- Nandi Veterinary Associates, New Freedom (717) 235-3798

## NEARBY FARRIERS:
- G. Lepley, York (717) 767-2433
- M. Wharton, York (717) 938-4323

# 28. Heritage Rail-Trail County Park
## York County Parks

**Lasting Impression:** A really nice, scenic, historical, and diverse rail-trail that extends miles into Maryland. Get your horse ready for tunnels!

**Location:** Heritage Rail-Trail connects from the city of York south into Maryland. The Heritage Rail-Trail is part of the York County Parks trail system.

**Length:** The Heritage Rail-Trail County Park consists of 176 acres and is 21 miles long.

**Level of Difficulty:** Easy, however, horses need to be comfortable with multiple trail users

**Terrain:** The trail is a 10' wide, multi-use trail with compacted stone and has wide shoulders. The trail is mostly flat. There are lots of shaded sections and some open stretches.

**Horse Camping:** No. (If you are visiting the area and don't mind the drive, one can camp at Michaux State Forest, or at Artillery Ridge Camping Resort in Gettysburg, and trailer over to this trail. This trail is about an hour (or less) drive from Michaux or Gettysburg.)

**Non-horse Camping:** No (however, the Indian Rock Campground is nearby)

**Maps and Info:** York County Parks, 400 Mundis Race Road, York, PA 17402-9721, (717) 840-7440, website: http://www.york-county.org. Maps are available that include detailed directions to each of the parking lots and the locations of the comfort stations. The maps were well stocked at both of the lots we visited.

**Activities:** Hiking, Biking, Horseback Riding Trails, and X-C Skiing (hunting may be permitted in certain adjoining areas during season)

**Fees for Trail Use:** None

**Permits for Trail Use:** None

**Comfort Station:** Yes. (Comfort stations can be found at the stations and several locations along the trail, including the Brillhart Station lot and the Seven Valleys lot.)

### DIRECTIONS:

There are a few areas to park along the length of the trail. One of the park representatives recommended the Brillhart Station section for equestrians. To reach the Brillhart Station lot, take I-83 to Exit #14 (Leader Heights Road/ Route 182). Travel west on Leader Heights Road for about .5 miles to Indian Rock Dam Road. (Leader Heights Road becomes Indian Rock Dam Road.) Follow Indian Rock Dam Road. After about 1.5 miles, slow down and begin to look for a left onto Days Mill Road. We did not see a sign saying "Days Mill Road" but there is a sign with SR3042 and a sign for Indian Rock Campground. Make a left on this road and travel about a mile. Once on Days Mill, bear right at the Y, go down a hill, see the RR signs, and travel to the parking lot on the left. This lot is a large, paved lot but does not have a separate designated equestrian area. However, equestrians are permitted to park here. We were able to test the trail at its peak as we visited on a summer holiday weekend when it was at its busiest. The lot had much activity with many bikers unloading and loading, however, we had no problem and had plenty of room. But, horses do need to be calm and comfortable with other trail activity. (Don't forget to clean up any horse droppings, as the lot is a paved multi-user lot.)

Another lot is the Seven Valleys parking area. Take I-83 to the Loganville Exit #10. Look for Route 214 signs. Travel on Route 214 through the town of Seven Valleys. Look for Eysters Machine shop and make a right into the lot. There are signs. The entrance to the Seven Valleys parking area is past the machine shop's parking and loading yard. The lot is a nice sized gravel section behind the shop and can fit a few horse trailer rigs, including larger rigs. (Large trucks have sufficient room to access the machine shop lot so larger trailers should also.) The lot is long vs. wide and will require some turning vs. pull-through. On the holiday when we visited, this lot did not have anyone parked there so there was plenty of room to unload and load horses. In addition, the machine shop was closed on the weekend so there was no business activity interfering with the entrance to the rail-trail lot. During the week, this access to the Seven Valleys lot could be partially blocked with machine shop operations. However, on a weekend, the Seven Valleys lot is probably the better lot to use when the machine shop is not in use. Plus on the weekend, this lot may be the more desirable of the two as it is more remote and further away from the busier sections near York. During the week, the Brillhart Station lot is likely the better choice for parking as there is much less activity during that time, and it is in a quiet location.

There are other lots where equestrian parking is permitted, but these two were the ones we visited. If choosing another lot, check with the York County personnel to ascertain that the lot can accommodate horse trailers. Note that the Richland Ave. section, north of the Brillhart Station lot toward the city of York, does not permit horse trailers.

**THE TRAILS:**
This is a really nice rail-trail! The trail is on a gradual railroad grade and is very easy. It is well done, well marked, and well maintained. There is excellent, solid footing of fine stone dust lining along most of the trail and there are mileage markers beside the path. The 10' wide trail parallels the intact but no longer used railroad bed. With a combination of the trail paralleling the intact railroad bed and the tunnel cut through solid rock, the path gives a very thrilling effect. One expects an old steam locomotive to come down the trail at any time.

The views are diverse and scenic. South of Brillhart Station, the trail passes between walls of rock and shale giving a dramatic appearance to the landscape. The railroad corridor travels along a rural country landscape with lots of changing scenery. Trees, providing shade in the hot weather, line much of the path. As you head south down the trail, the landscape opens up into farmland and the trail becomes less populated with decreasing activity. The pathway is also rich in history; there are old railroad stations to visit and various historical buildings along its route.

A must see is the Howard Tunnel. The tunnel is located just south of the Brillhart Station lot and is marked on the map. This is a scenic tunnel set against a background of rock and greenery. Bring your cameras as the tunnel offers a nice photo opportunity. (See the photo on the back cover.) We found the trail terrain to be wonderful, easy, and an ideal surface for a smooth ride. There are lots of picnic benches and tables along the way to enjoy a snack or lunch. We crossed over a few bridges and found them to be very well constructed. Also, do bring water for the horses to drink upon departure from and upon return to the parking area, as we did not encounter water that could be accessed directly from the rail-trail.

We very much enjoyed this trail but riders do need to be proactive and prepare for approaching bikes. This is a wide rail-trail with sufficient room for everyone, however, it is a popular trail with lots of activity. Although most of the hikers, bikers, and runners were very friendly and considerate, not every user chooses to travel, or knows to travel, a comfortable or sufficient distance from the horses. As with most of the rail-trails we visited, once you head away from the lot, the activity decreases quickly. From the Brillhart lot, we found the trail was less congested as we headed south away from the city of York. As indicated above, we did visit on a Labor Day weekend and probably experienced this trail at its peak period. It is likely to be much less active on a non-holiday weekend or on a weekday.

We have learned how many beautiful areas York County has to ride and we were grateful to York County for welcoming equestrians. All the locations that we visited had maps of the trails and large, gravel parking areas. The trails were clearly marked, nicely maintained, and clean. And the park staff was helpful, considerate, professional, and friendly. What a nice experience!

## HISTORICAL INFORMATION:
The Heritage Rail-Trail County Park is a newer park, just established in the late 1990's. Its length runs from within Maryland, to the Borough of New Freedom (in Pennsylvania near the Maryland border), to the city of York. Until recently, this was an active rail line and holds the distinction as being the nation's longest non-motorized trail that had active railroad use. The 10' wide gravel trail travels along side the railroad tract, with the rails still intact.

The Heritage Rail-Trail played a major role in history. In the 1800's, this was part of the Northern Central Railroad line, which connected Washington, D.C. to Harrisburg to New York State. The railroad quickly created growth and became central to the business economy along its route. As a result, the railroad was marked for destruction during the Civil War. With the goal of cutting Washington off, the Confederates targeted communication and transportation, demolishing bridges, and severing telegraph wires.

On his way to present the Gettysburg Address, President Lincoln traveled on the Northern Central. Many of the rural sections along the corridor still look like they did when Lincoln traveled along its path. The Hanover Junction station, where Lincoln was reputed to have been photographed, stands and has been restored to how it looked during the Civil War period. The New Freedom railroad station is also maintained and is listed along with the Hanover Junction railroad station in the National Register of Historic Places.

Operating since 1838, the 370 foot Howard Tunnel on the rail-trail holds the world record for the oldest, continuous functioning railroad tunnel. In the early 1970's, the Penn Central Railroad ceased to operate and severe weather inflicted major damage on the rail system. In 1990, the County of York acquired the rail line. By the end of 1999, the county had restored and completed construction of the trail system, and opened it for public use. Until just recently, the railroad still operated taking visitors on rides along the corridor.

The history of the railroad can be viewed at the displays and museums at the Howard Tunnel, Hanover Junction, and New Freedom train stations. Our thanks to Margie Lewis, Community Resource Coordinator, who was very helpful, graciously shared information on the York County Parks, and made us feel very welcome.

**THINGS WE LEARNED THIS RIDE**
- On this ride, I observed the seasoned bike riders and learned about the small (about the size of what the dentist uses in a patient's mouth) rear view mirrors that bikers attach to their helmets so they can see other trail users approaching from the rear. Those mirrors can come in handy for many trail uses. I wear a riding helmet and will be looking into getting one of those, as it can reduce turning around to check for approaching traffic. They appear to be a smart safety measure.

**ADDITIONAL INFORMATION:**
- York County Chamber of Commerce, website: www.yorkonline.org, (717) 848-4000
- York County Visitor Bureau, website: www.yorkpa.org, (888)-858-YORK

**NEARBY AND SURROUNDING AREA STABLES:**
- Artillery Ridge Camping Resort & National Riding Stable (overnight camping with hookups, trail rides, and stabling), Gettysburg (717) 334-1288

119

- Hickory Hollow Farm (trail rides, overnight stabling, and boarding), Gettysburg (717) 334-0349
- Windswept Stables (boarding, lessons, overnight stabling, and trailer parking), Columbia (717) 684-3975
- Rutledge (boarding only), Spring Grove (717) 225-3060
- Westfield Farm LLC (boarding, training, lessons, and possible emergency overnight stabling with Coggins and shot documentation), Dillsburg (717) 432-2828

**NEARBY VET SERVICES:**
- Greenglen Equine Hospital, Glen Rock (717) 235-4312
- Nandi Veterinary Associates, New Freedom (717) 235-3798

**NEARBY FARRIERS:**
- G. Lepley, York (717) 767-2433
- M. Wharton, York (717) 938-4323

# 29. Gifford Pinchot State Park
# DCNR
### (Department of Conservation & Natural Resources)

**Lasting Impression:** A beautiful, easy, quiet place to ride, conveniently located in close proximity to other interesting equestrian trails.

**Location:** Gifford Pinchot State Park is located near the town of Lewisberry, between Harrisburg and York, in northern York County, southcentral Pennsylvania. This park is within close driving distance to other equestrian trails such as the York County Trails, Gettysburg, or Codorus, and could be visited while en route to these other trails.

**Length:** The park consists of over 2,300 acres, of which there are several miles of equestrian trails that travel in various loops in the northern section of the park.

**Level of Difficulty:** Easy

**Terrain:** Some flat, some rolling hills, wooded hillsides

**Horse Camping:** No

**Non-horse Camping:** Yes

**Maps and Info:** Gifford Pinchot State Park, 2200 Rosstown Road, Lewisberry, PA 17339, (717) 432-5011, e-mail: giffordpinchotsp@state.pa.us. Call 1-888-PA-PARKS for general park info or for camping reservations.

**Activities:** Boating, Boat Rentals, Fishing, Biking, Hiking, Picnicking, Horseback Riding Trails, possible Hunting (during season), Camping, Ice Sports, and X-C Skiing

**Fees for Trail Use:** None

**Permits for Trail Use:** None

**Comfort Station:** Yes

## DIRECTIONS:
Take I-83 to the Lewisberry Exit #35 (connect via Route 382 north). Follow Route 382 north for 1.2 miles and look for Route 177 south. Take Route 177 south for 2 miles to Alpine Road. Make a left on Alpine (see the Gifford Pinchot sign). Travel about a half-mile on Alpine and you will see a gravel parking area on the right; there is a sign at the entrance. The entrance is narrow but we were able to get our large (50') rig in (with little room to spare). However, be careful entering this lot with low ground clearance rigs as there is a drop in the surface at the entrance to the lot! Due to the long length behind the wheels, we scraped the underside of our large trailer as we entered this lot. Once inside the lot, the parking area is of medium size and can accommodate larger rigs or a few small trailers.

## THE TRAILS:

We found these trails nice and leisurely in a quiet, wooded setting. There are many loops and they are marked as to where equestrians are permitted and not permitted. Do get a map, as it is helpful to keep from unintentionally going in circles.

There was very little other trail activity, the trail was easy, and we did not see any obstacles on the trails. One short section had some erosion but was easy to get around. As we found the trails to be peaceful and relaxing with little activity, this seemed like a good place to introduce a horse to trails.

Although this trail was worth the visit and ideal for folks who are looking for a short, leisurely ride; it is a shorter trail system. We did see many offshoots that had 'no equestrian' signs but the entrances looked very suitable to horses and exactly like the equestrian trails. If these trails are as nice throughout their length, maybe there is a possibility that some of these will be available to equestrians in the future, resulting in a longer equestrian trail system.

## HISTORICAL INFORMATION:

The park is named after Gifford Pinchot, a well educated politician and a founding father of the conservation movement. Born in the mid 1800's, he is noted for being the first American formally educated in forestry. Held in high esteem by President Theodore Roosevelt, Pinchot went on to become Chief Forester of the U.S. Division of Forestry. A combined effort of Roosevelt and Pinchot resulted in the administration and preservation of 200 million acres of forest.

But Gifford was unique and notable for many additional characteristics reflecting he was a man ahead of his time. To his much-deserved credit, Pinchot not only became governor of Pennsylvania; he worked long hours with a well publicized open door policy, making time for his entire public. He made the first Pennsylvania budget, reduced his own pay to meet the budget, eliminated debt, fought for employment positions during the depression setting precedent for the Civilian Conservation Corps, and was the first governor to employ women on his staff. Gifford continued to remain politically active and to fight for his causes during most of his life. This progressive man lived a long and productive life until passing away in 1946. In honor of Gifford Pinchot's valuable contribution to the national forest, the park was dedicated to Gifford Pinchot in 1961.

## NEARBY AND SURROUNDING AREA STABLES:
- Windswept Stables (boarding, lessons, overnight stabling, and trailer parking), Columbia (717) 684-3975
- Westfield Farm LLC (boarding, training, lessons, and possible emergency overnight stabling with Coggins and shot documentation), Dillsburg (717) 432-2828

- Artillery Ridge Camping Resort & National Riding Stable (overnight camping with hookups, trail rides, and stabling), Gettysburg (717) 334-1288
- Hickory Hollow Farm (trail rides, overnight stabling, and boarding), Gettysburg (717) 334-0349

**NEARBY AND SURROUNDING AREA B&Bs:**
- Pheasant Field B&B (overnight stabling, boarding, and trailer parking available), Carlisle (717) 258-0717

**NEARBY VET SERVICES:**
- Cumberland Valley Equine Services, Carlisle (717) 249-7771
- Greenglen Equine Hospital, Glen Rock (717) 235-4312

**NEARBY FARRIERS:**
- G. Lepley, York (717) 767-2433
- M. Wharton, York (717) 938-4323

# 30. Codorus State Park
# DCNR
### (Department of Conservation & Natural Resources)

**Lasting Impression:** Codorus State Park is a picturesque park and a fun place to ride, the result of a unique arrangement.

**Location:** Codorus State Park is located 3 miles southeast of Hanover, in York County, southcentral Pennsylvania. This is a nice trail to combine, while in the area, with a visit to nearby Gettysburg, Gifford Pinchot, Michaux, or the York County Parks.

**Length:** Codorus State Park contains over 3,300 acres with 7+ miles of equestrian trails. There were many newly cut trails during our last visit that we did not see on the map, so this amount has increased.

**Level of Difficulty:** Easy

**Terrain:** Easy, some flat, some rolling hills, gradual terrain, dirt or mowed grass, not rocky

**Horse Camping:** No. (As with the other York trail systems, we camped in Gettysburg and trailered to this trail.)

**Non-horse Camping:** Yes

**Maps and Info:** DCNR, Codorus State Park, 1066 Blooming Grove Road, Hanover, PA 17331-9545, (717) 637-2816, e-mail: codorussp@state.pa.us. Call 1-888-PA-PARKS for general park info or for camping reservations.

**Activities:** Boating, Boat Rentals, Fishing, Hiking, Picnicking, Swimming, Horseback Riding Trails, Biking (in a separate area from equestrian trails), Hunting (during season), Camping, Sledding, Ice Sports, and X-C Skiing

**Fees for Trail Use:** None

**Permits for Trail Use:** None

**Comfort Station:** Yes

### DIRECTIONS:

There are two areas to park. There is a nice, large lot that can be accessed as follows: Take Route 116 from Hanover, and make a right onto Route 216 east. Take Route 216 for 3 miles until you see the park. Within the park, go over the third bridge and make a left onto Sinsheim. There are lots of signs and the park is very clearly marked; just follow the signs. Parking is on the left. The lot has a wide entrance and parking area, which can accommodate large rigs or several rigs. There is also another lot: After the third bridge, travel to the intersection of Lakeview. Parking is at this crossroads.

### THE TRAILS:

Codorus is an old time favorite of ours and we have ridden it over a period of years. The parking area and equestrian trails are in the eastern side of the park.

124

Upon entering the designated parking area, we immediately feel welcome at this park due to the many equestrian signs and the well groomed lots.

These trails are nice! They consist of many interconnecting trails. The map is helpful; however, we found many new trails that were not on our map. The new trails were marked (already) and easy to follow. The trails are mostly wide stretches of mowed grass, or wide, dirt trails cut through the woods and logging type roads. The paths are gentle and leisurely. The nice trail surfaces and rolling fields of mowed grass make it a fun trail for a gait, trot, or canter. There are lots of wooded areas offering shelter from the weather, and also many open areas offering scenic views of the lake. The variety of mature trees surrounding the lake should be very colorful in the fall. Sometimes, in the internal sections, the trails can get a little confusing but usually the trails lead to Lake Marburg that serves as a point of reference or a sign or a landmark to help orient oneself. There are a few road crossings to continue along the trail. We visited on a Monday in mid September so they were not busy, but they are more likely to be busy on the weekends. These trails are very enjoyable and the park's attention to detail shows.

There are various locations to water the horses along the way. There is a nice place to have lunch along the trail or to stop and enjoy the view. This location has benches along the path; the large, grassy area down the center of the woods allows a scenic overlook of the lake.

## HISTORICAL INFORMATION:
Codorus State Park is the result of an interesting cooperative effort. The P.H. Glatfelter Paper Company of Spring Grove, PA purchased a portion of the Codorus land to build an earth fill dam to meet its water needs. The Glatfelter Paper Company owns the dam, and the surrounding property is owned by the Commonwealth of PA. In 1965 and 1966, the park land was purchased under "Project 70". Over the years, the park has been known by a few names. One of these names was Lake Marburg after the small town that was covered by the lake when the dam was built.

The funding for the park and recreational facilities was a result of the government's "Project 500" bond program and the Land and Water Conservation Fund. Currently, the Department of Conservation & Natural Resources runs the park.

## THINGS WE LEARNED THIS RIDE:
- If the lake is extremely low due to dry weather or drought conditions, and even though the shore appears to be firm ground, do not attempt to approach the lakeside. That bank was previously lake bottom and swallowed John's horse up to his knees like quicksand. I was quite concerned that both would get hurt but our horse kept it together and freed himself. Scary! On this very hot

125

day, we decided instead to look for the old, no longer used paved boat ramp roads leading into the water, which offered a solid surface to travel to the lake so the horses could have a drink. We will be more cautious of such conditions in the future!

- When crossing the bridge, upon seeing an oncoming vehicle, I trotted my horse to move him along. He kept spooking, turning his hindquarters to the road, and I couldn't figure out why. Although there was plenty of room, I didn't like this behavior along a road. Turns out, by trotting him, he was kicking up road stones which were bouncing off the metal road guard and making a noise. Not knowing what this sound was behind him, he was moving his hindquarters away from that noise toward the road. Next time, in this type of predicament, I will walk him across.

## NEARBY AND SURROUNDING AREA STABLES:
- Artillery Ridge Camping Resort & National Riding Stable (overnight camping with hookups, trail rides, and stabling), Gettysburg (717) 334-1288
- Hickory Hollow Farm (trail rides, overnight stabling, and boarding), Gettysburg (717) 334-0349
- Windswept Stables (boarding, lessons, overnight stabling and trailer parking), Columbia (717) 684-3975
- Rutledge (boarding only), Spring Grove (717) 225-3060
- Westfield Farm LLC (boarding, training, lessons, and possible emergency overnight stabling with Coggins and shot documentation), Dillsburg (717) 432-2828

## NEARBY VET SERVICES:
- Nandi Veterinary Associates, New Freedom (717) 235-3798
- Greenglen Equine Hospital, Glen Rock (717) 235-4312

## NEARBY FARRIERS:
- G. Lepley, York (717) 767-2433
- M. Wharton, York (717) 938-4323

# 31. Gettysburg National Military Park
# National Park Service

**Lasting Impression:** Ride the battleground at Gettysburg, a defining point in our nation's history.

**Location:** Gettysburg, Adams County, southcentral Pennsylvania

**Length:** 20+ miles. This may change. There has been discussion of the equestrian area that crosses Pickett's Charge being closed to horses or rerouted, and possibly the path through town to the Eternal Light being closed.

**Level of Difficulty:** Easy

**Terrain:** Most of the terrain is gentle and diverse with flat paths, rolling hills, meadows, open farm fields, and wooded sections. The trails are clearly marked with brown and white equestrian signs. Some paved road crossings are required to ride the complete loop. The surface is dirt, stone dust, or grass. There are not a lot of rocky sections, but there are a few rocky stretches around Little Round Top and at a couple of other locations, but they are passable. There is water along the trail.

**Horse Camping:** Other than special events, there is no public horse camping within the park. However, adjacent to the park, there is a full service campground with horse camping at Artillery Ridge Camping Resort. Corrals and stalls are available. Riding directly from the campground can access Gettysburg's trails.

**Non-horse Camping:** Special events. Non-horse camping is also at Artillery Ridge and other nearby campgrounds.

**Maps and Info:** National Park Service, 97 Taneytown Road, Gettysburg, PA 17325-2804, (717) 334-1124, website: www.nps.gov/gett/index.htm. Additional information available from the Gettysburg Travel Council (717) 334-6274 and the Chamber of Commerce (717) 334-8151. Details regarding guided horseback tours, equestrian camping, and Gettysburg Diorama are available at Artillery Ridge Camping Resort, 610 Taneytown Road, Gettysburg, PA 17325, (717) 334-1288, website: www.artilleryridge.com, e-mail: artilleryridge@earthlink.net.

**Activities:** Hiking, Picnicking, Biking, Horseback Riding Trails, Guided Tours, Guided Horseback Trail Rides (at Artillery Ridge National Riding Stable), Special Events, and Historical Reenactments. Hunting is normally not permitted, however, special herd reduction hunts may take place; check with the park for that information.

**Fees for Trail Use:** None

**Permits for Trail Use:** None

**Comfort Station:** Yes, at McMillan Woods, and at various locations throughout the park

127

## DIRECTIONS:

To McMillan Woods equestrian day parking: Take Route 30 to Seminary Ridge Road (west end of Gettysburg). The turn for Seminary Ridge Road is at General Lee's headquarters. Head south on Seminary Ridge Road for one mile. Seminary Ridge Road becomes Confederate Avenue. Continue straight. Come to a McMillan Woods Youth Group Campground sign. Make a right; travel to the end of the road. The equestrian parking and trailheads are at this location. Note: we met some equestrians that commented they felt Route 30 was difficult to haul on due to traffic, width, turns, etc. An alternate is to approach from the south as follows: If traveling from Route 15, the Visitor Center, or the Artillery Ridge Camping Resort, take Route 134/Taneytown Road north to Route 116 west. Take Route 116 to (Seminary Ridge) Confederate Avenue into the park. Make a right on the gravel road following signs to McMillan Woods. The lot is large and has room for several rigs.

To Gettysburg National Military Park Visitor Center (Due to crowds and limited parking, do not bring horse trailers to the Visitor Center.): From the north, take Route 30 to the town of Gettysburg. In Gettysburg, look for South Washington Street to Taneytown Road (Route 134). Take South Washington Street; travel straight and South Washington Street becomes Taneytown Road (Route 134). Go a short distance; the Visitor Center is on the right on Taneytown Road. Or, if traveling from the south, take Route US 15 to Route 134 north. Route 134 becomes Taneytown Road. Travel between 2 and 3 miles on Route 134/Taneytown Road; the Visitor Center is on the left.

To Artillery Ridge Camping Resort and National Riding Stable: If coming from the north, continue from the Visitor Center above on Taneytown Road. Artillery Ridge is just south of the Visitor Center on the left (east) side. Or, if traveling from the south, take Route US 15 to Route 134 north to Taneytown Road (about 2 miles). Artillery Ridge Camping Resort and National Riding Stable is on the right. Campers and day riders (fee) can park at the campground and ride directly from the campground onto the trails. The trailhead is on the opposite side of the road from the campground office.

## THE TRAILS:

Gettysburg National Military Park is a popular park with multiple-use trails. The trails pass over open fields, through woodlands, across streams, and by historic homes and markers. This is a beautiful, yet sad place where so many lives were lost. One can sense what transpired here long ago while traveling from monument to monument and reading the descriptions. The park has been so well preserved that it feels like a step back in time, and perhaps not such a long time ago after all. This is a special place, a major turning point in our nation's history.

Bridle maps of the park are available, helpful, and recommended as they indicate the location and name of various historical sites. Maps, rules, tours, and other park information can be obtained at the Visitor Center or at the nearby campground at Artillery Ridge. Riders are requested to stay on the equestrian trail and not to ride up to the monuments to prevent damage. The park also asks riders not to exceed a walk throughout the park. The trails are marked and easy to follow; there are signs directing riders. (The map helps in case there is a detour or you miss a sign. During our most recent visit, a section of the trail near Big Round Top was closed to equestrians. Riders are directed to an alternate route along the road before the trail can again be picked up. This closed section was one of my personal favorites, so I am hoping it will be re-opened to horseback riders in the near future.) Some road crossing is necessary. There is lots of activity within the park, especially buses full of very expressive, energetic children on group trips. Horses need to be comfortable with this type of activity. Except for a few areas, much of the park's equestrian trails are some distance from the bus and tourist stops, which helps minimize any interaction. Our horses didn't seem to have a problem, but it is well advised to bring horses that are seasoned trail horses.

There are lots of beautiful vistas overlooking the surrounding countryside; much of it still looks like it did in 1863. As you ride, you will also have a good view of the adjoining picturesque Eisenhower Farm, home to Dwight D. Eisenhower. We really enjoy visiting this park, and what more appropriate way to see it than on horseback!

**ARTILLERY RIDGE CAMPGROUND DESCRIPTION:**
When John and I have visited Gettysburg, we have always stayed at the commercial campground at Artillery Ridge Camping Resort (aka Gettysburg Horse Park). Artillery Ridge can accommodate about 60 horses and that number is growing. The campground has a variety of campsites including large pull-through sites for very large rigs and convenient access to the equestrian trails at Gettysburg. Artillery Ridge is one of our favorite horseman's camps as we have always found it clean, organized, nicely maintained, and professionally run. It is a full service facility with box stalls, corrals, showers, hookups (water and electric), laundry, bike rentals, guided horseback tours, cabin rentals, pool, arcade, movie pavilion, camp store, gift shop, diorama, historical reenactments, museum, equestrian clinics, a round pen, and a large, fenced arena to warm up your horse! There is even a dump station that big rigs can access and has a smart design allowing drainage from either side. Full service horseman's camps like these are hard to find in this region. Plus there is so much to see locally if the weather is not suitable for riding. But don't forget your negative Coggins as it is required and is checked. Pets are permitted.

During our stay at Artillery Ridge, we visited the Gettysburg Diorama. The Diorama is a miniature HO scale model of Gettysburg as it was during July of 1863, with an explanation of the three days of the battle as the events unfolded. We found this very helpful in understanding the layout of the battlefield for our ride. The room of the diorama also has an interesting museum, which houses many original Civil War Artifacts including cavalry saddles. And the campground has a neat, new feature for horseback riders! This is a must do to truly appreciate what transpired on the battlefields. Artillery Ridge Campground has produced an audiotape with headset, detailing the ride from Artillery Ridge campground into and through the park describing the events of the battle and the significance of the landmarks, all timed to when you will be riding past them. (Sorry, gaited horse folks may have to periodically pause as the tape is geared toward a Quarter Horse walk.) Not only did the tapes recap what we learned at the Gettysburg Diorama, but also gave a compassionate account of the sacrifice and personal perspectives of the men of both the Union and Confederate armies. There are also heartfelt stories of the people, along with some music of the time. Both of us enjoyed the old marching music, as it was fun to ride and listen to, and seemed to match the rhythm of our horses' hoof beats. Then the audio wonderfully concludes with the Gettysburg address, reminding the listener that the outcome of the war was consistent with our founding fathers' intention that this nation was created on the basis that all men are created equal and our nation would remain united and indivisible. Closing with a "United We Stand" statement and the Battle Hymn of the Republic, the tape gave a very moving reminder of what our great country is truly about. We felt we got so much more out of this visit by both viewing the diorama and listening to this audio tour. If you like the audio tour, make sure you tell Ray Starner (see photo) who was instrumental and influential in the creation and the availability of the tapes. Ray, a very friendly man, is the General Manager who runs this busy campground. Just look for him overseeing the camp operations on his four-wheeler.

As this is a very popular campground; reservations are recommended. While making reservations, do confirm what specific paperwork (i.e., Coggins) is needed upon arrival. The campground also permits equestrian day parking for a nominal fee. Horse rentals, guided tours, and weekend packages are available. This is a nice destination for equestrian folks with non-equestrian family members too, as there is something for everyone to do.

Just a short distance down the road from the campground is the National Park's Visitor Center. There is an excellent, huge, comprehensive museum (free) at the Visitor Center. This is a must see! There are uniforms, rifles, guns, cannons, and personal artifacts, just about everything from the battle at Gettysburg. We found one of the most interesting displays to be the personal furniture of nearby residents, showing bullet holes through the wood. The Visitor Center is a good option for a rainy day, but try to visit on off peak hours.

## HISTORICAL INFORMATION:

Gettysburg National Military Park is home to the scene of one of the bloodiest and most decisive battles of the American Civil War. On three days in July 1863, the Union and Confederate armies fought a battle that would end with General Pickett's disastrous charge. Over 152,000 men fought in the battle with 550 cannons, plus other weapons, in a 25 square mile radius resulting in over 50,000 human casualties and the death of 5,000 horses. (I was also astonished to hear that a total of 1.5 million horses were lost as a result of the Civil War!)

Although today Gettysburg is a peaceful site with rolling fields, scenic meadows, and old homesteads, statues of marble and bronze stand as reminders and tributes to those who lost their lives in battle. Visitors can walk, ride, or drive to these monuments to understand what took place in July 1863.

## THINGS WE LEARNED THIS TRIP:

- Take the high ground. (If you take the tour, you will not forget this.)
- Do take the audio headphone tour to really get the most meaning out of the visit.
- Wilderness primitive camping does have its merits, but after many days of doing that, we especially appreciate a full service horseman's camp like Artillery Ridge, where we felt the horses could be safe and comfortable while we indulged ourselves at the variety of nearby attractions and excellent restaurants.
- And on an important note, we were reminded of the immense sacrifice that many made to establish this great country today, as we know it.

## NEARBY OR SURROUNDING AREA EQUESTRIAN TRAILS WITHIN AN HOUR DRIVE FROM GETTYSBURG:

- Codorus
- Michaux
- Cumberland
- Gifford Pinchot
- York County Trails: Heritage Rail-Trail, William Kain, Spring Valley, Rocky Ridge

## NEARBY ATTRACTIONS:

- Gettysburg National Military Park Visitor Center & Cyclorama Center on Taneytown Road. (Be sure to visit the museum at the Visitor Center.)
- Historic town of Gettysburg
- Eisenhower National Historic Site
- And there are lots more. For additional information, see the Gettysburg Convention and Visitor's Bureau website at www.gettysburg.com or www.gettysburgcvb.org. They can also be reached by calling (717) 334-1166 or (800) 337-5015.
- If you like historic restaurants, one of our favorites is the Springhouse Tavern at the Dobbin House in Gettysburg (717) 334-2100, website: www.dobbinhouse.com.

This building served as a station for the Underground Railroad in the 1800's, and the crawl space is depicted in the room on the second floor of the entrance to the Springhouse Tavern. This room is open for visitors to view.

## NEARBY STABLE AND FULL SERVICE HORSEMAN'S CAMP:
- Artillery Ridge Camping Resort & National Riding Stable (overnight camping with hookups, trail rides, and stabling), Gettysburg (717) 334-1288

## NEARBY STABLES:
- Windswept Stables (boarding, lessons, overnight stabling, and trailer parking), Columbia (717) 684-3975
- Hickory Hollow Farm (trail rides, overnight stabling, and boarding), Gettysburg (717) 334-0349

## NEARBY VET SERVICES:
- Emmitsburg Veterinary Hospital, Emmitsburg, MD (301) 447-6237

## NEARBY FARRIER:
- B. Buxton, Gettysburg (717) 337-5959

# 32. Tuscarora State Forest & The Iron Horse Trail
## DCNR
### (Department of Conservation & Natural Resources)

**Lasting Impression:** A big, beautiful, rugged area to camp and ride.

**Location:** Tuscarora State Forest is located in southcentral Pennsylvania near the town of Blain, in Perry County. The forest extends into Franklin, Cumberland, Huntingfon, Juniata, Perry, and Mifflin counties. The Tuscarora State Forest contains The Iron Horse Trail, a rail-trail that is linked with the Tuscarora equestrian trails.

**Length:** This is a large place; the forest consists of over 90,000 acres. A total number of riding miles was not listed; however, individual equestrian trail lengths total over 75 miles, including the 10-mile stretch of the Iron Horse Trail. Plus there are many more miles of additional trail riding on the dirt/gravel State Forest roads.

**Level of Difficulty:** Easy to Difficult

**Terrain:** This area has it all and is diverse with terrain consisting of flat stretches, rolling hills, steep climbs, gradual ascents, wooded trails, open areas, easy footing, and some very rocky sections. There are many really nice trails in Tuscarora State Forest. Except for the Iron Horse Trail, most of the Tuscarora trails we rode were easy or moderate, but there are some very challenging trails too. We did not ride the Tuscarora Trail but were told some parts were very steep and rocky. The Bistline Trail had some rocky sections too. At the time of our visit, sections of The Iron Horse Trail were very difficult or impassable. The Iron Horse Rail-Trail surface was extremely rocky and rugged, with many detours due to growth or erosion. When improved or finished, this rail-trail should be a really nice trail as it travels through some scenic forest land. Overall, we found much of the trails to be gradual, but some of the power lines can be a steep climb or decline. Usually, there was a good view of what could be expected along the power line prior to riding it. Due to the varied terrain, horses should have shoes. We found borium to be helpful.

**Horse Camping:** Yes, camping application and reservations are required

**Non-horse Camping:** Yes

**Maps and Info:** To obtain equestrian maps, information, camping application, and reservations; call (717) 536-3191 or write Tuscarora State Forest, R.D. #1, Box 42-A Blain, PA 17006. Applications and reservations can be faxed to (717) 536-3335. E-mail is at fd03@state.pa.us. At this writing, a revised, more detailed equestrian map and information packet is being developed. Do call ahead for maps as this is a big trail system and maps may not be at the equestrian trailheads. Also, the maps provide topographic information, which is useful for this mountainous region. For information regarding the four State Parks, call 1-888-PA-PARKS. For information regarding the Iron Horse Trail, contact the PA Rails-to-Trails Conservancy at (717) 238-1717, website: www.railtrails.org. The positive tone of the brochure and nice remarks of the folks at the forest district office reflected a genuine interest in working with equestrians. Comments were said to be welcomed and "appreciated". I was told this area has a lot of faithful followers and that the equestrians have expressed a lot of interest in Tuscarora. Also, local volunteers have been active in marking the trails. My impression was that there was a cooperative, joint effort being made by both the officials of the forest and the equestrians. Great to hear!

**Activities:** Hiking, Biking, Horseback Riding Trails, Horse and Non-horse Camping, Fishing, Picnicking, and X-C Skiing. Hunting is permitted during season. State Parks in the Tuscarora area also offer swimming and boating.

**Fees and Permits for Trail Use and Horse Camping:** There is no fee for camping or trail use, however, an application, permit, and reservations are required in advance for motorized camping or non-motorized camping for more than one night. Permits must be placed on the vehicle where they can easily be seen.

**Comfort Station:** There is an outside toilet at Shaeffer Run. Additional facilities are at the State Parks. Colonel Denning State Park and Fowlers Hollow State Park offer dump stations. Before inquiring if there will be a usage fee, check the dump station out in advance (without the whole rig) as there may not be sufficient room for large units.

## DIRECTIONS:

Take I-81 to Wertzville Road Route 944 Exit #61. Go 8 miles to Sterretts Gap. (While traveling the 8 miles, you will come to a split in the road; continue going straight bearing right. After bearing right, you are still on Route 944.) Route 944 climbs up the mountain (we didn't find this to be a difficult climb). You will then come to a stop sign, which is Sterretts Gap. At Sterretts Gap, Route 944 becomes Route 34. Bear right; follow Route 34 north for about 4 to 5 miles. Route 34 will join PA 850 west. There is a Dromgold sign and PA 850 will turn to the left. Bear left and take PA 850 west for 10 miles. PA 850 will wind in and out of small towns; follow signs saying PA 850 west. (There is a sharp right in Landisburg.)

Continue into Loysville and a stop sign at Route 274. Make a left on Route 274. Stay on Route 274 into the town of Blain (it is about 9 miles to Blain). Continue past Blain for about another 5 to 6 miles. Pass the Forest District Office on the right. About .25 miles past the district office, look for a somewhat narrow dirt and gravel road on the left called Upper Buck Ridge Road. (There is a Fowlers Hollow green park sign.) Make a left onto Upper Buck Ridge Road. Proceed on Upper Buck Ridge Road for about a mile. This is a winding country road and passes a Christmas tree farm. Look for a dirt and gravel road to the right, which is Hemlock. (There is a State Forest sign.) To access horse camps #67 & #66, make a right on Hemlock. Site #67, Alfarata Trail, is the first left, and Site #66, Rising Sun, is at the top of the mountain on the right. (A vehicle that can handle a short but pretty good climb is needed to reach Site #66.) Red numbered markers indicate where camping is permitted. There are various camping sites for non-equestrians along this route and

134

throughout other locations in Tuscarora. To access the day parking, continue on Upper Buck Ridge to Fowlers Hollow State Park. Enter the Fowlers Hollow State Park. There is a large loop at the entrance on the left where equestrian day users can park. (This is where the water spigot is located that campers can use.) Ride toward the picnic area and follow signs to the trails.

To reach the Iron Horse Trail, travel on Hemlock toward Big Spring State Park. There is a small lot on the right just before Route 274. We had our larger rig and proceeded to the intersection of Route 274 and Hemlock, made a right on Route 274 and parked in a large, gravel lot on the right. We also proceeded down to site #62, which is on the left side of Route 274 near Shearer Dug Trail. (Sections of Site #62 were under development during our visit, and its permitted use may change. Check with the office first.) The Iron Horse trail has an interesting tunnel and can be accessed on foot from Big Spring State Park.

**THE TRAILS:**
The area is huge with numerous days of riding available! There is a North Block and a South Block. Both have many equestrian trails and equestrian camping. We visited the south section but were told the north section has some nice riding too. Most of the equestrian trails, camping area, and trailheads described in this article are in the south section in the vicinity of Fowlers Hollow State Park and Big Spring State Park. But there are many other trails to explore, too numerous to describe here. Information on other camping options and trails can be obtained from the State Forest Office.

The Tuscarora region also contains four Natural and Wild Areas: Hemlocks Natural Area, Hoverter and Sholl Box Huckleberry Natural Area, Frank E. Masland, Jr. Natural Area, and the Tuscarora Wild Area. In addition, there are four State Parks: Colonel Denning State Park, Big Spring State Park, Fowlers Hollow State Park, and Little Buffalo State Park.

The Tuscarora equestrian trail system consists of many loops and offshoots. The trails are multi-use and bikes are permitted along with hiking. Both day use and overnight use is permitted. The trails are divided into four groups: Fowlers Hollow State Park Trailhead, Showaker Ranger Headquarters Trailhead, Hickory Ridge Area Trails, and Henry's Valley Area Trails. Each of these four areas consist of several trail systems. Most of the trails are marked with colored blazes. The map and brochure, which can be obtained from the State Forest Office, list each trail's length, description, marker details, and miles. There are also many dirt or gravel forest roads that can be ridden. We visited for four sunny days in May and we only encountered one vehicle while on horseback. We did not see anyone on the trail yet the trails were used. However, we did see several equestrians at the campgrounds and some equestrian day users. So the trails are getting plenty of use; it is just the large area can absorb the users and still retain a feeling of having the forest mostly to oneself. There are thousands of acres to ride, mostly nice, wide trails, old logging roads closed to public motorized use, or park gravel roads. There are some sections that are rocky but many sections are wonderful, easy stretches without rocks. Where there were rocks (other than the Iron Horse Trail), we found those trails passable. The trails are well marked with lots of signs and markings on the trees. If the trails are no longer showing markings, you may have traveled off course. We ended up on an outlying trail, which did not have markings, however, it wasn't difficult to backtrack and return to the main trails (especially when we ran into a bear). Take a bridle trail map and a topo map.

Occasionally, some of the trails are closed for maintenance or seeding, so observe signs. We rode a loop from Site #66, Rising Sun, at the top of the mountain which varied from easy to moderate with just a few more challenging sections. We took Hemlock Road to Twig Trail. Twig was rocky but pretty and passable. The trail could get a little narrow yet it was not too bad. Then we traveled from Twig to Fowlers Hollow Road and made a left on Fowlers Hollow Road. We proceeded on Fowlers Hollow Road and made a right on Bastille Trail. This is a pretty trail by a stream and a footbridge, but Bastille is extremely rocky. (An alternate is to stay on Fowlers Hollow Road into Fowlers Hollow Camp.) Then we road Bastille to Hart Ridge Trail which was a nice trail. We made a right on Bastion Trail, a very nice trail with wide, grassy stretches, a watering hole, and it travels past site #68, the equestrian camping area. (This open area is a shale pit and is located just before the gate area. This looked good for day parking and can be used for overnight camping, but we didn't feel this was as nice as the other sites for overnight as we did not see where the horses could be picket tied within close distance and on the same side of the road as the camping area.) We backtracked on Bastion a short distance toward Fowlers Hollow State Park Picnic area. This is a beautiful area with lots of streams to water the horses, pines, and shade. From Fowlers Hollow, make a left, cross the river, then a right onto Alfarata Trail. (Follow signs.) This is a nice, easy stretch back to camp. We continued on Alfarata, made a right on Perry Lumber Trail, passed campsite #67, crossed Hemlock Road, took a left on Rising Mountain Trail and headed back to #66, Rising Sun.

We then changed campsites to #67, Alfarata, and rode some easy, leisurely loops that included Alfarata, Beaston, Hart Ridge, Perry Lumber, and Fowlers Hollow Road trails. We found these trails to be some of the nicest.

To leave more time for exploring, we chose to trailer over to the Iron Horse Trail. (You can ride to the Iron Horse Trail, which is in the northwest section of the Tuscarora equestrian trail systems.) This trail is marked by red blazes and has views of the old railroad beds. Some remnants still remain and can be seen along the trail. We did not ride the whole trail as we found it too rough to continue. Although it

136

was undeveloped during our visit, we were told that there are plans for improvements to this trail, and it should be much more equestrian friendly sometime in the future. The State Forest Office or the PA Rails-to-Trails Conservancy can be contacted regarding progress on this trail.

The State Forest Office said there is a new equestrian map in the works. Hopefully, that will be available soon, as it will be very helpful because much of the trail system has changed and expanded. We passed many trails that we did not see on the map.

Sometimes, like many of the State Forest lands, the area is logged. We did not notice any logging on the weekend, but during the week there was some equipment in operation on one of the trails. Usually, there are alternate paths to take around the lumbering area. However, during our visit, the machine operators were very considerate and shut down their equipment to politely let the horses pass. And they even left the trails in very good order! If logging activities concern you or frighten your horse, check at the State Forest Office as to the time and location of planned logging and substitute paths to take.

**EQUESTRIAN CAMPING:**
Motorized camping is marked with a red, carsonite post indicating the number of the site. Maps and info regarding the sites can be obtained from the State Forest Office. Sites need to be left clean; and manure scattered. Ask the State Forest Office where they want the manure. We were told another site was closed due to improper manure removal. Although there are many other sites for equestrian camping at Tuscarora, we were told some of the following sites are the favorites of frequent visitors.

Site #67, Alfarata Trail, is a large, open gravel lot with easy in and out access, lots of turn around space, room for big rigs and groups, bordering trees and shade to picket tie the horses, tie posts, a high/dry area for the horses, and direct access to many of the trails. This was one of our favorite campsites for its convenient access to trails and an easy entrance to the camping area.

Site #66, Rising Sun, is on Hemlock Road at the top of the mountain, which offers a beautiful vista of the rising and setting sun. (We went when the leaves weren't fully on the trees and we could see quite a distance.) This is our favorite campsite for its remoteness and beauty. Visiting off-season, we had the mountaintop to ourselves. Although this site can only fit one rig, it has plenty of room for a large rig. The trick is getting the rig into it. The site requires good backing skills and high ground clearance; we had to pull past the site, unload the horses, and back in with the wheels on the shoulder to offer enough room for the back of the trailer to clear the uneven ground. However, it was well worth it once we got in. We were at a secluded spot at the top of the mountain (had great cell phone reception too). It was really a scenic camping site not just a lot. There were lots of trees to picket tie to and the trail goes directly out the back of the site. Riding down the State Forest Road can access other trails. (This was a quiet road during our off-season visit.) There is a great view riding down the road from camp. This camping location does require some riding down and back up the mountainside to network with the lower trails, but also has direct access to the higher trails. We chose to stay here for 2 days and then moved to the Alfarata Trail site to be closer to the lower trails, sort of the best of both worlds.

Site #68, Shale Pit (take Upper Buck Ridge to Couch Road), offers lots and lots of room for big groups and has central access to the lower trails. Not as attractive as the other sites, the lot is a gravel or shale lot with mounds of shale bordering it and a steep hill in the back. With good drainage, solid terrain, lots of space, and convenient location, this could be easily fixed up into an exceptional equestrian group camping area. There are trees surrounding the lot but there is a significant hill bordering the lot, making it more difficult to find a spot where the horses could be picket tied close to the camping area. However, there were equestrian day users at this lot when we visited and they said this was one of their choice sites for camping.

There used to be a picturesque, large lot with corrals at the centrally located Showaker area, but that is no longer used due to the land being soft lowland and rigs getting stuck in it. This area has been allowed to return to its natural state.

There is a large, newly cleared area by Site #62 (off of Route 274) that provides access to the Iron Horse Trail and other Tuscarora trails. This lot is at the "connector trail" which snowmobilers use to ride from the trails in the Northern Block of Tuscarora to the Southern Block. Some of these trails are open to horses. When the site and the Iron Horse Trail are finished, and if this site is open to equestrians, this could be an ideal site to access the Iron Horse Trail.

Picket tying is permitted; however, horses are not permitted to be tied to trees or close to trees where they can do damage. Wrapping of the tie lines is recommended to protect the tree bark. Horses are not permitted to be tied near wetlands. Dogs are permitted at the State Forest campgrounds but should be kept under control. Bring your own water. Although there is water along the trail, there is none at camp. At Fowlers Hollow there is a stream for watering the horses. There are also restroom facilities and a frost-free water unit at the day parking area at Fowlers Hollow.

There are fee campgrounds at Fowlers Hollow State Park and Colonel Denning State Park for non-horse campers. These have drinking water, restrooms, and dump stations. Permits for these locations can be obtained at the Colonel Denning State Park Office or at the self-registry in the campground.

## HISTORICAL INFORMATION:

The Tuscarora State Forest is part of the Tuscarora Mountain range. The mountains were named after the Tuscarora Indians who lived in this area in the early 1700's. Originally, the higher areas of the forests consisted of chestnut and oak. However, most of the area was heavily lumbered and cleared by several lumber companies in the early 1900's. An interesting note: we were told that Tuscarora, near Amberson Ridge, was the sight of one of the region's last cattle drives in 1902.

The state first started acquiring portions of the Tuscarora State Forest in 1902. The price at that time was $1.72 an acre! In the 1930's, the Civilian Conservation Corps (CCC) began work on the area constructing the roads, trails, camping areas, bridges and early park facilities.

With four Natural and Wild Areas and four State Parks, the Tuscarora State Forest is a large area to visit with many scenic vistas and attractions. One unique area is the Hoverter and Sholl Box Huckleberry Natural Area. Near New Bloomfield in Perry County, this is a 10-acre area containing an unusual cluster of box huckleberry. This colony is actually a single plant estimated to be 1,300 years old! A must see is the Giant Hemlock Natural Area which is 120 acres of virgin timber. Trees reaching 123 feet or diameters up to 50 inches have been reported. The trees are huge. One estimated age was 280 years. No riding is permitted in this area, as it is a natural area. But you can drive past it on Hemlock Road or hike in this forest. At one time, hemlocks were only valued for their bark, which was used in the tanning of leather. The wood was not considered useful and once stripped of its bark, was left lying on the forest floor. This area has been saved from that end and preserved for all to enjoy.

The Tuscarora is home to the Iron Horse Trail, portions of which were converted to trail by the US Youth Conservation Corps and overseen by the DER, Bureau of Forestry in the early 1980's. The northern section (north of Route 274) of the Iron Horse Trail was formerly the Path Valley Railroad grade. The southern section was the Perry Lumber Company Railroad. After the Perry Lumber Company Railroad ceased operations in 1906, the Commonwealth of PA acquired the lands, which became the first significant Tuscarora State Forest purchase.

We found the surrounding communities of the Tuscarora Forest, with their rural, rolling landscapes of Amish and Mennonite farms, reminded us of the old Lancaster County countryside.

## THINGS WE LEARNED THIS RIDE:

- At the time of our visit, we concluded one needed an iron horse to ride the full length of the Iron Horse Trail due to its tough terrain. However, we look forward to returning to ride the whole trail when it is completed as it travels through some very pretty areas.

- We learned what tolerant and cooperative horses we have when they patiently waited for us to pull out thorn bush branches caught in their tails or when a wrong turn produced a long staircase that they had to walk down to continue on the trail. (Whoever said *"just* a trail horse" was never a *real* trail rider!)
- While riding the outskirts of the main trail system, we learned what the sound of a bear being unhappily disturbed sounds like (growl, grunt, thrash, thrash). Luckily, he was shy and our horses were brave.
- How big a Great Horned Owl is up close.
- Bring an extra map when riding large areas in case one pops out of one's (John's) pocket during a canter.
- Before you jump off your horse, check where your feet will land as there may be a rock there. (Ouch!)
- And importantly, John and I discovered lots of beautiful trails that Tuscarora has which we had not discovered on our previous visits. We had been under the very mistaken impression that there was mainly road riding and power line riding. Our thanks to the very friendly and helpful folks at the Tuscarora ranger station who patiently answered our many questions.

**NEARBY STABLES:**
- Windy Ridge Acres (boarding, trail riding, and overnight stabling available), Newport (717) 567-7457

**NEARBY B&B:**
- Pheasant Field B&B (overnight stabling, boarding, and trailer parking available), Carlisle (717) 258-0717

**NEARBY VET SERVICES:**
- Cumberland Valley Equine Services, Carlisle (717) 249-7771

**NEARBY FARRIERS:**
- There is an Amish farrier one mile east of Blain on Rural Route 17. There is a sign out front (no phone).
- R. Grochalski (limited availability), Carlisle (717) 243-9097
- J. Ross, Carlisle (717) 697-8831

# 33. Cumberland Valley Rail-Trail
# Cumberland Valley Rails-to-Trails Council, Inc.

**Lasting Impression:** Ride through picturesque farmland in the rural Pennsylvania countryside with miles of wide open spaces and scenic views of the surrounding mountains.

**Location:** The rail-trail is located in Cumberland County near Carlisle and currently runs from Newville to Shippensburg. Not far from Michaux, Tuscarora, and Gettysburg, this trail makes a nice day ride and weekend combo visit with one of these other areas.

**Length:** The trail offers 11 miles (22 round trip) of scenic trail riding.

**Level of Difficulty:** Easy

**Terrain:** During our visit, the trail surface was a surface of mostly dirt and grass with some ballast. We found this surface easy and leisurely to ride. The trail is in the process of development and may have cinder or another surface in the near future making it even more gentle. There is one steep road crossing when traveling from Newville to Oakville, but we found it appeared more challenging than it actually was, and was not difficult once we were ascending or descending it. Nor did the road appear to be heavily traveled. The abrupt embankment is a result of the demolition of the old railroad bridge. The Cumberland Valley Rail-Trail is mostly flat and travels through farms and the countryside. There are trees and brush bordering the path, providing some shade, but there are lots of open areas exposed to the sun. In the heat of the summer, you may want to plan your trail ride for a cooler time of the day.

**Horse Camping:** No, but there is camping at nearby Tuscarora State Forest. We camped at Tuscarora and drove to this trailhead. One can also camp at Michaux State Forest or Artillery Ridge Campground at Gettysburg (see those chapters) and travel to this location to ride this trail.

**Non-horse Camping:** No

**Maps and Info:** Cumberland Valley Rails-to-Trails Council, (717) 860-0444, P.O. Box 531, Shippensburg, PA 17257, www.cvrtc.org, e-mail: info@cvrtc.org. For the PA Rails-to-Trails Conservancy, call (717) 238-1717, www.railtrails.org. They also have a newsletter along with their website; both are a great source of information. The members of the Cumberland Valley Rails-to-Trails Council were very helpful in answering inquiries regarding trail developments and providing recommendations. This is a great group to support. We are thankful for CVRT's dedicated work to establish this nice rail-trail, and we are also grateful to nearby Shippensburg University that has been a very significant contributor to the development of this rail-trail.

**Activities:** Non-Motorized Uses Only, Fishing, Hiking, Biking, Horseback Riding Trails, and X-C Skiing. Hunting is not listed as a trail use, but exercise caution as adjoining areas may have hunting during season.
**Fees for Trail Use:** None
**Permits for Trail Use:** None
**Comfort Station:** We were told of plans for a comfort station to be built at Newville; there is a comfort station at Shippensburg.

## DIRECTIONS:
Newville: Take I-81 to Newville Exit #37 (old Exit #11) PA 233 to Newville. Or travel along PA 233 to Newville. In town, look for Vine Street. Turn onto Vine Street following signs for PA 533 west. (If traveling north on 233, make a left on Vine, if traveling south on 233, make a right). Vine Street will become Fairfield Street, which is 533W. As the road leaves town, make a left on Cherry Street and travel to the end. Make a right; you will see McFarland Street. Parking is on the left side of the street, on the grassy area opposite the houses. The trail leads out from the back of the grass parking area. This is a very quiet back road and the grass area has ample room for a few large rigs or several 2-horse trailers. To exit, we did not have to turn our big rig but rather just pulled out and circled around the corner to exit. There were no structures on the lot during our visit, but some friendly local folks informed us that there are plans for a pavilion and comfort station. These people lived across from the Newville parking area and told us how they used to see the trains go by and now enjoyed watching the equestrians. They made us feel very welcome. We double-checked that no horse droppings were left in the lot to keep their view pleasant and riders welcome.
*Note: We traveled from the north at Tuscarora and headed south to the Cumberland Trail along Route 233. Route 233 is extremely steep approaching from this direction. Instead, traveling from the south and heading north on Route 233 to the Cumberland Trail is a much easier approach, with a more gradual terrain. Check the roads and topos before traveling.*
Oakville: There is parking at Oakville also. We rode to this lot but did not drive to it. Per the CVRTC, this trailhead parking can be reached from PA 533 or US 11 by traveling west on Oakville Road into the small town of Oakville. Park along the rail-trail in the marked area. There is also a picnic area at Oakville.
Shippensburg Township Park: Modifications are planned for this lot to accommodate equestrian parking. At the time of our visit, it was recommended that equestrians not park at this location nor start their ride from this lot due to a difficult steep crossing at Britton Road. Instead, it was recommended that riders travel from Newville to Britton Road. Plans are for a ramp to be constructed which will permit riding for the full length of the trail. The CVRTC website can be contacted to determine if this crossing is completed, view the latest developments, and obtain directions to parking.

**THE TRAILS:**
This rail-trail is a relatively new trail. At the time of our visit, we found the trail to be wonderfully primitive in a very rural setting. The trail stretches from Newville to Shippensburg in diverse settings. Crossing both wooded and open farmland areas, the trail offers diversity with views of the surrounding mountain ranges and pretty Pennsylvania countryside including Amish farms. Trees, fragrant honeysuckle, and other growth border most of the trail and offer some shade in the morning and late day. The borders of the trail are home for a variety of birds. The abundance of colorful birds was amazing. Plus, there is lots of wildlife in the brush, including the local ground hogs. In one section toward Newville (near Bulls Head and Nealy Roads), it is ground hog heaven and riders need to be extremely careful as the ground hogs keep making holes right on the trail. The CVRTC does fill these in but the ground hogs are persistent. On one short section of the trail, we felt like we were in a pole bending contest dodging the holes. But don't let this deter you, just exercise caution. This is a lovely trail; and with increased use and development, the ground hogs will likely move off the main trail.

There is no water along the trail so bring your own. But there is plenty of really nice timothy grass growing on and along the trail if your horse needs refreshment. Sometimes the trail appears to end but actually winds around a detour. Look around and you should be able to see where the trail continues. (On one part of the path, we encountered an electric fenced area directly in front of us. We were headed south and made a right. The trail continued along what appeared to be a farm driveway but actually was the continuation of the trail.)

There are lots of farm animals, including many Amish draft horses, along the rail-trail that watch as you pass by their pastures. On some of the other farms, farmers waved from their tractors, greeting us as we passed by. We rode this trail in early May when a light breeze offered a cooling effect. It was a weekday and we had the trail to ourselves. If you like an easy rail-trail that travels through open, spacious, rural farm country with miles of views, you should enjoy this trail. Our ride was reminiscent of traveling the old farm lanes of years ago. We would like to return on a cool day in the fall to view the panoramic vista of colors of rolling farmland set against the backdrop of the surrounding mountain ranges.

**HISTORICAL INFORMATION:**
The Cumberland Valley Railroad was formerly established in the 1830's and operated along this route, providing a needed link between Shippensburg, Chambersburg, Harrisburg, and ultimately to points south and east. The Cumberland Valley Railroad was one of our nation's leading railroad services to offer a sleeper car. The operation was run with much pride and tight quality controls. The line was acquired by the Pennsylvania Railroad which eventually

became Conrail. In 1995, Conrail donated the Cumberland Valley Trail to the Cumberland Valley Rails-to-Trails Council.

**THINGS WE LEARNED THIS RIDE:**
- There is still beautiful, rolling farmland looking like it did 50+ years ago.
- Cinder trails are nice, but rail-trails can be just as beautiful in their natural state of grass and dirt (but without the railroad ties).
- Fill up with diesel (if you use diesel) before traveling to some of these remote, rural locations.

**NEARBY STABLES:**
- Windy Ridge Acres (boarding, trail riding, and overnight stabling available), Newport (717) 567-7457

**NEARBY B&B:**
- Pheasant Field B&B (overnight stabling, boarding, and trailer parking available), Carlisle (717) 258-0717

**NEARBY VET SERVICES:**
- Cumberland Valley Equine Services, Carlisle (717) 249-7771

**NEARBY FARRIERS:**
- R. Grochalski (limited availability), Carlisle (717) 243-9097
- J. Ross, Carlisle (717) 697-8831

# 34. Michaux State Forest DCNR

### (Department of Conservation & Natural Resources)

**Lasting Impression:** Camping and riding in Pennsylvania's scenic State Forest with lots of potential for so much more.

**Location:** Michaux State Forest is located in Franklin, Cumberland, and Adams Counties in southcentral Pennsylvania, located not far from Gettysburg National Military Park and Codorus Park (you can make a combined vacation and trailer to nearby trails).

**Length:** The forest sits on over 82,000 acres. The equestrian trails consist of over 30 miles of equestrian-marked trails and roads. In addition, horseback riders are permitted on the many multi-use adjoining trails, such as the old logging roads, gas lines, wood roads, and snowmobile and ATV trails. Horses are also permitted on all roads within Michaux State Forest, except Old Forge Picnic Area, the Rocky Knob Trail, the Beaver Trail, the Appalachian Trail, the Buck Ridge Trail, or any areas indicated as closed to horses. There are 130 miles of State Forest roads to ride; we rode some of the dirt Forest roads to link to other trails and they were nice to ride.

**Level of Difficulty:** Mostly easy to moderate. We did not encounter a lot of rocky sections, however, there was one stretch that was difficult to impassable. The trails we rode were generally gradual, and the underground gas line right-of-ways varied from gentle to steep.

**Terrain:** The terrain varies from low land along stream beds to mountainous areas. There are wooded dirt trails, dirt logging roads, dirt/gravel State Forest roads, and nicely mowed grass gas lines. (I do not usually favor riding gas or power lines but some of these were the best maintained right-of-ways that I had seen, sometimes as nice as the regular State Forest trails, and they offered awesome views.) Except for the area by the gas lines, most of the trails were wooded.

**Horse Camping:** Yes, but camping is primitive. Bring your own water. We camped at the Teaberry lot, which was a very big area and had lots of room for large groups. This location could accommodate a club or group ride. Trails may be accessed directly from camp. Equestrians preferring amenities can camp at the nearby full service Artillery Ridge (Gettysburg) Horseman's Camp, and day trailer over. (Artillery Ridge is about 50 minutes from the Michaux Teaberry lot and easy to get to.)

**Non-horse Camping:** Yes

**Maps and Info:** Maps, info, and permits can be obtained from the District Forester, Michaux State Forest, 10099 Lincoln Way East, Fayetteville, PA 17222, (717) 352-2211. The office brochure recommends calling the office for planning group rides, or if in need of assistance with trail or camping questions.

**Activities:** Boating, Fishing, Hiking, Picnicking, Swimming, Biking, Horseback Riding Trails, Hunting (during season), Snowmobiling, Golf, Horse Camping, and Non-horse Camping

**Fees for Trail Use:** None

**Permits for Trail Use:** None. However, a permit for camping is necessary prior to arrival. Permits are issued free of charge by calling (717) 352-2211.

**Comfort Station:** There are no facilities at the Teaberry Lot, but there are comfort stations at the State Parks.

## DIRECTIONS:

To Michaux State Forest: Take I-81 to Route 30 east (Stoufferstown). Travel east on Route 30 until you see signs for the Route 233 intersection (near Caledonia Park). Or, if traveling from the east, take Route 30 west to Route 233 intersection. (The Forest Office is located just east of the Route 30 and Route 233 intersection.) To access the trails and the Teaberry lot (from Route 30), head south on Route 233. Travel 4.2 miles on Route 233 to a stop sign. Make a left on South Mountain Road. Proceed 5.1 miles on South Mountain Road to the Teaberry (camping) Lot and trailheads. During the 5.1 miles, you will need to note the following to find the lot: South Mountain becomes Cold Spring Road. Pass the intersection of Antietam Lane, a "private" sign, and Newman Road. At this crossroads, continue straight. The road does not look like a through road, but it is. Travel to the top of the mountain. The road winds and is sometimes bumpy but navigable. Pass the yellow gate on the left. Shortly after the gate, look for the Teaberry lot, which is a big gravel parking area on the left. The trailheads lead directly out from the back of the lot and on the opposite side of the road. Information is posted at the lot.

## THE TRAILS:

This is a pleasant area to ride a variety of types of trails, and the area is large and extensive. Due to bad weather, we could only cover about 6 to 7 hours of riding. Those trails that we were able to ride, we enjoyed.

The trail varies; there are dirt forest roads, grass and dirt trails through the woods, old logging trails, and some really nice trails with great views along the cleared, underground gas line trails. Brown and white signs with the emblem of a horseback rider mark the equestrian trails. Maps should be obtained prior to arrival. The maps correspond with numbered posts at the trail intersections. Sometimes there are gaps in the markers or the markers are situated a short distance from the road and you have to be careful not to miss them (i.e., marker #19 is set way back past the yellow gate so you have to ride past the gate to look for it, and can not see it from the connecting road). Other signs are sometimes after the intersection vs. before.

We rode from the Teaberry lot, crossed the road to marker #25 riding Rock Road to High Road and passing marker #13. The trail traveled quite a distance along the unpaved Forest Road, but the road was hardly traveled during our visit and there was lots of room if a vehicle did pass. The road is lined with woods and many trails branch out from the road. We passed the gas line, which offered a panoramic view. We enjoyed riding down the one gas line to the overlook. (On some adjoining trails there are white blazes, which indicate the Appalachian Trail. Horses are not permitted on the Appalachian Trail.) We then returned to the road and traveled up the hill to the other side of the gas line trail to pick up the return loop from markers #14 to #19, onto #22 and #26, and back to the lot. There are alternate routes if you prefer to do less road riding. Again, the road was just like a spacious trail and we found it enjoyable. We did not encounter any "on the edge riding". Most trails were of a wide width.

The mountainous area offers views of the surrounding areas, including the South Mountains. The gas line paths that travel through Michaux are some of the nicest we have seen or ridden and there are many vistas! They are attractive, long grassy stretches, nicely maintained. The gas lines offer lots of alternate riding and also a means of connecting between different trails. Overall, we did not find the trails to be rocky. However, there was one rocky section between markers #22 and #23 that was extremely difficult to pass. We were traveling in a northerly direction and chose an alternate path around this obstacle by traveling to the right. Look around; the rocky sections usually have an area to go around them, but some require careful navigation without a bypass. There is lots of wildlife including herds of deer, turkey, colorful birds, and snakes. (We did not encounter any snakes but we did see snake hunters. That was proof enough that there were lots of snakes in the area, as this was the only place in our equestrian travels where we encountered snake hunters on the trail.) There is some water on the trail, but not a lot. Bring water to provide to the horses upon departure and return.

Some time after our visit, we were told that there are many more trails than what was reflected on the State Forest map, including at other locations in the Michaux State Forest. The folks that shared this information with us indicated that they were nice trails. We enjoyed what we had visited and plan to return and explore more of this scenic area. We will likely bring a group of friends to camp with, as there is ample room for numerous rigs.

## CAMPGROUND DESCRIPTION:
Motorized units or trailers with horses can park or camp at the Teaberry lot, which has a shale base and grass open area. Organized groups must contact the office prior to their arrival. This lot is located with immediate access to the horse trails and snowmobile trails. The Teaberry lot is primitive, yet functional. If fixed up, this could be an exceptional camping area. Due to its remote location, distance from the

main Michaux Park activities, and minimal supervision, this area is attractive to various types of other unauthorized users. With increased equestrian use, management presence, and amenities such as water and restrooms, this could be an awesome camping area as it is in a nice location with lots of room, and there are some very nice trails.

Camping with horses is allowed but a permit is required. The permit is free and can be obtained at the office (see above). Permits can be obtained up to 90 days in advance. There are hitching poles to tie horses to or run picket ties through, however, one pole was vandalized prior to our visit so they may not be available. There were plenty of trees surrounding the lot to picket tie the horses to. Horses can be picket tied, but are not permitted to be tied directly to trees or where they have access to damage the trees. There is a large fine if damage does occur.

As camping is primitive and there are no facilities, campers must bring their own water. This is a "take in, take out" camping arrangement so garbage, sewage, etc. must leave with the campers. The office mentioned that contained rigs emptying tanks at the camping areas resulted in closing some areas to campers in the past. A list of rules is provided at registration. Please leave camping areas clean, and be mindful of the regulations so as not to ruin it for future users of the Forest. Unfortunately, in our travels, we have encountered isolated locations where others (unauthorized users) have littered. If equestrians or other campers encounter this, they may be well advised to keep the office informed so that there is not the mistaken impression that they have not taken out what they brought in.

Facilities are at the nearby Pine Grove Furnace and Caledonia State Parks, including fee non-horse camping, comfort stations, and dump stations. Check with the Forest Office to confirm that horse campers (with permits) are allowed and that there is sufficient room to access the dump stations. It has been our experience that, often, the larger equestrian rigs do not have sufficient room to access these dump stations in the non-equestrian camping areas. Unloading of horses is not permitted in the non-equestrian campgrounds.

## HISTORICAL INFORMATION:
Michaux State Forest was named after two French botanists, Andre Michaux and his son Francois Andre Michaux. Michaux State Forest consists of Caledonia State Park, Pine Grove Furnace Park, Old Forge Picnic Area, and Monto Alto Park. Michaux State Forest has grown quickly over the years and has become a popular recreational destination. Michaux State Forest is overseen under the "multiple-use concept" of forestry. It is both a recreation area and a managed forestry area, producing various wood products, providing a home for wildlife, promoting preservation, and serving numerous other functions. The State Forest is run by the Department of Conservation and Natural Resources.

**WATER:**
Don't forget the water. It is not provided and campers must bring their own.

**NEARBY STABLE AND FULL SERVICE HORSEMAN'S CAMP:**
- Artillery Ridge Camping Resort & National Riding Stable (overnight camping with hookups, trail rides, and stabling), Gettysburg (717) 334-1288

**NEARBY STABLES:**
- Hickory Hollow Farm (trail rides, overnight stabling, and boarding), Gettysburg (717) 334-0349

**NEARBY AND SURROUNDING AREA B&Bs:**
- Pheasant Field B&B (overnight stabling, boarding, and trailer parking available), Carlisle (717) 258-0717

**NEARBY AND SURROUNDING AREA VET SERVICES:**
- Emmitsburg Veterinary Hospital, Emmitsburg, MD (301) 447-6237
- Cumberland Valley Equine Services, Carlisle (717) 249-7771

**NEARBY FARRIER:**
- B. Buxton, Gettysburg (717) 337-5959

# 35. Big Pocono State Park & The Old Railroad Trail
## DCNR (State Park)
## & Pennsylvania State Gamelands (adjoining)

**Lasting Impression:** A scenic, rugged ride high on the top of Camelback Mountain
**Location:** Big Pocono State Park is in northeastern Pennsylvania, near Tannersville in Monroe County.
**Length:** The park contains over 1,300 acres and approximately 3 to 4 miles of trails, plus possible adjoining trails on State Gamelands (numerous miles) including the Old Railroad Trail (8 miles) if permitted. (Gameland riding may be subject to change; check if horses are permitted prior to arrival.)
**Level of Difficulty:** Within the State Park, moderate due to rocky sections. Outlying sections can vary from easy to difficult. I was informed that plans for improvements of the State Park trails are in progress.
**Terrain:** Conditions are varied. Sections are flat, some have climbs, and terrain is often very rugged, as this is the top of the mountain. Settings fluctuate from wooded to open stretches.
**Horse Camping:** No
**Non-horse Camping:** Not within the park
**Maps and Info:** DCNR, Big Pocono State Park, c/o Tobyhanna State Park, P.O. Box 387, Tobyhanna, PA 18466-0387, (717) 894-8336, e-mail: tobyhanna.sp@al.dcnr.state.pa.us. Call 1-888-PA-PARKS for general park info or for camping reservations. For adjoining State Gameland information, call the Pennsylvania Game Commission Northeast Region Office (877) 877-9357. See the State Gamelands chapter for more information and contacts.
**Activities:** Hiking, Picnicking, Horseback Riding Trails, and Hunting (during season). At this writing, bikes were not listed as an official, permitted activity. However, the trails are expected to be upgraded for ease of use and there is a chance of expansion along with a possibility that bikes may be allowed. Check with the office prior to your visit.
**Fees for Trail Use:** None
**Permits for Trail Use:** None
**Comfort Station:** Yes

**DIRECTIONS:**
Take Interstate 80 to Exit #299 (old Exit #45) at Tannersville. Take PA Route 715, follow signs to Camelback Mountain. Pass Camelback Mountain resort area and continue to the top of the mountain. You will see signs for Big Pocono State Park. Note the approach to the park is on a steep grade. If your truck is marginal in pulling power, do not attempt it. Trailer parking and the trailhead is located near

the park entrance on the west side of the park on Rim Road. As you travel up the mountain, the parking area is on the left side, a short distance from the Big Pocono State Park signs. This is a multi-use, paved, medium sized lot with room for large rigs. There is no separate area designated for equestrians.

## THE TRAILS:

The region is rugged as Big Pocono State Park is situated on Camelback Mountain. There are three trails: the North Trail (red blaze), the South Trail (yellow blaze), and the Indian Trail (orange blaze). The equestrian trail is on the South Trail. While riding, you will see the Big Pocono Fire Tower that is used for monitoring any fire activity in the surrounding areas. The tower has been named a historical structure.

The park equestrian trail system is a short trail system, which travels along the rim of the mountain. During our visit, we traveled to some outlying sections that had overgrowth, making it awkward to ride. Because of its short distance, this is a trail system that may be considered too far to travel a long distance to. As a result, I debated whether to include it in this book. However, it is in a beautiful setting with many vistas and one to watch if expansion is ever considered. The trail is even more beautiful during a fall foliage ride and during the spring when the mountain laurel are in bloom. Future possibilities exist, as there are many undeveloped adjoining lands. These include the old railroad path and State Gamelands. At the time of this writing, information was not yet available as to whether these State Gameland trails will be open to equestrians. However, if the State Gamelands are designated as being open to horses, there may be quite a bit of riding available. Be alert for four wheelers and dirt bikes in areas bordering the State Park as we did encounter a few during our ride.

In the past, about once a year, local riding clubs obtained permission and sponsored a ride that traveled in many nearby adjoining lands, including the rail-trail. This too will depend on future land restrictions, but if continued, is well worth joining as the club travels through some very scenic sections of the area and through some of the more gentle terrain. Watch for advertisements in local equestrian publications.

## HISTORICAL INFORMATION:

The park land used to be owned by Henry Cattell in the early 1900's. Mr. Cattell so enjoyed the view from Camelback Mountain that he built a stone cabin and generously left it open for all to share. Anyone could use it and they too could take in the breathtaking view. After Henry Cattell's death, the Pennsylvania Game Commission acquired the park.

151

In the 1950's sections of the park were leased to commercial ski operations. Camelback Ski Corporation currently operates the ski facilities. The PA Department of Forests and Waters, now DCNR, purchased a portion of the gamelands. In 1954, the park was officially opened. During this time and for years to come, the Cattell Cabin was utilized as a park office and museum. The park continues to be operated in a joint effort between DCNR and the commercial ski operation.

Nearby attractions include numerous Pocono resorts, shopping outlets, and recreation and natural areas. Some of these are Gouldsboro State Park, Hickory Run State Park, Tobyhanna State Park, and the Delaware Water Gap National Recreation area. Of these, the Delaware Water Gap National Recreation area permits riding on the Conashaugh View Trail. See that chapter for more information.

## NEARBY OLD RAILROAD TRAIL:
Adjacent to the Big Pocono State Park is the Old Railroad Trail; a rail-trail that extends from Big Pocono State Park to Crescent Lake for over 8 miles. The surface is mostly crushed stone and an easy ride. (Check in advance for restrictions.)

## NEARBY AND SURROUNDING AREA STABLES:
- Misty Hill Acres (boarding, emergency overnight stabling, and trailering), Lehighton (610) 681-4994
- Carson's Riding Stables (guided trail riding), Mt. Pocono (570) 839-9841
- Pocono Adventures (guided 45-minute and 2-hour trail rides; no boarding), Mt. Pocono (570) 839-6333

## NEARBY AND SURROUNDING AREA VET SERVICES:
- E. Balliet & Associates, Northampton (610) 262-3203
- L. Wessel, E. Bangor (610) 588-9467

## NEARBY AND SURROUNDING AREA FARRIERS:
- J. Kleintop, Lehighton (610) 681-4994, cell (610) 393-8363
- B. Gannon, Kunkletown (610) 381-3213

# 36. Pohopoco Tract Recreation Area
# DCNR
### (Department of Conservation & Natural Resources)

**Lasting Impression:** Scenic trail riding in the Poconos without the steep climbs. Best to visit when it is off-season to ATV's.

**Location:** Pohopoco is located in northeastern Pennsylvania, Monroe County, in the Delaware State Forest Region of the Poconos. It is about 9 to 10 miles north of Broadheadsville across from the Pocono International Raceway.

**Length:** 15 miles

**Level of Difficulty:** The trail ranges from nice and easy to very difficult due to rock clusters. If it weren't for the rocks, this would be easy.

**Terrain:** The terrain varies from flat, old farm roads, to gradual dirt climbs, to very rocky stretches. There are many rocky sections, but there are also some sections that are not or are less rocky. If riders avoid the rocky sections, this can be an easy, leisurely ride.

**Horse Camping:** Camping is not permitted in the Pohopoco trail area. But, motorized horse camping is permitted at the Maple Run Road lot (just off of Route 402, about 5 miles south of I-84) and the Burnt Mill Road lot (just off Route 402, about 10 miles south of I-84) of the Delaware State Forest area. These two locations are gravel lots and are primitive. It is necessary to trailer from these lots to the Pohopoco Tract. The Pohopoco trails can not be accessed directly from the Maple Run Road lot or the Burnt Mill Road lot.

**Non-horse Camping:** Not within Pohopoco, but camping is permitted at the above lots

**Maps and Info:** PA Bureau of Forestry, Delaware State Forest District, HC1 Box 95A, Swiftwater, PA 18370-9723, (570) 895-4000, website: www.dcnr.state.pa.us. During our visit, there was a stocked supply of maps and info at the trailhead; there were also maps at the Forest Office trailhead.

**Activities:** The Pohopoco Recreation Area is open for four seasons and is a multiple-use trail system. Only during certain seasons are certain users permitted on the trail. Make sure you check with the office before traveling to this trail to ascertain that it is open to horseback riders, and to determine what other types of users may be sharing the trail. Currently, horseback riding is permitted April through October. ATV's, hiking, biking, hunting, and snowmobiling are also permitted during certain months. This area is popular with ATV's, but in April, part of May, and October, ATV's are not permitted.

**Fees for Trail Use:** None

**Permits for Trail Use:** None

**Permit for Camping Required**: For the Maple Run Road lot or the Burnt Mill Road lot: Yes, obtain at Bureau of Forestry, Delaware Forest District, HC 1 Box 95A, Swiftwater, PA 18370-9723, (570) 895-4000
**Comfort Station:** No

## DIRECTIONS:
Take Interstate 80 to Blakeslee Exit #284, PA 115. (Pohopoco is located near the Pocono Raceway.) Take 115 south for about 5 miles. The entrance is off Route 115, marked by a brown Delaware State Forest sign indicating Pohopoco Tract. Parking is on the right just off of a gravel road. Pohopoco can also be reached from the south by taking Route 209 to Broadheadsville. At Broadheadsville, take Route 115 north for about 9.5 miles, then look for the brown sign on the left. Parking is on the left. The lot is a large, gravel lot with sufficient space to pull around. There is room for big rigs or a group of rigs.

## THE TRAILS:
The Pohopoco Recreation Area is situated in the Pocono region of Pennsylvania with many views of the surrounding mountain ranges. The visibility is even better when the leaves are not on the trees, and the vistas offer miles and miles of beautiful scenery. The trails are very well marked with numbered posts corresponding to the map at all intersections. The equestrian trails are mostly wide trails or dirt farm roads, traveling through woods, rhododendron, and brush, and offering lots of opportunity to see wildlife. We saw many deer and turkey during our visit.

We departed from the parking area, traveling along the eastern section. As you ride out from the lot and look back, there are quite a few sections offering a panoramic view of the surrounding mountain region. There is a lookout by markers #3 and #5, but sections of this trail are rocky. Horses should have shoes. Most of the rocky sections we found passable. However, the Miller Trail, although it offers some nice vistas, was extremely rocky, way too rocky for our comfort level. But there are alternate, non-rocky, or less rocky areas such as the Old Farm Trail, which is a dirt road, and Jack's Trail. Jack's Trail, trimmed by rhododendron, was one of our favorite trails which we would like to visit when the flowers are in bloom. Most of the trail terrain was very gradual, without steep climbs. There wasn't much water on the trail, so riders should bring their own water to provide to their horses before and after the ride.

This day-use trail system is open four seasons to various users. Again, current regulations should be obtained from the above number prior to arrival to determine the best time to visit. At the time of this writing, trails are open to equestrians from April through October. We visited this trail in late April when ATV's were not permitted on most of the trails. Since this trail is a favorite for many ATV enthusiasts, and can get quite populated with ATV's, equestrians may prefer to visit during April, early May, or October when the trails are closed to ATV's. The schedule may change so check with the Pohopoco office. During our visit, surprisingly, we did not see any hikers or bikers actually on the trails, and the trails were extremely quiet other than one ATV. We weren't sure if he was a renegade or if he was riding on adjoining trails where ATV's may have been permitted. However, he was very courteous and cautious around the horses.

At certain high altitude locations we could hear the distant sounds of the Pocono Raceway, but most of the trails felt far away from any noise or traffic. However, you may want to choose a different time to visit this trail system when nearby, larger races are scheduled. We really enjoyed our visit and had a nice, leisurely ride.

**HISTORICAL INFORMATION:**
The Pohopoco fire tower was constructed in 1934, providing a panoramic vista of 50 miles. The tower is still in operation during fire seasons. Currently, the Pohopoco Recreation Area is managed by DCNR and the Pennsylvania Bureau of Forestry, Delaware State Forest District.

**NEARBY AND SURROUNDING AREA STABLES:**
- Misty Hill Acres (boarding, emergency overnight stabling, and trailering), Lehighton (610) 681-4994
- Woodlands Stable & Tack, Inc. (by appointment only: lessons, trail rides, pony parties, tack store, camp, limited boarding, and possible emergency overnight stabling), Gouldsboro (570) 842-3742
- Carson's Riding Stables (trail riding), Mt. Pocono (570) 839-9841
- Pocono Adventures (guided 45-minute and 2-hour trail rides; no boarding), Mt. Pocono (570) 839-6333

**NEARBY AND SURROUNDING AREA VET SERVICES:**
- E. Balliet & Associates, Northampton (610) 262-3203
- L. Wessel, E. Bangor (610) 588-9467

**NEARBY AND SURROUNDING AREA FARRIERS:**
- J. Kleintop, Lehighton (610) 681-4994, cell (610) 393-8363
- B. Gannon, Kunkletown (610) 381-3213
- K. Martin, Allentown (610) 791-2375

# 37. Promised Land State Park
# DCNR
### (Department of Conservation & Natural Resources)

**Lasting Impressions:** A nice fall or cool summer ride in the Poconos, lots of shaded trails, and this park keeps getting better each visit. DCNR has been making some very nice improvements to the trail surface and trail markings.

**Location:** Promised Land State Park is in northeast Pennsylvania near Canadensis in Pike County.

**Length:** The park is located on 3,000 acres and over 12,000 acres of State Forest and natural preserves surround the Park. Estimates of length indicate about 24 miles of trail.

**Level of Difficulty:** Easy

**Terrain:** Some flat, some rolling hills, grass, dirt, and rock

**Horse Camping:** Horse camping is not permitted in the area surrounding the Promised Land State Park. However, motorized horse camping is permitted (no fee) at the nearby Maple Run Road lot (off Route 402 about 5 miles south of I-84) and the Burnt Mill Road lot (off Route 402 about 10 miles south of I-84). The camping is primitive and without facilities. From the camping lots, riders can ride the back roads, power lines, and ATV trails. Or, riders can trailer over to the Promised Land and Conashaugh View Trail (Delaware Water Gap) trailheads.

**Non-horse Camping:** Yes, at Promised Land State Park

**Maps and Info:** DCNR, Promised Land State Park, R.R. 1, Box 96, Greentown, PA 18426, (570) 676-3428, websites: www.dcnr.state.pa.us or www.state.pa.us, e-mail: promland.sp@state.pa.us. Call 1-888-PA-PARKS for general park info or for camping reservations. There are a few maps; make sure you request the latest DCNR map with the marked intersections. Maps are available at the trailheads.

**Activities:** Boating, Boat Rentals, Fishing, Hiking, Picnicking, Horseback Riding Trails, Swimming, Biking, Hunting (during season), Camping, Snowmobiling, X-C Skiing, and Ice Sports

**Fees for Trail Use:** None

**Permits for Trail Use:** None

**Permit for Camping Required:** Maple Run Road lot and Burnt Mill Road lot: Yes, obtain at Bureau of Forestry, Delaware Forest District, HC 1 Box 95A, Swiftwater, PA 18370-9723, (570) 895-4000.

**Comfort Station:** Yes (see map for locations)

**DIRECTIONS:**

Day Parking: To approach the north lot, take I-84 to the Route 390 interchange, Exit #26. Take Route 390 south for 1.4 miles. Trailhead parking is on the right at Cross Cut Trail. The lot is a nice sized gravel lot, and can hold a few rigs and still have room for other users to park. This lot was well stocked with maps and the DCNR ranger was even stocking them while we were there. There is another lot in the southwest section, which we did not ride from nor visit. Directions provided to us were to travel on Route 507 to Newfoundland, where Route 507 and Route 447 meet. Turn onto Route 447 (if headed south, make a left, if headed north, make a right onto Route 447.) Go a short distance and make a left onto Hemlock Grove Road. Take Hemlock Grove Road to Roemerville Road; make a right onto Roemerville Road. Proceed onto Sawmill Road. Go to the top of the hill on Sawmill after a sharp right. If you choose this lot, confirm these directions with the office prior to your visit.

## THE TRAILS:

Most of the equestrian trail is on the west and north side of the park. The trail winds in and out of wooded trails, offering a cooler ride in the summer and a variety of foliage color in the fall. The trail also joins sections of the lake. There are places where horses can access water along the trail. Surrounding the park is the Delaware State Forest.

We rode this with a group of friends in the fall and the colors were spectacular. We have also visited in the spring. Due to the forested area and lake effect, I would expect that this trail would be a nice cool ride in the summer. The trails do have some rocky sections but most are passable. The trails are multiple-use so riders must watch for approaching bikes. During our fall and spring visits, we did not encounter many bikes. In addition to the designated equestrian trails, riders are permitted to ride on ATV trails, road systems, and power lines in the area. Much wildlife can be seen as you ride the trails, especially early in the morning before the park gets active.

The park terrain, like other Pocono locations, was once formed by glacier action, which resulted in plateaus of flat rock. Thus, many of the trail surfaces have a low, rock surface. Crushed stone has been laid on portions of the trail helping to minimize rocky sections and providing drainage. This is an excellent trail improvement. Another smart trail feature is that the trail intersections are marked with numbered posts that correspond to the DCNR map. This really helps users stay on course. During our spring visit, there had been an abundance of rainfall. There were wet areas but the turf was mostly solid due to the gravel and stone base. Horses should have shoes, as some terrain is rugged. Although there are lots of nice grassy stretches, and fine stone fill has been added in some places, there are also occasional rocky sections. However, we did find those areas to be passable. A few years ago, a tornado severely damaged the woodlands. This area is now beginning to recover much of its former beauty.

## HISTORICAL INFORMATION:
Legend has it that the name Promised Land came from the land being "promised land" to the Shakers who originally settled in the area in the late 1800's. When the land was determined to be too hard and rocky to be productive as farmland, the disappointed Shakers abandoned the land but left the mocking label. This location also attained historic significance as Civil War Union deserters sought refuge there.

In the early 1900's, the Commonwealth of PA acquired the land with the intention of returning it to a natural area for the public to enjoy. The park was opened in 1905 and the facilities were later expanded by the Civilian Conservation Corps (CCC) in the 1930's.

While visiting the park, stop by the park office and ask for a copy of *After the Wind Died Down*. The booklet tells of a tornado that ravished the park in 1998, trapping 500+ people. Incredibly, there were no serious injuries!

Nearby attractions include Bruce Lake Natural Area, the Stillwater Natural Area, the Delaware Water Gap National Recreation Area, Lake Wallenpaupack, Big Pocono State Park, plus others as listed in the Delaware State Forest brochure available from DCNR (see above). Southeast of the Promised Land State Park is the Stillwater Natural Area.

## NEARBY AND SURROUNDING AREA STABLES:
- Malibu Ranch (dude ranch, guided trail rides or b.y.o. horse trail riding, overnight stabling, boarding, guest accommodations), Milford (800) 8-Malibu
- Misty Hill Acres (boarding, emergency overnight stabling, and trailering), Lehighton (610) 681-4994
- Fernwood Riding Stable, Bushkill (570) 588-9500 x4280
- Carson's Riding Stables (trail riding), Mt. Pocono (570) 839-9841
- Pocono Adventures (guided 45-minute and 2-hour trail rides; no boarding), Mt. Pocono (570) 839-6333
- Woodlands Stable & Tack, Inc. (by appointment only: lessons, trail rides, pony parties, tack store, camp, limited boarding, and possible emergency overnight stabling), Gouldsboro (570) 842-3742

## NEARBY AND SURROUNDING AREA VET SERVICES:
- E. Balliet & Associates, Northampton (610) 262-3203
- L. Wessel, E. Bangor (610) 588-9467

## NEARBY AND SURROUNDING AREA FARRIERS:
- J. Kleintop, Lehighton (610) 681-4994, cell (610) 393-8363
- B. Gannon, Kunkletown (610) 381-3213

# 38. Conashaugh View Trail
# Delaware Water Gap Equestrian Trail
# National Park Service

**Lasting Impression:** The Conashaugh View Trail is a beautiful trail through dense woods that are situated high above the Delaware River; this trail is one of my personal favorites for a day trip.

**Location:** The Conashaugh View Trail is located in northeastern Pennsylvania near Dingmans Ferry and Milford.

**Length:** The Delaware Water Gap National Recreation area covers 70,000 acres. The Conashaugh View Trail offers 10+ miles of trails for equestrians to ride plus forest gravel/dirt roads and possible adjoining trails.

**Level of Difficulty:** Moderate, with some more challenging sections

**Terrain:** The Conashaugh View Trail is mostly in woodlands with a few open sections. As the trail winds around the mountainous terrain, there are some climbs and declines. Riders and horses should be fit and comfortable with varied terrain. There were two sections we found to be more challenging. One was the section between markers #4 and #5. This section can be bypassed by riding the tract between #6 and #9. Also, the approach to the "loop" at marker #6 is steep. However, improvements are being made to this approach. (We could not find the physical marker for #6 during our last visit, which may be due to work being done on the trail.) The trails traveling through the steeper areas usually are wide, and offer the opportunity to switchback within the width of the trail to minimize the climb/descent and to proceed along the trail slowly. Doing this, we did not have any problem. Some sections get a little rocky, but there was dirt in between the rocks for the horses to pick through. We also did not find this to be an obstacle.

**Horse Camping:** Horse camping is not permitted at the Conashaugh View Trail. However, equestrians can camp with their horses at the nearby Maple Run Road lot (off Route 402 about 5 miles south of I-84) and the Burnt Mill Road lot (off Route 402 about 10 miles south of I-84). There are no facilities and camping is primitive.

**Non-horse Camping:** Non-horse camping is available at various nearby areas; see the website for more information.

**Maps and Info:** Maps and info can be obtained at the Park District Ranger Station at Dingmans Ferry, Park Headquarters, (570) 588-2451, or the Dingmans Falls Visitor Center, (570) 828-7802. Website: www.nps.gov/dewa

**Activities:** Hiking, Horseback Riding Trails, and Hunting (during season). *Nearby areas have camping, biking, fishing, swimming, boating, snowmobiling, ice sports, and X-C skiing.*

**Fees for Trail Use:** None

**Permits for Trail Use:** None

**Permit for Camping Required:** Maple Run Road lot and Burnt Mill Road lot: Yes, obtain at Bureau of Forestry, Delaware Forest District, HC 1 Box 95A, Swiftwater, PA 18370-9723, (570) 895-4000

**Comfort Station:** Yes, there is a portajohn at the trailhead

## DIRECTIONS:

From the north, take I-84 to Exit #34 (old Exit #9) Dingmans Ferry, Route 739 south. Take Route 739 south for 11.5 miles. Make a left on Milford Road and continue as below. (Note: This is an alternative to the southern approach which we use on our return trip to avoid the heavy weekend flea market traffic at Marshall's Creek on Route 209.) If approaching from the south, take I-80. At Stroudsburg, take Exit #309, Route 209 north. Follow Route 209 north for 23.5 miles. Make a left on Route 739 north. Take Route 739 north for 2.5 miles to a stop sign at Milford Road. Make a right on Milford.

On Milford, travel 1.2 miles to Long Meadow Road. (See church.) Turn right on Long Meadow; travel a total of about 2.2 miles on Long Meadow to the parking lot on the right. *Along the way, pass the brown Delaware Water Gap signs. The road becomes gravel and will turn left. (As you turn, note there is a trailhead marker on the side of the road.) Pass a large, fenced pasture on the left. Just after the fenced field, make a right into the trailhead lot.* The lot is large and can fit a group of rigs. It is a big grassy area with room to pull through if no other vehicles are there. (The grass was high during our last visit, so do not miss it.) There is a trailhead bulletin board and portajohn. We did not see any maps, so obtain a map prior to arrival.

## THE TRAILS:

The trails are beautiful and riders should enjoy them. But, also be mindful to observe and abide by the rules for equestrian riders. This area was difficult to obtain permission for equestrian use, and riders do not want to lose it. Officials ask that riders stay on marked trails, do not tie horses to trees, use bridges over wet areas, and do not let horses drink from streams to prevent erosion to wet areas and river banks. It is recommended to bring one's own water and to water the horses before departing and upon returning to the parking area. Maps can be obtained in advance so riders can follow the course and stay on the trail. If equestrian riders cooperate, there may be a possibility of expansion. We always found this trail well worth visiting. It is a beautiful trail in spring (rhododendron in bloom), summer (shaded and cool), and fall (bright foliage). In the winter, bald eagles return to this area and can be spotted in mid-morning or late afternoon.

There are trail markers at the intersections that coincide with the map. There are also red and silver equestrian markers on the trees marking the trails. To access the trailhead at #1, ride out of the lot, make a left, pass the fenced pasture, travel

160

down the gravel road (where the road makes a right) to the trailhead marker on the left. We made a left and rode in numerical sequence from #1 to #8 and returned from the loop back to #7, #6, #5, #4, then to #9 and back to #1. Since #5 to #4 have some steep sections, an alternate is to ride from #6 to #9 on the return. We rode #6 to #9 some years ago and it was not as steep, but we did not re-ride that section on our most recent visit. Conditions may have changed.

The trail winds down wooded paths, old fence rows, and old dirt farm roads. The trail starts off easy to moderate and descends down a nice, wide trail to an overlook near #3. As you travel from #2 to #3, you will notice an old, unoccupied farm with a wonderful stone barn. The trail turns away from the farm to the left. This must have been a very attractive farm in its time as the building's architecture has lots of character and personality. As you descend down this wide stretch, the trail makes a sharp left. Do not go straight as it drops off. This location offers a nice view of the Delaware River and the valley below. After this stretch, there are small bridges along the trail to cross. One of these looked like it was beginning to weather, so riders (as always) need to assess if the bridges are suitable and safe prior to crossing. (This location offered alternative bypasses.) There is lots of growth along the trail, but the trail is worn enough that it is easy to follow.

Once at the top of the approach to the "circle" (markers #6, #7, #8), the trail levels off for a very nice ride through woods and fields. We visited in June and there was a variety of scenery, many pretty wild flowers, high grasses with tips the color of mauve, and tall sections of fine, pale green grass blowing in the breeze at the base of the woods. On the return between #6 and #4, the landscape was even more captivating with babbling brooks and small waterfalls throughout the forest. The final stretch between #9 and #1 is mostly easy, but is a narrow path through high grass in scenic fields of rolling hills and pine trees scattered throughout. The fields lead back to the lot.

Although there were a few horse trailers in the lot, we did not encounter anyone out on the trail, nor did any vehicles pass when we rode the short distances on the gravel roads. Although this is a popular equestrian trail system, during this visit and our prior visits, we found the trail to feel very secluded and peaceful. It is used but does not seem to be over used. There is much wildlife to encounter. Deer watch from the side of the trails as riders pass. We saw many deer including a mother with a set of speckled twins. Bird watching is also excellent. We saw some bright, colorful birds in the brush and hawks circling overhead. Also a pleasure, we enjoyed the picturesque rows of stone walls which still remain that once bordered pastures and properties. An amazing amount of labor to produce those stone walls! The Conashaugh View Trail is a unique trail system. We really enjoy our visits and hope to return soon to enjoy its scenic and rugged beauty.

## HISTORICAL INFORMATION:
The original dwellers in the area were the Lenape Indians. Later, in the 1800's, the Delaware Water Gap was used as a resort destination with an abundance of large hotels catering to wealthy individuals. Visitors would come for weeks at a time to escape from the heat of the cities during the summer. In 1965, The Delaware Water Gap National Recreation Area, which is part of the National Park Service, set aside the 70,000 acres as a public recreation area. The area includes both land in Pennsylvania and land in New Jersey. Although the hotels are long gone, the area is still popular as a weekend getaway.

Visit the PA District Ranger Station information center located just south of Dingmans Falls (where Route 739 intersects), off of Route 209, to obtain more information. Besides the trails, there are over 200 miles of road to see by auto which includes scenic views of the gap, waterfalls, wildlife, historic areas, and places to stop and picnic.

The equestrian trail is the result of years of hard work by many individuals and groups. These include the Delaware Water Gap Equestrian Advisory Committee and the South Wayne Trail Riders who worked with the Delaware Water Gap National Recreation Area to establish the first equestrian trail in the Delaware Water Gap National Recreation Area. The trail was officially opened in June of 1995 on National Trails Day. Often, National Trails Day is still celebrated at this equestrian site. Usually, more information about this trail system can be obtained at that time.

## NEARBY AND SURROUNDING AREA STABLES:
- Misty Hill Acres (boarding and emergency overnight stabling), Lehighton (610) 681-4994
- Fernwood Riding Stable, Bushkill (570) 588-9500 x4280
- Carson's Riding Stables (trail riding), Mt. Pocono (570) 839-9841
- Pocono Adventures (guided 45-minute and 2-hour trail rides; no boarding), Mt. Pocono (570) 839-6333
- Malibu Ranch (dude ranch, guided trail rides or b.y.o. horse trail riding, overnight stabling, boarding, guest accommodations), Milford (800) 8-Malibu

## NEARBY AND SURROUNDING AREA VET SERVICES:
- E. Balliet & Associates, Northampton (610) 262-3203
- L. Wessel, E. Bangor (610) 588-9467

## NEARBY AND SURROUNDING AREA FARRIERS:
- J. Kleintop, Lehighton (610) 681-4994, cell (610) 393-8363
- B. Gannon, Kunkletown (610) 381-3213

# 39. D&H Rail-Trail
# Rail-Trail Council of Northeastern Pennsylvania

**Lasting Impression:**   Ride easy trails offering gorgeous views of the Moosic Mountain range and the Lackawanna River.   Visit the nearby architectural wonder, the Starrucca Viaduct, which is still in operation today.

**Location:**   The D&H Rail-Trail is mostly in Susquehanna County, in northeastern Pennsylvania, running from Simpson to Lanesboro.

**Length:** 38 miles plus additional connecting trails and the O&W Rail-Trail

**Level of Difficulty:**   The main rail-trail, the finished section, is easy.   There are many offshoots and also some unfinished sections further north that may be more challenging.

**Terrain:**   At the time of our visit, the terrain consisted of ballast and cinder.   The trail is mostly flat or gradual.   *There are a few sections that have missing or deteriorating bridges, and may require a departure from the flat railroad grade.*

**Horse Camping:** No

**Non-horse Camping:** No

**Maps and Info:**   For info or to support this organization, contact: Rail-Trail Council of Northeastern PA, P.O. Box 123, Forest City, PA 18421-0123, (570) 785-7245, e-mail: tccrail@epix.net, websites: www.nepa-rail-trails.org and www.railtrails.org.

**Activities:**   Fishing, Hiking, Biking, Horseback Riding Trails, and X-C Skiing.   Snowmobiling has been allowed; check before arrival.   Carriage driving has been permitted, as the surface is ideal; check with the above contact for more information.   Hunting is not listed as a trail use, but be cautious during hunting season as adjoining areas may have hunting.   During our visit, ATV's were permitted on some sections of trails. They are no longer permitted.

**Fees for Trail Use:** None

**Permits for Trail Use:** None

**Comfort Station:**   There was a portajohn at the Forest City lot during our visit.   Many improvements to the trail are being made and there may be additional facilities in the future.

**DIRECTIONS:**

Route 171 runs parallel to most of the rail-trail, and the rail-trail can be accessed at the many towns along its path from Route 171.   To approach the southern end of the trail at Simpson, take I-81 to Route 6, east Carbondale exit.   (At this point, follow the Route 6 Expressway not the Business Route 6).   This is called the Governor Robert P. Casey Highway.   Travel on the Expressway for about 12 miles to Exit #6, Carbondale.   Now follow signs for Business Route 6 east.   Go a short distance to a light.   Make a right at the light, continuing on Business Route

163

6. Follow Business Route 6, which winds through the town of Carbondale, to Route 171 north (will be about a total of 16 miles from I-81 to Route 171). Travel through Simpson. Just before the bridge and the military tank, make a right on Reservoir Street. Parking is on the left and the trailhead begins further down the road on the left. It is marked but was a bit overgrown during our visit, so you may have to look for it. (Watch where the hikers and bikers travel and follow them to the entrance.) This is a very small lot and can only fit one 2-horse trailer rig and really is more suitable to hikers and bikers. There are better areas for equestrians to park. There are also trailheads at Forest City, Thompson, Uniondale, and Starrucca.

To reach the other parking areas, continue on Route 171 north. To reach the Forest City lot, cross the bridge at Simpson and continue north on Route 171. Make a right on 247 north (at the Mini Mart) and travel to the bottom of the hill. Make another right by the Vision 2000 Industrial Park sign. Travel the entrance into the park for a short distance; the trailhead parking is on the right. There are trailhead signs, fencing, and landscaping to mark the trailhead. We found the parking area at Forest City to be the roomiest, the largest, and most suitable for horse trailer parking. The size of the lot permits room for a few rigs, larger rigs, or groups; and the lot is away from the main roads. (As many nice, aesthetic improvements have recently been made to this lot, be sure to clean up the manure and not let the horses damage the landscaping and flowers.) This lot appeared to be a newer lot and was not marked as parking on our map.

Since this is a long rail-trail, there are other trail access points where a horse trailer may fit. There is a lot suitable for a few 2-horse rigs at the trail access point in Uniondale. This is at the intersection of Skyline Drive and Main Street in Uniondale, on the west side of the bridge by Stillwater Lake. (Take Route 171 toward Uniondale; at the north end of Stillwater Lake, head west on Skyline Drive toward Uniondale, the lot is on the left.) Although not as big as Forest City, this access point would be our choice to park as it is further north and the trails have less ATV's north of Uniondale. We noted that this section was posted that no ATV's were permitted. There is also an access point in the small town of Thompson, which could fit one standard 2-horse trailer rig, possibly two. Just look for a charming old train station which is now an ice cream takeout stand; the train station is next to the trail. There is some parking behind the stand at the trail access point. (Let's keep good relations; check we are not blocking the store's lot, leave room for customers to access the ice cream store, and clean up all droppings. This is a good opportunity to buy one of their delicious ice cream cones!) We found this town to be a nice, quiet town away from some of the southern, busier sections of the trail. Further north is Starrucca. The Starrucca trailhead is one block from the Starrucca intersection. Look for the Nethercott Inn in the heart of Starrucca (if heading north, make a left at the Inn), take Little

Ireland Road up the hill a short distance. Parking is on the right. This section is more primitive and overgrown, but one or two small rigs can fit in this isolated lot. Before departing for these northern most lots, call ahead to make sure the bridges are open and not under construction.

Further north of the town of Starrucca is the Starrucca Viaduct. This is a huge architectural wonder (see photo in the O&W chapter). Built in the mid 1800's, this is still an active rail line today. Even if you do not ride this far north, take a drive up Route 171 toward Lanesboro to see it. You can not miss it. Heading north, make a right following signs to the park. Travel under the viaduct; there is ample room for parking at the trailhead just past the viaduct. We visited the viaduct but we did not ride south from it, so we can not comment on this section of the trail. We were told that there are 3 unimproved bridges on the D&H, north of Stevens Point and Brandt.

To approach the D&H Rail-Trail from the north, take I-81 to the Great Bend exit (new Exit #230, old Exit #68). Follow to Route 171, heading toward Susquehanna and Lanesboro. The trail begins at the Starrucca Viaduct in Lanesboro.

**THE TRAILS:**
The Rail-Trail Council indicated that equestrians seem to prefer the trails north of Uniondale for both the D&H and the O&W Rail-Trail systems. Starting at Simpson, the O&W Rail-Trail runs alongside the D&H Rail-Trail. The southern section of the trail offers panoramic views of the Moosic Mountain range and the Lackawanna River. A newly constructed area is Panther's Bluff, which consists of 1,500 acres of scenic hiking paths with views of waterfalls. Loop rides can be made due to the two rail-trails running parallel for several miles. (However, see the ATV note below.) Plans are for a trail extension into New York and for a link with the Lackawanna Heritage Valley Trail, to ultimately connect to Wilkes-Barre via Scranton. It should be noted that a trail system linking Bristol, PA to Wilkes-Barre is intended. If that occurs, there will be trails connecting from Bristol, PA into New York State!

The rail-trail travels through some beautiful areas of Pennsylvania. As you travel north on the rail-trail, there are some good views of the surrounding countryside including lakes and mountain ranges. The small towns are charming. During our first two visits, we brought our bikes to make sure the ATV usage wasn't too heavy. Also, we were told that some of the bridges were not usable and some sections of the trail primitive, and we weren't sure of parking. However, we were happy to see the nice, improved section at Forest City with the large parking area, the maintained lot at Uniondale, and the many signs marking the trails. We concluded that the trails, terrain, and parking lots were very suited to equestrians. But, we also found that, after visiting the trails, we spent hours driving the countryside and small towns enjoying their beauty and tranquility. There are some really pretty, quaint towns nestled in these mountain ranges! The scenic Route 6 (our own "Route 66"), Pennsylvania's longest and one of its most charming and picturesque roads, travels throughout these parts.

During our visit, attractive landscape improvements were being made to this trail. We visited the D&H Rail-Trail from Simpson toward Burnwood, and the trail was mostly a wide, level, two-lane width railroad grade of cinder and ballast. The finished sections have a nice top of cinder, and there are mileage markers and the trail is very well marked. There are woods and brush bordering the trails. There is shade in the early part of the day on most of the trail. But, due to the width of the trail, it gets a lot of sun mid day so this is likely a better place to ride on a cooler day. We went on overcast days in July and August and it was not too hot. Many of the adjoining trails and connecting O&W Rail-Trail have more shade but also had many ATV's. South of Uniondale, the trail passes Stillwater Lake offering views of the lake and surrounding countryside.

Bring water for the horses for before and after the ride because many sections of the trail do not have access to water. There are some places to water the horses in the northern sections of the trail. In Starrucca, there are waterfalls to enjoy.

This trail is in various stages of completion. We found that, while traveling straight north from Simpson to south of Burnwood, there were excellent, wide bridges to cross along the main path, and continuing was no problem. But there are a few bridges that are in very poor condition and usually were blocked or obviously not suited for use. Do not attempt to cross any of these bridges. The map indicates where the trail is still under construction. (Three bridges near Simpson are not usable or safe. Also, a bridge is planned for Buck's Falls in 2003.) From Simpson to south of Burnwood, the trail was continuous and easy. (On this stretch, we did not need to go around any bridges; in fact they were built like a fort. But the adjoining trails had the old, unusable bridges mentioned above.) We did find the trail was busier in the southern section below Forest City, and more ideal for horses toward Uniondale and points north. There is sufficient equestrian parking at Uniondale. The trail crossed this lot and riders can travel north to Uniondale and onward where the trails are less traveled. This would allow for hours of riding. The trails become more primitive as you head north and are not yet completed (just) south of Thompson. Motor sports and four wheeling are very popular in this area of Pennsylvania. Many sections of the D&H were posted as closed to motorized vehicles. At the time of our visit, some sections permitted ATV's and some sections prohibited ATV's. However, the neighboring O&W had many sections that were not posted and appeared to permit ATV's; plus, there are many connecting loops of trails between the two rail-trails. We saw more ATV's in the southern most section of the D&H Rail-Trail, below Forest City, and the adjoining O&W Rail-Trail. We rode on two different Sundays, and observed that the early part of the day was quiet, and by afternoon there were numerous four wheelers. On the O&W, which is more primitive and overgrown, limited visibility and high ATV usage can be a dangerous mix with horses. We found the best section to ride was Forest City (from the big lot) north, where we only encountered one ATV on the trail; or Uniondale north, where we did not encounter any. Unlike the more primitive adjoining trails, the D&H Rail-Trail was wide with room for other users and had good visibility. Forest City was clearly posted as closed to motorized vehicles, except licensed ATV's. Further north, toward Uniondale, the trails were posted as closed to ATV's. Sections of the D&H do travel close to the O&W, and you may hear or see four wheelers, but they should not be traveling down the trail in these posted sections. We did not see any violators along this section of the D&H. We did see hikers and bikers, but due to the wide width of the trail there was lots of room for everyone.

Please note, the above trail description was written as we experienced it during our visit. Since our visit, we were notified that ATV's are no longer permitted on the D&H or the O&W Rail-Trails. In time, as this becomes communicated and enforced, the ATV usage or encounters on the trails should not need to be a consideration for hikers, bikers, and equestrians.

**HISTORICAL INFORMATION:**
The Erie Railroad Company built the D&H (Delaware & Hudson) Railway, from Carbondale to Lanesboro, to carry the coal being produced in the surrounding areas. Service began in 1870. By 1888, the O&W (Ontario & Western) section was completed to transport the large quantities of coal being produced along that branch.

In the 1990's, work began to restore the trail and transform the rail-trail to a multi-use trail system. One of these groups, the Rail-Trail Council of Northeastern PA, formed a non-profit corporation in 1991 with the purpose of acquiring and improving old railbeds. They have been successful in acquiring 38 miles of the D&H trail and securing an 8-mile easement of the O&W trail. Improvements to current trails are continuously in the works, along with plans for future trails and expansion.

Along with the Rail-Trail Council of Northeastern PA, thanks go to the National Park Service who first identified the D&W and the O&W as having potential for transformation to recreational rail-trails. There have been numerous other contributors. Much gratitude and appreciation go to these many individuals, groups, and corporations who helped these trails become available for all to enjoy. Also, thanks to Lynn Conrad of the Rail-Trail Council of Northeastern PA who corresponded with me regarding these trails and was very helpful.

After seeing all that the Rail-Trail Council of Northeastern PA was doing for these trails, we joined their organization. For an amount of their own choosing, sponsors can help support this hard working group. They are creating the great trails of today and tomorrow. (See 'Maps and Info' above for contact information.)

## THINGS WE LEARNED THIS RIDE:

- Look a little further for the trailhead; if you can't find it, just look for and follow the other trail users. During our first visit to the Simpson lot, we almost left thinking there was no access point. The lot was somewhat overgrown and we could not see where the rail-trail began. We even went up to the bridge to see if we could see it from overhead. As we were getting ready to leave, I watched a passing biker disappear into the woods down the road. Ah, ha! Kind of like following the other traffic in a detour in unfamiliar areas. We then discovered another trailhead marker down the road and a nice, wide trail. Parking was not at the actual trailhead but a short distance down the road from where the path began.

## FOR ADDITIONAL AREA INFO:

- Pocono Mountains Vacation Bureau, (800) 762-6667, website: www.poconos.org
- PA Rails-to-Trails Conservancy, (717) 238-1717, website: www.railtrails.org

## NEARBY STABLES:

- Quiet Hill Farm (boarding and possible overnight stabling), South Gibson (570) 756-2657
- Diamond in the Rough Farm (carriage services including wedding & events, horse sales, and emergency *only* overnight stabling), Thompson (570) 727-3091
- Triple W Riding Stable (B&B and riding stable, *Triple W's horses only, no overnight stabling or outside horses*), Honesdale (570) 226-2620

## NEARBY B&B:

- Green Meadows Farm, Susquehanna (570) 727-3496, (888) 325-3229

## NEARBY VET SERVICES:

- Ark Mobile Vet Service, Montrose (570) 278-9717
- Carbondale Veterinary Hospital, Carbondale (570) 282-0744
- H.J. Nebzyboski, Pleasant Mount (570) 448-2214

# 40. O&W Rail-Trail
# Rail-Trail Council of Northeastern Pennsylvania
### (Simpson to Stillwater)
## & Private Interests (Stillwater north)

**Lasting Impression:** More great scenery on a rail-trail that is not just linear. This rail-trail has lots and lots of possibilities!

**Location:** Buckingham to Preston and Poyntelle, Wayne County, northeast PA

**Length:** 13 miles, 8 miles of which the Rail-Trail Council of Northeastern Pennsylvania has acquired

**Level of Difficulty:** Easy to moderate to more challenging. This rail-trail was still primitive during our visit, and not yet developed. The bridge in Browndale is not functional; riders must follow the path to the side to cross the stream.

**Terrain:** Some flat, some rolling hills, wooded, intervals of ballast and rocky surfaces but passable

**Horse Camping:** No

**Non-horse Camping:** No

**Maps and Info:** Rail-Trail Council of Northeastern PA, P.O. Box 123, Forest City, PA 18421-0123, (570) 785-7245, e-mail: tccrail@epix.net, websites: www.nepa-rail-trails.org and www.railtrails.org. Interested individuals can write the above address and, for a nominal fee, become a member of the Rail-Trail Council. The Council provides newsletters on updates on the trails and helps promote and support trails including purchase, maintenance and expansion of the rail-trail system. The newsletter should be especially informative regarding developments on this primitive trail system.

**Activities:** Fishing, Hiking, Biking, Horseback Riding Trails, Snowmobiling, and X-C Skiing. Hunting is not listed as a trail use, but adjoining areas may have hunting during season.

**Fees for Trail Use:** None

**Permits for Trail Use:** None

**Comfort Station:** We did not see any during our visit but check the nearby D&H Rail-Trail at the Forest City lot. As this is an unfinished rail-trail, there is the possibility that additional facilities may be added in the future.

## DIRECTIONS:
Much of the O&W Rail-Trail and the D&H Rail-Trail run parallel to each other. At the time of our visit, most of this rail-trail was undeveloped. For equestrians looking to explore this trail, they may be better off parking along the D&H Rail-Trail (see the D&H chapter) and branching onto the O&W. Trail connecting points can be viewed on the D&H Rail-Trail map.

**THE TRAILS:**
The Rail-Trail Council of Northeastern Pennsylvania owns the section from Simpson to Stillwater. North of this section is privately-owned and is primitive. This section has been in use, but check prior to your visit that riding is still permitted. Be considerate, and respect no trespassing signs.

This is a trail to watch as it is not yet developed. It has great potential. Like the D&H, this rail-trail travels through beautiful country offering miles of wonderful scenery including woodlands, rolling farmland, mountain ranges, lakes, and streams. Currently, it is much more primitive and rugged than the leisurely D&H. The terrain is not flat and there are lots of loops intermingled along the trail which deviate from the straight path the railroad once took. But these loops make the trail more fun and interesting too. However, the loops also make the trail attractive for ATV users. During our visit, the ATV's were still permitted on this rail-trail and the trail was heavily traveled by ATV's. This should change after the implementation of the new regulations prohibiting ATV usage. In the meantime, equestrians may prefer to visit on off peak times. Possibly, during the week may be quieter and safer. Future plans by the Rail-Trail Council of Northeastern Pennsylvania are to utilize the loop trails of the O&W and grade the O&W.

**HISTORICAL INFORMATION:**
In the 1880's, the Erie Railroad Company built the O&W (Ontario & Western) branch of the railroad to transport the large amounts of coal being produced in the area. (See the D&H trail chapter for more info.) By the 1940's and 1950's, the need for coal decreased and the railroads became no longer used.

In the 1990's, the Rail-Trail Council acquired adjoining land and easements to the O&W. The O&W parallels the D&H, offering many loops to ride which is an advantage over most standard rail-trails that can offer only linear travel.

**NEARBY STABLES:**
- Quiet Hill Farm (boarding and possible overnight stabling), South Gibson (570) 756-2657
- Triple W Riding Stable (B&B and riding stable, *Triple W's horses only, no overnight stabling or outside horses*), Honesdale (570) 226-2620
- Diamond in the Rough Farm (carriage services including weddings & events, horse sales, and emergency *only* overnight stabling), Thompson (570) 727-3091

**NEARBY B&B:**
- Green Meadows Farm (B&B, overnight stabling, boarding, possible future guided trail rides, and prospective future horse campground), Thompson (570) 727-3496, (888) 325-3229

**NEARBY VET SERVICES:**
- Ark Mobile Vet Service, Montrose (570) 278-9717
- Carbondale Veterinary Hospital, Carbondale (570) 282-0744
- H.J. Nebzyboski, Pleasant Mount (570) 448-2214

# 41. Lackawanna State Park
# DCNR
### (Department of Conservation & Natural Resources)

**Lasting Impression:** What a pretty park! A very pleasant trail system in a rural setting. Once a site of horse races and fairs during the Colonial Period.

**Location:** Lackawanna State Park is located in northeastern Pennsylvania, just north of Scranton in Lackawanna County.

**Length:** The park contains over 1,400 acres. The surrounding areas are rural with views of the Endless Mountain Region, making the park feel even larger. A direct round trip trail ride is just about 5 miles, but due to the mountainous terrain, and time taken to enjoy the scenic vistas and the beauty of the park, there are quite a few leisurely, enjoyable hours of wonderful riding.

**Level of Difficulty:** Moderate

**Terrain:** Generally good terrain of a dirt surface through woodlands, some road crossing, not a lot of rocks, climbs (but not overly steep or on the edge), possibly some wet low-lying areas in the northeast section

**Horse Camping:** No

**Non-horse Camping:** Yes

**Maps and Info:** Lackawanna State Park, R.R. 1, Box 230, Dalton, PA 18414-9785, (570) 945-3239, e-mail: lackawanna@dcnr.state.pa.us. DCNR website: www.dcnr.state.pa.us. Call 1-888-PA-PARKS for general park info or for camping reservations.

**Activities:** Boating, Boat Rentals, Fishing, Hiking, Picnicking, Swimming, Biking, Horseback Riding Trails, Hunting (during season), Camping, X-C Skiing, and Ice Sports

**Fees for Trail Use:** None

**Permits for Trail Use:** None

**Comfort Station:** Yes

**DIRECTIONS:**

To reach the southwest lot, take I-81 to Exit #199. Take Route 524 west for 2.5 miles to the entrance to the park. There is a sign. Continue a short distance to Route 407, make a left (head south). Travel a short distance and you will come to a hard turn to the right. (This is opposite the Lackawanna State Park sign and the Abington equestrian trail marker on the left.) Make the sharp right turn. (Pass another marked Abington equestrian trail sign on the left marking the trailhead.) Travel a short distance and you will see the boating area and restrooms. Equestrians can park at this location on the left. The lot is of medium size, can fit a few 2-horse or medium sized trailers. Equestrians may need to back their rigs to turn around. There are two trailheads near this location (as described above). There is also an additional lot at the end of this road. Although the road is a dead-end, there is pull-through room or turn around room sufficient for hauling a medium sized (3-horse or stock) trailer.

Northern section of the park: There is also horse trailer parking in the northeast section of the park, which the park brochure mentions. However, we felt the southern access point was roomier and had easier access to the trails. In case the lot is full, or as a matter of preference, the north lot can be reached by taking I-81 to Exit #201, East Benton. Take Route 438 west to Wallsville Road. Travel about a mile and begin to look for the first lot on the left on Wallsville Road. This is a small to medium sized lot (can accommodate two or three 2-horse trailers), and you must ride along a frequently traveled, paved road with little shoulder to access the entrance to the trail system. There is a second lot just down Wallsville Road on the left side by the entrance to the trail. To access this lot, make a left on Cole Road and a right into the dirt lot. It is not suitable for large rigs with living quarters but can accommodate a few 2-horse trailers. There is some room, but not much to pull in and turn around. To reach the trail, cross the bridge and the trail begins on the right. There is an old sign marking the trailhead, but this trailhead was very overgrown during our first visit and did not look as if it was used. It appears the other (southern) end of the park (described above) has become the more favored of the access points as the trails are well used and most of the paths are cleared.

**THE TRAILS:**
We visited this trail twice, once on a hot summer day, and the second time on a cold Sunday in November while light flurries were falling. We had not heard of this trail system before our research for this book so we took our bikes to make sure the trails were suitable to horses and that there was sufficient parking. This trail system appears to be popular with local folks but, otherwise, seems to be a well kept secret (until now as I would like to share it). This is at the edge of the Endless Mountain Region of Pennsylvania and there is some beautiful country here. In the summer, the woods are cool and refreshing. On a winter-like day, the serenity, beauty, and scenery of the woods set against the lake and mountain ranges were tranquil and captivating. Although it was not crowded during our summer visit, I think I preferred it on the still of that November day. In the earlier part of the day, we, along with the herds of deer, had the woods to ourselves. Into the afternoon, we shared the woods with small groups of friendly mountain bikers. Mountain bikers frequent the trails, so horses need to be comfortable with passing bikes. But, there is some challenging uphill terrain that can slow everyone down. Descending is another thing and one has to keep alert for approaching bikes.

Lackawanna is Indian for "the meeting of two streams". Lackawanna Lake meets Kennedy Creek at Route 407. The trails wind around both of these lakes.

Lackawanna Lake is interesting, and is a popular fishing area as it has both cold-water species and warm-water species of fish. The equestrian trailheads are marked with signs that read "Abington Riding Trail". Once within the woods, due to many interconnecting hiking, biking, and equestrian trails, the map helps to keep you on course. However, it should not be easy to get lost as the lake and the roads serve as reference points.

The Abington Riding Trail travels in a loop in the southwest section of park on the opposite side of the boat mooring area and the parking area. This was our favorite part of the trail as the paths zigzag through the mountainside, and through quiet woods, divided by old stone walls with traces of former homesteads. When the leaves are off the trees, the trails offer views of Lackawanna Lake and the surrounding countryside. The trail then returns to the boat mooring and parking area, makes a right, crosses Route 407 and ascends up the opposite side of the road (by the Lackawanna State Park sign and Abington Riding Trail sign) into another loop. This section also travels through forest and the terrain provides a workout. This trail system seems to be a good place to condition a horse for mountainous terrain without exposing them to too much, and there are plenty of places to rest along the way. Most of the trails are wide enough with room to pull over and let others pass. The path meanders on the hillside and eventually descends onto Route 524. During both of our visits, we found the road to be quiet and easy to cross. The trail makes a slight right on Route 524 and then a quick left onto Rowlands Road. Rowlands Road is a dirt road and connects with the Kennedy Creek Trail and back onto the Abington Riding Trail. During our first visit, we traveled along the section of the Abington that borders Kennedy Lake. This lowland can be wet. If it is wet, riders can turn around and return to the rest of the trail that travels in mostly higher, dryer locations.

The surrounding area is exceptional as knoll of mountain after mountain frames the view. We have returned to this area just to take in the scenic landscape. A visit to this trail system can be combined with a nearby visit to the D&H or O&W trails. The Lackawanna State Park offers a contrast to the rail-trail with lots of climbs for variation, heavy woods, and canopied trails.

**HISTORICAL INFORMATION:**
At one time, Lackawanna Valley was the site of a major Indian trail connecting Pennsylvania to New York State. Later, this trail became a travel route used by settlers and was eventually called old Route 407. In the late 1800's, the population had grown and the Woodland Ponds Trail area became the site of horse races and fairs. The Woodland Ponds camping area was where the races were held. In the early 1900's, the D.L.&W. Railroad purchased the park land. The intention was to build a water holding basin, however, the basin was never built. Later, in the 1940's, the land was purchased by a coal operation employer and leased

1940's, the land was purchased by a coal operation employer and leased to his employees. By the 1960's, the Commonwealth of PA acquired the land and the park was officially opened in 1972. Currently, the park is run by DCNR.

For nearby riding, see the D&H and the O&W Rail-Trail chapters. Other nearby attractions include the Steamtown National Historic Site, Archbald Pothole State Park, and Salt Spring State Park. At Archbald Pothole, one can view the world's largest glacial pothole. At Salt Spring, waterfalls and huge hemlocks can be enjoyed along with various other park recreation and programs.

Thanks to Don Anderson of DCNR who was very friendly and helpful. Don generously took the time to answer our questions regarding the equestrian trails and parking, and made us feel welcome. Also thanks to the Abington Hills 4H and Riding Club and other local individuals and groups, who we were told have contributed much to these trails.

**THINGS WE LEARNED THIS RIDE:**
- Could it be that sometimes the exit numbers not only change but also disappear? Maybe we have been on the road too much. John, without me, drove up to this area in the prior winter and took directions for us to return, but we could not find that original exit number which was one of the newer numbers. This happened to me at another trail location. Perhaps we are mistaken, but it seems that, during the renumbering project, there were some additional changes. Hopefully, no more changes were made after our visit and after I have written the directions in this book. We do compare to the exit numbers on the Penn DOT website which is helpful. We have tried to include further descriptions and names of places, along with the exit numbers, in the event of changes or if we have misread or got it wrong.

**NEARBY:**
- North of Lackawanna are two rail-trail systems: the D&H Rail-Trail which runs over 30 miles from Stevens Point to Simpson in mostly Susquehanna County, and the O&W Rail-Trail that runs 13 miles from Preston Township to the Delaware River in Wayne County.

**NEARBY AND SURROUNDING AREA STABLES:**
- Bailey Hollow Farm (boarding and overnight stabling), Dalton (570) 563-1664
- Triple W Riding Stable (B&B and riding stable, *Triple W's horses only, no overnight stabling or outside horses*), Honesdale (570) 226-2620
- J&L Pocono Stables (boarding, lessons, and possible overnight stabling available), just off Route 380, Moscow (570) 842-5094

175

**NEARBY VET SERVICES:**
- Abington Veterinary Center, Inc. (for emergencies, trailer to office), Clarks Summit (570) 585-2006
- Carbondale Veterinary Hospital, Carbondale (570) 282-0744
- H.J. Nebzyboski, Pleasant Mount (570) 448-2214

**NEARBY FARRIERS:**
- L. Stanek, Moscow (570) 842-3766, (570) 842-5437 fax
- Timber Horse Shoeing, Moscow (570) 842-7096

# 42. Ricketts Glen State Park
# DCNR
### (Department of Conservation & Natural Resources)

**Lasting Impression:** A wonderful park with standing trees over 500 years old and fallen trees over 900 years old!

**Location:** Ricketts Glen State Park is located in the northeast/northcentral part of the state. It is located about 30 miles north of Bloomsburg, near the town of Benton, and spans the counties of Luzerne, Sullivan, and Columbia.

**Length:** Ricketts Glen State Park consists of over 13,000 acres with over 9 miles of designated trails, plus miles of connecting dirt roads and possible riding in adjoining state gamelands and surrounding areas.

**Level of Difficulty:** Mostly easy, some sections are moderate due to rocky patches

**Terrain:** Toward the center of the park, the terrain is cinder or stone dust. Outlying trails are dirt or sand. The trails vary from flat to rolling hills. Many of the trails are cleared paths through the woods. Although there are some rocky sections, we found them passable.

**Horse Camping:** No

**Non-horse Camping:** Yes

**Maps and Info:** Ricketts Glen State Park, R.R. 2, Box 130, Benton, PA 17814-8900, (570) 477-5675, e-mail: rickettsglen@dcnr.state.pa.us. Call 1-888-PA-PARKS for general park info or for camping reservations. For State Gamelands info, see the State Gamelands chapter.

**Activities:** Boating, Boat Rentals, Fishing, Hiking, Picnicking, Swimming, Horseback Riding Trails, Hunting (during season), Camping, Snowmobile Trails, X-C Skiing, and Ice Sports. At this writing, bikes are only permitted on roads open to vehicles.

**Fees for Trail Use:** None

**Permits for Trail Use:** None

**Comfort Station:** Yes

## DIRECTIONS:

There are a few approaches to the park. One approach is to take I-81 to Exit #170, follow Route 309 north (Wilkes-Barre direction). Travel 8 miles, passing Dallas, and come to a Y. Route 309 north goes to the right and Route 415 north goes straight. Do not turn right; head straight on Route 415 north for another 3 miles. Look for signs for Route 118. Come to a light (after traveling a total of 11 miles from I-81), make a left on Route 118 west. Travel on Route 118 for about 17 miles to Red Rock (pass Ricketts Glen State Park signs). Make a right onto Route 487 north. We were told the grade is about 18%. Rigs will need to be able to handle a steep climb. We did not experience any problems but we were hauling

177

our 2-horse trailer, not our larger rig; and we were pulling with a heavy-duty truck. To avoid the steep approach, the park can be accessed by traveling to Dushore and heading south on Route 487 to the park entrance.

At the top of the mountain, see the Ricketts Glen State Park entrance. If traveling from the south, make a right. Follow the State Park Road, pass two parking lots on the left, and travel toward the direction of the loop of cabins on the map. At the end of the park road there is a lot with picnic grounds and access to the beach. This is where equestrians park. The lot is very large with ample room to travel the circle of the loop, with no backing required. We drove the full circle of the loop and parked in the corner of the loop away from the picnic area. The lot is paved and there is no separate, designated equestrian area. Due to this being a shared location, the ranger did stress that droppings should be cleaned up immediately and we gladly complied. However, although this is an excellent lot, we are hoping that a less central area nearby will be designated as an equestrian parking area. This is a really nice park and we wouldn't want to see a few riders who neglect to clean up ruin it for other riders.

Finding the trail from the lot is a little tricky. We did not see markers in the lot. We had to stop and flag down a passing DCNR vehicle to ask where we should ride. Although the lot was not crowded, the parking area is central to the picnic grounds, cabins, hiking trails, and beach access so we did not want to bring the horses where we should not. To reach the trailhead, ride from the parking lot; make a left at the entrance and head toward the cabin area. Travel a short distance down the paved park road passing cabins, hiking trails, etc. (It is a good idea to scatter any droppings along the way on this paved, central shared-use area.) Come to the gated trailhead, which is marked and has a stone dust surface. Continue straight, then come to an intersection. Look for equestrian signs to the outer trails. Follow signs to Cherry Run Trail or Mountain Springs Trail. Orange blazes or triangles will begin to mark the trails.

**THE TRAILS:**
Once away from the parking lot and the busy cabin area, we seemed to have the trail to ourselves. There are many cleared paths winding through mature woods and lots of huge wild cherry trees that have somehow avoided being cut into lumber. The equestrian trail is in a loop that begins at a dam by Lake Leigh. There are numerous signs at this intersection. The DCNR map lists the trail information, which includes the name of the trail, length, blaze color, and level of difficulty. The map also indicates which trails are open to equestrians. The map is helpful and, also, there are signs at various intervals of the trail indicating the name and direction of the trails. However, the signs seem to drop off in the outer reaches of the trails, so do bring the map.

Traveling clockwise on the map, take Cherry Run Trail which heads north to Fish Commission Road. Cherry Run Trail is a nice trail through the woods. We found it easy to follow. There are some climbs but the terrain we encountered was mostly gradual. Overall, the trails were not very rocky. There are a few sections with a cluster of rocks but we found these passable. We took Cherry Run and made a right on Fish Commission Road, which is a dirt road with lots of shoulder. We visited on a Sunday in early August, and this road was not busy. It was a very hot day, though, and mid day this road gets lots of sun. Luckily, there were many places to water the horses along the trails. The road is sand and has an easy footing. There are a few miles of riding along this road, but we found it to be a nice ride with views of The Meadows and various wetlands.

The Fish Commission Road borders State Gameland No. 57. From the road you could see that there appeared to be some nice looking trails heading into the State Gamelands. If you choose to extend your ride, check with the State Gamelands prior to your visit to see if horseback riders are permitted to ride these trails. A map can be obtained (nominal fee) from the Game Commission; ask for State Gameland No. 57. There are several dirt pull-off areas along the Fish Commission Road, sufficient to park a rig and with access to the eastern section of Ricketts Glen State Park and the Game Commission land. We were thinking this could be a more desirable location for horse trailer parking as it was away from the main park activity. We will be inquiring with DCNR if there is a possibility that this section of the park can have a designated equestrian parking area.

When we approached the end of Fish Commission Road, we saw an orange ribbon and made an (early) incorrect left onto what was clearly a trail, and appeared to be a very scenic one too. But there were no signs indicating this was not the equestrian trail or what trail this was. I was really enjoying the view as we rode; however, the path eventually narrowed and became overgrown. It looked like at one time it continued on and was a nice, wide trail. But trees had fallen and growth blocked the path. We kept looking for the place to pick up the correct trail. We came to what was once a crossing, and now was just the ruins of an old bridge. We knew we needed to cross the river; so we crossed upstream and picked up an old railroad right-of-way on the other side. It was quite overgrown and not enjoyable as it was a 'duck and dive' trail. But it could be a really nice multi-use trail if cleared, and it wouldn't take much to get it into shape. Finally, we approached the right trail and got back on course, and the trees again had blazes. We were now on the Mountain Springs Trail, passing wonderful views of Mountain Spring Lake. We saw lots of waterfowl including heron. I especially enjoyed the ride along the lake.

Mountain Springs Trail continues for a few miles and returns to the intersection at the dam. There are some rocky sections along the way, but there was dirt in between the rocks for the horses to pick through; we didn't find the rocks to be an impediment. The last stretch is a pretty, wooded, wide trail with waterfalls to the left. On a hot day, the temperature cools as you enter this area. This section of the trail approaches the Glens Natural Area, but access into the heart of the natural area is by foot only via the hiking trails. The Glens Natural Area is a popular destination as it offers a panoramic view where you can stand "on the edge" to view the deep gorges of Glen Leigh and Ganoga Glen. The surrounding woods contain huge trees over 500 years old with 5 foot diameters! The rings of trees lying on the forest floor have reflected ages of up to 900 years! Also within the Glens Natural Area are numerous waterfalls. The names of the falls are listed on the DCNR map along with the height. The equestrian trail will pass the eastern tip of this area giving a glimpse of the beginning of the falls. This is a really nice section of the trail and made us want to return to explore the Glens Natural Area on foot. After riding past the waterfalls, the trail returns to the main intersection and the dam. We made a left at the foot of the dam and headed back to the cabin area and the parking lot.

## HISTORICAL INFORMATION:
The park is named after Colonel Robert B. Ricketts who fought and survived the Battle of Gettysburg. Colonel Ricketts owned over 80,000 acres of land. Lumbering companies eventually acquired much of his land. In the 1920's, the PA Game Commission purchased 48,000 acres of this land from the lumber companies. By the 1930's, plans were made for a national park. However, the outbreak of World War II interrupted these plans, and the park again changed ownership.

Additional acquisitions were later made, and some of the more scenic areas were sold to the Commonwealth of PA for the State Park. Other purchases were also completed which together comprise today's park. In the 1940's, the park was opened. By 1969, the Glens Natural Area had become a registered National Natural Landmark and in 1993, it was made a protected State Park Natural Area.

## THINGS WE LEARNED THIS RIDE:
- If there are consistent tree blazes and all of a sudden they stop, immediately go back and check that you didn't miss your trail.
- We also learned, while trying to find the trail, that if in the vicinity of an old homestead or just crossing off trail due to whatever circumstance, pull the sunglasses off and look closely as old fencing may be laying on the ground which could cause harm. We did not have an incident as I had dismounted and walked ahead with the intention to check out the area. I was checking the firmness of the ground in order to cross the river and came across the old wire fencing. I was glad I did dismount, as it was much easier to see on foot.
- And we experienced that when a brochure says, i.e., "9 miles of trails", they may mean only the trail length and may not be counting the connecting roads. Each map is different and it helps to look at the mile scale for comparison. We had left later than usual, expecting a shorter ride and ended up returning

well after what we expected. And, we had gotten off course adding to the time! We were, however, glad that there was a longer combined length of trail and road to ride. We really enjoyed our visit to Ricketts Glen State Park and look forward to returning. Next time we would like to bring our bathing suits to enjoy the beach after a long ride.

- After speaking with one park representative about horses in the park, we came to realize that cleaning up after one's horse before leaving is not enough. We have not had any problems and always clean up upon departure, but in a heavily used multiple-use area, the manure left all day or for a few hours until return could cause complaints by other users, jeopardizing use of the area in the future. Complaints from other users also can put added pressure on the DCNR, because they must respond to them. In a multi-use area, riders should clean up immediately, and not let the manure lay until before they leave. A few minutes spent to clean up without delay can go a long way for good relations between equestrians, other users, and those that manage the parks and trails.

## NEARBY STABLES:
- Drake Hollow Stables (feed, hay, overnight stabling, trailer parking, and motels nearby), Dushore (570) 928-7101
- Spotted Horse Riding Stable (boarding, lessons, guided trail rides, and emergency overnight stabling), Dushore (570) 924-3210

## NEARBY VET SERVICES:
- D. Fine, Larksville (570) 287-9085

## NEARBY FARRIERS:
- R. Minnier, Dushore (570) 924-4606
- D. Treaster, Dushore (570) 924-3210

# 43. The Tiadaghton State Forest & The Black Forest
# DCNR
### (Department of Conservation & Natural Resources)

**Lasting Impression:**  A must visit in June when the mountain laurel are in bloom!

**Location:**  The Black Forest region and the Black Forest Trail ("BFT") of the Tiadaghton State Forest are located mostly in the northwest section of Lycoming County, (slightly east) central Pennsylvania, close to the town of Slate Run.  The Black Forest Trail is just south of the Pine Creek Trail (Pennsylvania Grand Canyon) in Tioga County and is part of the West Block of the Tiadaghton State Forest.

**Length:**  There are well over a hundred miles of trails to ride throughout the Black Forest/Tiadaghton State Forest region.  Equestrians are permitted to ride anywhere that horses are not prohibited or posted as not permitted. Looking at the Tiadaghton Forest Fire Fighter's map and the tree blazes, horses are permitted on many sections of the blue trail (blue blaze) and a few connecting sections of the Black Forest Trail or red trail (orange blaze).  The prohibited areas are often areas posted "for foot traffic only" due to their being considered environmentally sensitive or not suitable for horses.  Much of the blue trail is open to horses unless posted otherwise.  However, many portions of the Black Forest Trail, a 42-mile loop, are for foot traffic only.  But there are some linking trails (i.e., where the orange and blue marked trails meet) where horses are permitted.  There are also lots and lots of State Forest (dirt or gravel) roads to ride.

**Level of Difficulty:**  Easy to difficult, depending on the trail

**Terrain:**  The terrain varies greatly.  There are flat sections, rolling hills, wide grassy stretches, old dirt logging roads, converted railroad right-of-ways, some climbs, easy level ground, rugged surfaces, mostly wooded paths, streams, high land, and some wet lowlands.  We did not encounter steep climbs on the blue trail but were told the red trail had some abrupt mountainous terrain.  There are many really nice trails in the vicinity of the Black Forest Trail in the Tiadaghton State Forest, but you need to know where to ride.

**Horse Camping:**  Yes

**Non-horse Camping:**  Yes

**Maps and Info:**  Maps, info, and Letters of Authorization for group rides can be obtained from DCNR, Bureau of Forestry, 423 East Central Avenue, South Williamsport, PA  17702, (570) 327-3450. Also, forest or camping questions can be answered at (570) 321-0974 or write Jim Hyland at JHyland@state.pa.us.  *Jim Hyland, a Forester at Tiadaghton, was extremely helpful, professional, and pleasant during my queries.  Jim has done extensive work in the support and maintenance of the Bureau of Forestry trails, including the equestrian trails.*

*Jim has worked closely with the Pennsylvania Equine Council to establish trail systems, including that of nearby Bald Eagle State Forest. Jim deserves special mention and thanks.* Maps, info, the Black Forest Trail booklet, and the Tiadaghton Forest Fire Fighter's map can also be obtained from Fin, Fur, and Feather (570) 769-6620 at website: www.finfurandfeather.com, Pine Creek Outfitters (570) 724-3003, or Tiadaghton Forest Fire Fighter's Association at Box 5091, S. Williamsport, PA 17701. We found the Tiadaghton Forest Fire Fighter's map, a long, narrow map, to be very useful and is the one referred to in this chapter. Ask for this map and bring it with you on the trail. It reflects the Black Forest Trail/red trail (orange blaze) and the blue trail (blue blaze). Note that the Tiadaghton Forest Fire Fighter's map has numbers on it, which correspond to the small Black Forest Trail book (small fee) also produced by the Tiadaghton Forest Fire Fighters. The Black Forest Trail book gives detailed descriptions and history of the trail.

**Activities:** Hiking, Biking, Horseback Riding Trails, Hunting (during season), X-C Skiing, Fishing, and Snowmobiling

**Permits and Fees for Trail Use:** None

**Permits for Camping:** Yes, but no fee. Permits will not be issued more than 90 days in advance, and are issued at the South Williamsport District Office listed above.

**Comfort Station:** There were no comfort stations at the Gas Well Campsite and we did not see any along the trails that we rode. However, there are restrooms at the nearby State Parks.

## DIRECTIONS:

Take Route 220 to the town of Jersey Shore. From Jersey Shore, take Route 44 north (Pine Creek State Park exit). Take Route 44 north for 17 miles to Haneyville. Route 44 is windy and has some significant climbs. *(You will pass the southern entrance to the PA Grand Canyon Rail-Trail in Waterville. This section is a nice scenic section for hikers and bikers. Equestrians are not permitted at the southern end of the rail-trail. Throughout Route 44 there are lots of places to pull off, park, and hike.)* Come to a T in Haneyville. Make a right at the stop/right turn sign. Stay on Route 44. To reach the Old Gas Well Campsite, continue on Route 44 for 12 miles and look for Manor Fork Road on the right. There is a sign that says "Recreational Parking". Slow down as Manor Fork Road travels down through a series of mature evergreen trees bordering the entrance resulting in a tight turn. (We were able to make the turn in our large rig.) Make the right onto Manor Fork Road. There are some park buildings at the end of the pine row. Take Manor Fork Road to where there is a gate. Bear left at the gate. Travel slowly and look for a dirt/gravel road to the left. (The total distance is just a few tenths of a mile off of Route 44.) The Old Gas Well Campsite is at the end of the dirt/gravel road on the left side. (We were unsure this was the turn, we stopped the rig, and walked the short distance to make sure this was the place.) There is plenty of room to turn around within the Old Gas Well Campsite. The Old Gas Well Campsite is one of the most popular locations for equestrian campers, especially for those traveling in groups or for campers who have large rigs. There are other sites to camp at in close proximity to the Black Forest Trail but they are smaller and sometimes these sites change. Contact the Forest Office to provide the latest information on alternate sites and adjoining trailheads.

Warning: Do not travel south on Route 44 from Galeton. This is extremely steep and windy; this route can 'do a truck in' and be hard on the horses. Instead, approach from the south on Route 44 as described above.

## THE TRAILS:
This trail system is a must see about the third week in June (around Father's Day) as the Black Forest Trail and the neighboring trails are covered in blankets of mountain laurel. This is the most mountain laurel we have seen on one trail system.

The trails are very diverse as they consist of hiking paths, cross-country ski trails, snowmobile trails, old railway right-of-ways, and logging trails through valleys and mountainous terrain. The BFT is a loop, which begins and ends in a pine farm approximately a mile from Slate Run. There are many beautiful vistas where the BFT and the adjoining trails overlook Slate Run, Pine Creek, Morris Run, and other surrounding sites. There are some places to water the horses along the trail and in some low-lying wetlands. The trails are well marked. The Black Forest Trail ("red trail" on the map) is marked with orange circles; adjoining trails have blue circles or rectangles. DCNR indicated that trails not permitting horseback riding are posted as such. Maps with topo info should be obtained prior to departing.

Trails vary from extremely easy and leisurely to rough and challenging. We found the following loops to be mostly easy:
- The first day we went for a short ride out through camp, through the pine area (left side as you drive into the lot). We rode the Baldwin Gasline Trail to the White Birch Vista, which is an old dirt and grass logging path, and backtracked for our return. (Some of this trail joins the "red trail" but was not posted as closed to horses.) We found it to be suitable for horses and easy to ride. Bring your camera! There were lots of beautiful vistas on both sides of the trail. There is, however, a trail that goes to the left called "Slide" trail. The name provides a clue that it is for foot traffic only. We did not visit this trail but were told that it is a dangerous trail for horses.
- The next day we rode out the entrance to the camping lot to Manor Fork Road, made a left, traveled a short distance down Manor Fork, made a left on Harrowed Trail. Harrowed Trail is a scenic, wide stretch of old logging grade, easy to ride, and full of mountain laurel in the spring. Take Harrowed

Trail, cross Route 44, and take the George Will Trail loop. The George Will Trail (blue trail) will join with the BFT (red trail). Return toward Route 44 by following the George Will Loop to the Ruth Will Trail. (The Will family contributed much to the establishment and preservation of these trails.) As you come off of the George Will Trail loop, avoid the section on the map between 21.13 and 21.50. Here, the blue/red combo splits at 21.13, with blue (George Will Trail) to the left and the red trail (BFT) marked by orange blazes to the right. Keep to the blue as the red changes back to foot traffic only and can be very challenging (rocky and ravines) for horses. Taking either trail leads to the ruins of a small stone building, which is an old pump house. Note the metal roof with the narrow gauge railroad track as support beams. After this section, there are metal grids used as bridges. These are not the sturdy, wooden bridges usually seen on equestrian and multi-use trails, but rather springy metal plates-not very horse friendly. Usually, we found room to pass on the side of them as many horses may take some convincing to cross them. We hope they will be replaced with safer, solid wooden bridges. Ride the Ruth Will loop and cross over Route 44 to Naval Run. Come to a fork; bear left. Loop back to the road. Cross the road, pass the buildings to the left. Enter the pine area toward camp. Most of this ride was easy except for a few short sections that were wet lowlands.

- Another loop can be accessed by heading out the entrance to camp. Make a left on Manor Fork Road, left on Harrowed Trail, cross Route 44, and ride north on the trail that parallels Route 44. Basically, we rode the blue trail in a clockwise direction. It circles around the border of the Black Forest Inn property. Pick up the Blackberry Trail west (left), ride a short distance, make a right on Sentiero Di Shay to Little Daugherty Trail, and back to Sentiero Di Shay to the Pine Bog Trail. (The Pine Bog was our least favorite part of the trail. It is a bog. If your horse can not handle wet or mud, or there has been recent rains, avoid this section. We were able to cross it but it had deep, wet spots with some rocks. This is, however, not a long section and the trail returns to higher ground.) Take Pine Bog or an alternate back to Route 44, cross over Route 44, ride south on the trail that parallels with Route 44 south. (Pine Bog can be avoided by taking the green trail back to Manor Fork, making a right on Manor Fork, and heading back to camp along Manor Fork. We obtained this alternate from the map and did not ride this substitute route.) Cross back over Route 44 and pick up the Harrowed Trail or one of the others back to camp.

Frequent visitors told us that there are lots of other trails and camping areas within the forest. Some of these folks found nice trails, and then requested and received permission from the Forest Office to camp at designated locations with direct access to those trails. Start at the established Old Gas Well Campsite and explore. Although, be forewarned that experienced travelers of this area advised and cautioned us not to ride east of Algerine Wild Area or north of the Algerine Wild Area on the red trail/BFT as it is a foot path and dangerous to equestrian travel. As a whole, they indicated the blue rectangle or circle trail is more suitable for horses.

## EQUESTRIAN CAMPING:

A favorite location for many equestrians is the Old Gas Well Campsite. Camping is primitive. This is a nice, clean camping area with a private feel but is only a short distance off of Route 44. Large groups and many long rigs can fit. There is plenty of room, including room to turn around without backing. The camping area is basically a big, gravel and grass lot with trees bordering the open area. Dogs are permitted. There are plenty of trees for picket tying or room for portable electric fence corrals. (Steer clear of the abundant mountain laurel, as we have been told that it can be extremely irritating or toxic to a horse if eaten.) Campers can set up camp on the border of the woods for shade. Our favorite site was just to the right upon entering the camping area. We backed in and had a nice, grassy area for the horses to graze, and a secluded and shady area to camp. Camping does require a permit but there are no specific assigned sites.

Horse campers are requested not to tie horses to trees and to scatter manure, leaving a clean campsite and following the "Leave No Trace Outdoor Ethics". Let's not wear out our welcome; the Forest Office asks campers to be extra cautious and not allow animals access to where they can damage trees. Equestrian groups of more than 10 people must get a Letter of Authorization from the DCNR office.

There are three State Parks within the Tiadaghton Forest District: Little Pine State Park, Ravensburg State Park, and Susquehanna State Park. These are not open for equestrian camping, but the Little Pine State Park is closer to the equestrian camping area, and individuals with a permit may be able to access park facilities including campgrounds, swimming area, bathhouse, and restroom facilities. For permission and information on Little Pine State Park in Waterville, call (570) 753-6000.

## WATER:

Bring sufficient amounts of water. Although there are some streams on the trails, there is no water at the equestrian camping area. However, often along Route 44, there are pipes coming out of the rocks, which are bursting with spring water. As you pass these locations, you will see people filling up containers. One of these sites is 6 miles north of Jersey Shore, along Route 44 on the right side as you travel north. There is a stream to water the horses, not far from camp, at the old pump house where the George Will and Ruth Will Trails meet. We chose to refill our tanks at a nearby commercial campground. Often, when asked, campgrounds will permit you to fill your tanks (sometimes for a nominal fee). We were not charged a fee so we made sure we made a few purchases at their camp store to show our appreciation. Also, we have found that State Parks' camping areas usually have water. But in this were as close to the equestrian camping area as some of the commercial campgrounds were.

## HISTORICAL INFORMATION:

The Black Forest Trail System is part of the Tiadaghton State Forest. The Tiadaghton State Forest contains over 215,000 acres and derives its name from the Iroquois name for Pine Creek. Tiadaghton is divided into three blocks, the South Block, the West Block, and the East Block. The West Block, located in the Pine Creek Valley, comprises most of the Tiadaghton State Forest and contains the Black Forest Trail. The Black Forest obtained its name from the thick, dark woods of coniferous trees that were native to the area.

Much of the Tiadaghton State Forest was acquired from the lumber companies in the early 1900's. The Civilian Conservation Corps built foot paths and road systems in the 1930's and the Bureau of Forestry built sections of the trail and now manages the system. Many of the original facilities had to be rebuilt due to extensive damage and flooding caused by Hurricane Agnes in 1972.

Although we did not have the pleasure of personally meeting Bob Webber during our visit, we were told that he was a primary contributor to these trails and generously dedicated years and years of his time to their establishment and maintenance. Many thank you's to Bob. Also, thank you to fellow trail rider, Terry Mort of Ohio, for taking the time to tell us what trails to ride.

## THINGS WE LEARNED THIS RIDE:
- Be careful when setting aside doggie jerky treats for your dog, that someone does not mistake them for human beef jerky treats, as they can look the same (sorry Garth).
- Beware of any trails that transverse through areas with "bog" in the name.
- Above all, we learned this region is awesome when the mountain laurel are in bloom. The laurel blankets much of the forest borders and mountainside. This area must also be beautiful in the fall due to the variety of trees including beech, cherry, maple, ash, and birch.

## NEARBY VET SERVICES:
- Lewis Vet Clinic, Jersey Shore (570) 398-2729
- Laurel Highland Farm & Equine Services LLC, E. Early, Williamsport (570) 326-1134
- Troy Veterinary Clinic, Troy (570) 673-3181

## NEARBY FARRIERS:
- S. Sims, Loganton (570) 725-3910
- T. Andrews, Cogan Station (570) 326-3807

# 44. Tioga State Forest,
# Home of The Grand Canyon of PA, &
# The Pine Creek Rail-Trail
# DCNR
### (Department of Conservation & Natural Resources)

**Lasting Impression:** Trail ride the Grand Canyon of PA! Big, bold, beautiful. If you know where to ride, this place is great fun. Can't wait to return and explore more.

**Location:** Tioga State Forest is located in northcentral Pennsylvania near Wellsboro in Tioga, Bradford, and Lycoming Counties.

**Length:** There are well over a hundred miles of trails with many days of riding within the Tioga State Forest. This is an unmarked and sometimes confusing territory where you need to bring a compass, maps, and a GPS if you have one. Other than an occasional sign or orange blaze indicating snowmobile trails, the State Forest trails are not clearly marked. Although the DCNR's map is very helpful and a necessity, it reflects some of the trails but does not reflect all of the trails, nor the detail on the trails or mileage. Check with the local outfitters for the availability of an updated map, including snowmobile maps. (Pine Creek Outfitters is on Route 6 just west of the canyon and may have maps.) Numerous discussions with various DCNR offices informed and confirmed that horseback riding is allowed on State Forest land, except on designated hiking trails and trails specifically closed to horses. Horses are permitted throughout the Tioga State Forest, except for the trail called the "West Rim Trail" which travels along the edge of the canyon, the lower section of the Pine Creek Trail, and areas posted as closed to horses. (In our travels, we did not see any areas posted as closed to horses. We also did not see the "West Rim Trail" posted as closed to horses, so you need to know to avoid it.)

The Tioga State Forest is home to the PA Grand Canyon. The PA Grand Canyon is 50 miles long with the Pine Creek Trail winding in a deep valley at the base of it. The designated riding area is along the Pine Creek Trail. The Pine Creek Trail is expected to be a length of over 60 miles when completed. Horses are permitted on the 9 mile (18 mile round trip) stretch between Ansonia and Tiadaghton. This section travels through the heart of the scenic PA Grand Canyon.

The Tioga State Forest, encompassing the PA Grand Canyon, has additional trails that locals and others have established in the surrounding mountains. Often, these trails lead out from the nearby stables. Call or stop by and talk to these folks. Many are very helpful, provide maps, or recommend guide services.

**Level of Difficulty:** The Pine Creek Rail-Trail, which travels through the heart of the Grand Canyon of PA, is easy. Horses will need to be comfortable with passing bicyclists and hikers (who pass on a separate, designated parallel trail). In contrast, the surrounding mountainous area of Tioga State Forest contains a diverse and huge trail system, with varying degrees of difficulty and complexity. These trails can fluctuate from easy, to moderate, to rugged.

**Terrain:** The railroad grade along Pine Creek is flat to gradual with a surface of cinder (may be paved also) on one side for hikers and bicyclists, and dirt/gravel on the other side for equestrians. Of the surrounding mountain trails that we sampled, we found most of the terrain varied from easy, grassy stretches, dirt logging roads, forest (dirt and/or gravel) roads, and trails with a dirt surface. Overall, we did not encounter much rock on the wider trails and logging roads; generally the terrain was very good and numerous trails were exceptional in terrain and beauty. Some of the side trails do have rocky stretches; we found them rugged but passable. There are a few very rough trails; these can be bypassed. We visited in late spring and the trails south of Route 6 (west side of the canyon) had lots of water beside the path and, occasionally, there was water running across the trails. Logging activities can also affect and interfere with the smooth terrain. However, the overall surface was firm and passable. We revisited in the fall, after heavy recent rains, and rode the north side of Route 6 (west side of the canyon). In spite of the recent wet weather, the main trails were high, dry, wide, and of solid footing. Except for the Pine Creek Rail-Trail, almost all of the trails we encountered were wooded and canopied.

**Horse Camping:** Primitive, non-motorized camping is permitted in sections of the State Forest, including some portions of the Pine Creek Rail-Trail. The Tioga State Forest does permit motorized camping along pull-offs on forest roads. A permit (free) must be obtained prior to arrival. There are no designated camping areas. We searched for functional areas for camping or day parking in the block of forest south of Route 6 and west of the canyon near Colton Point. Finding a large enough area to pull off was not that easy. We were told many riders ask for permits to camp along the O'Connor Trail. However, upon visiting the O'Connor Trail, we found the dirt roads approaching this area to have tight turns and no location to turn around. We only saw one or two possible pull-offs but they were small and on soft terrain. Although situated in a central location to the trails, we did not feel comfortable with suggesting this location. However, we did find a roomier, higher, dryer area near Refuge Trail (see below) which could accommodate 2 to 3 rigs. This location appeared to be ideal for day parking or camping, as it is central to many trails. Most of the roads do not have sufficient shoulder space for a rig. Drivers of large rigs also need to be cautious when exploring, as many of these forest roads are dirt, of narrow width, and inadequate to travel on while hauling.

Late in our research process, we were told that a favorite camping area for equestrians is in the area north of Route 6, near the ASAPH Wildlife Area off of ASAPH Road, at the loop at the end of Hesselgessel Road. We rode trails within close proximity and they were outstanding. We believe this may be a choice camping location. Unfortunately, although we had wanted to visit and camp at this location, the early onset of winter weather prevented us from doing so. We will have to do so next riding season.

There are nearby campgrounds and equestrian facilities that can accommodate horse camping, lease horses, and/or offer guide services. During our visit, we stayed at Woodlands Campground (formerly Fromes), (814) 435-8279, located along the Pine Creek near the PA Grand Canyon. They permit pets and camping with your horse. Woodlands Campground is situated close to many nice Tioga State Forest west rim trails, and is a short trailering distance from the Pine Creek Rail-Trail which is located on the east shore of the Pine Creek.

For campers or travelers who are not visiting with their own horses but want to ride, The Mountain Trail Horse Center in Wellsboro, (570) 376-5561, has convenient access to trails and offers guided horse tours on their horses. Upon inquiry, we were told this facility does not accommodate camping with one's own horse. Further away, near Covington, is Tanglewood Camping, (570) 549-8299. Tanglewood is a campground, which advertises that they accept horses and pets, and offers camping with hook-ups and cabin rentals.

**Non-horse Camping:** Yes, both within the State Forest and surrounding areas. Contact the Forest Office for rules, limitations, and regulations. There are also many nearby motels and accommodations; contact the Wellsboro Chamber of Commerce for more information.

**Maps and Info:** Obtain the map and information from DCNR, Tioga State Forest, One Nessmuk Lane, Wellsboro, PA 16901, (570) 724-2868, e-mail: fd16@dcnr.state.pa.us. Other local info, including maps, can also be obtained from Pine Creek Outfitters, Wellsboro, (570) 724-3003, e-mail: pinecrk@clarityconnect.com; and Fin, Fur, & Feather, Haneyville, (570) 769-6620, website: www.finfurfeather.com. Again, since trails are not marked, a map is essential. A topo map and GPS is helpful also.

**Activities:** Boating, Boat Rentals, Fishing, Swimming, Rafting, Hiking, Picnicking, Biking, Horseback Riding Trails, Hunting (very popular during season), Camping, and Ice Sports

**Permits and Fees for Trail Use:** None

**Permits for Camping:** Yes, but no fee. Contact the district office for more information.

**Comfort Station:** There are comfort stations at the State Parks.

**DIRECTIONS:**

Pine Creek Rail-Trail parking lot (ride the valley of the Pennsylvania Grand Canyon): From Wellsboro, take Route 6 west past the Route 362 junction and continue over the bridge. Just past the bridge (when your rear wheels leave the bridge get ready to make a

190

right), there is an "Ansonia" sign and an old white church with a steeple and a cemetery on the north or right side. Make a right at the church onto a dirt and gravel road. This is Marsh Creek Road. Go about .25 miles and look for brown signs on the right indicating horse trailer parking. This is a large, open, grassy lot in a rural and scenic setting with views of the surrounding mountains. The lot can hold large rigs or several standard 2-horse trailers. There is plenty of turn-around room. The Pine Creek Trail starts south of the lot and is marked with two signs, one indicating where equestrians are permitted to ride and one where they are not. The trailhead has a map posted, but the rail-trail is easy to follow as it is a finished, wide trail of even gravel and adjoining dirt surface. (Rail-trails are usually very easy to follow; however, we have been on some unfinished rail-trails that, over the years, have become difficult to follow due to growth, erosion, development, or other factors.) Primitive camping is allowed along the Pine Creek Rail-Trail. There is an area below Tumbling Run, along the Pine Creek Rail-Trail, that seemed suited to primitive camping, and also was a good place to water the horses.

West rim of the Tioga State Forest, south side of Route 6: There are many trails in the Tioga State Forest. We visited some on the west end of the rim, located southwest of the intersection of the Pine Creek and Route 6, just off of Route 6. To reach these we traveled about 14 miles west of Wellsboro to Woodlands (formerly Fromes) Campground. If staying at the campground, take the railroad grade on the far (west) side of the campground, just south of Route 6. The old railroad bed is in a low-lying area, which does get a lot of water, but this is for a short distance. Travel along this to Route 6, make a left, cross the bridge, and continue as indicated below. (Note: Just before the bridge, the end of the railroad bed comes out on Route 6. As you approach this area, exercise extreme caution as this road can be busy.) Or, if not staying at the campground, travel along Route 6, pass the Woodlands Campground and Fromes Restaurant (will also see the Antler's Inn), turn left, and go over the bridge.

After the bridge, make another left onto a dirt road. Travel along the dirt road and travel past the cabins. (We found this road to be quiet with very little traffic.) Proceed down the dirt road; come to a fork in the road. To the left accesses trails in the forests, and to the right continues along the dirt road passing various trails and pull-off areas within the forests. Day parking is permitted along, but off, the dirt road and not blocking gates. Overnight parking is permitted with a permit, but it is hard to find a sufficient pull-off area that is not in front of a gate. And searching for an ideal location with a large rig can be tricky within the State Forest due to the winding, dirt, narrow, and sometimes steep roads. We felt one spot was suitable to camping. To reach that location, we traveled approximately 18 miles west of Wellsboro along Route 6. We made a left on SR3001 in Gaines Township. Route 3001 is the main road into Watrous. (You will see signs to Pine Creek Vista Campground.) Follow SR3001 south, the road winds, stay on the main road, cross the bridge. Travel 5 miles. Along the way, SR3001 becomes Route 310, which becomes Cedar Mountain Road. Make a left on Thompson Hollow Road. Travel on Thompson Hollow Road for a mile; come to a fork. Bear left on Thompson Hollow (do not turn toward Mill Run Road). Follow signs to Painter Leetonia Road. Travel 2.6 miles to Painter Leetonia; make a right on Painter Leetonia. Travel .8 miles on Painter Leetonia to a sharp turn in the road and a sign saying "Refuge Trail". At this trailhead, there is sufficient room to park 2 or 3 medium sized rigs for day parking or overnight camping. This is an ideal location to access the upper west rim trails including the Colton Point area. We chose this approach as it can be accessed in a larger rig. There are other ways to access this location, but (again) a word of warning: due to the dirt surface, narrow width, abrupt grade, and tight turns of the roads, this is not an area to explore while hauling. We disconnected and proceeded to check the roads before choosing this approach as suitable for hauling.

Yellow gates identify certain State Forest Trails, and some are just obvious trails that have been blazed and used over the years. Most are not on the map. It helps to obtain a topo map from the local outfitters or enlarge the (green) DCNR Tioga State Forest map as a point of reference. During our visit, the trails were not yet marked and signs were a rarity. If the trails are marked, maintained, and a few designated equestrian trailer parking and camping areas established (like they have at the Tuscarora State Forest), the Tioga State Forest trail networks could be an absolutely awesome trail system and camping area, one of Pennsylvania's finest.

West rim of the Tioga State Forest, north side of Route 6: We accessed these trails by riding from the rail-trail leading from Woodlands Campground. Day riders can park along the State Forest Trails within this area also. From Woodlands, the north side is not easy to access as riders must cross busy Route 6, and proceed along the dirt road (Mill Run Road) near the Antler's Inn. Riders need to avoid private lands and remain on the dirt access roads until within the State Forest area. Look for yellow forest gates marking the entrance to the State Forest Trails.

We were told that these trails can also be accessed, without crossing Route 6, from the ASAPH Wildlife Area and the Hesselgessel Road camping location mentioned above. (The following directions were provided to us. Due to the arrival of snow we were unable to personally confirm the following information or view the campsite setting.) To travel to this spot, take Route 6, head west from Wellsboro, come to ASAPH signs and look for ASAPH Road. Make a right on ASAPH Road (heading north) and travel toward the ASAPH Wildlife Area. The road will bear to the right; make a right onto Hesselgessel Road. Travel on Hesselgessel Road to the loop on the end. We were told this loop is a popular area for equestrian camping and day parking, and has convenient access to these northern trails. I have included this as it sounds like an ideal location to set up camp.

## THE TRAILS:

The Pine Creek Trail, east shore of the canyon: There are two parallel paths along the east rim of the Pine Creek, one is a stone dust surface for bikes and hikers, and one is a dirt terrain for equestrians. If heading south from Ansonia, the equestrian trail is to the right. The rail-trail is well marked as to where equestrians and non-equestrians are permitted. DCNR does patrol the trail to ascertain that users are adhering to the appropriate designated trails. This is an old railroad trail with excellent views of the Grand Canyon of PA and surrounding mountains. The rail-trail has been very nicely finished with wonderful, easy, level ground and is well maintained. The ride is pleasant and leisurely. This is a great place to bike or hike too! The contrast of rock, greenery, and waterfalls offers an interesting trail ride with dramatic landscapes. All sorts of wildlife can be seen including deer, turkeys, eagles, coyotes, herons, hawks, beavers, and otters. The multiple-use rail-trail currently open is part of a larger 60+ mile planned route. There is a 20-mile section completed from Ansonia to Rattlesnake Rock; equestrians are permitted on the 9-mile stretch between Ansonia and Tiadaghton, which travels in the heart of the canyon. Another segment runs from Rattlesnake Rock to Waterville. More sectors are planned to be opened for other trail users from Ansonia to Wellshoro Junction and Waterville to Jersey Shore, which will total over 60 miles. Dogs are permitted on the trail right-of-ways, parking lots, and campgrounds, but need to be on a leash.

The trail travels along the bottom of the canyon and does offer some shade along the way, depending on the time of day and section. But mid day the sun shines directly into the canyon so it may be better to visit in the early morning or late day during hot weather. The Pine Creek does offer some cooling effect. There are some areas to access Pine Creek and water the horses along the route. However, since there are only a few that are located down stream, bring water to provide upon departure and return. We visited the canyon in the late spring and returned in the fall when the canyon, with its variety of foliage, is a spectacular sight with a rainbow of colors for miles and miles. Even riders who aren't fond of straight rail-trails should enjoy this one. The mountain ranges and scenery are beautiful.

West rim of the Tioga State Forest, south side of Route 6 (We rode trails in the west rim in the southwest corner where Route 6 and the Pine Creek Trail meet, between Colton Point and Route 6.): Since riding is permitted in much of the State Forest, there are many informal trail systems within it, and we could not find specific published information on how to find the equestrian trails or where to park. The Tioga State Forest is an area where riders must be comfortable exploring and have a good sense of direction. To park for day use, rigs must either stay nearby or must search to find a pull-off area within the State Forest. (In our other travels, we have inquired with local businesses, stables, or campgrounds that had convenient locations, and perhaps the only roomy access, if we could park for a day or night to get into the trails. Just nicely asking has provided good opportunities and well situated locations.

Some will allow day parking for free. Depending on the circumstances, we may offer to pay a nominal fee for their courtesy, especially if we stay longer.) Riders are permitted to ride on the State Forest lands, including that west of the canyon, but are not permitted on the West Rim Trail. The West Rim Trail is not marked as off limits to horses but horses are not permitted. (So, if you see "West Rim Trail", do not ride it.) We were told that many portions of the West Rim Trail are dangerous and on the edge, and not suitable to equestrians or mountain bikers.

This section of trails can lead to some of the overlooks. Near Colton Point or some of the other vistas, some of the trails may permit equestrians to approach public viewing areas. In any public scenic overlook, riders should dismount, have another rider hold their horse, and walk to the designated viewing area. At these locations, it is important that all droppings are scattered and that horses not harm or disturb the foliage or landscaping. Respecting these areas will help allow horseback riders to remain welcome in these sections. When we visited Susquehannock Creek State Park (see that chapter), the park had tie rails near the overlook. We realized this also served as an area where local Amish could secure their horses, but we liked the idea of the tie rails as it provided a place to tie the horses so we too could enjoy the view without being concerned about the above factors. For both the equestrians and the parks, this may be a very good feature for the parks to consider.

The Tioga State Forest is a nice destination to spend a week riding on the wide variety of trails, including old logging roads, dirt roads, or trails established by other use. Of the trails we sampled, we found these trails to be beautiful, wide wooded trails, easy to moderate to ride, generally gradual, with little or no rocks, mostly not "on the edge", and overall just a wonderful pleasure. However, it is possible to run into obstacles such as downed trees. At the time of our visit, these trails did not have equestrian markings nor designated parking areas. Nor, can we name or describe many of the trails we rode because they were not marked on the map or on the trail. We found it helpful, while exploring, to refer to the map and the main State Forest dirt roads as a reference. Hopefully, there will be the initiation of trail markings and the establishment of access points in the future.

West rim of the Tioga State Forest, north side of Route 6: There is additional riding on the north side of Route 6 which can be accessed from Mill Run Trail (near the Antler's Inn), off of Route 6. During our second visit, we rode from Woodlands Campground, along the rail-trail, crossed Route 6, and picked up the dirt road up to Mill Run Trail. (To avoid private properties, we followed the short distance of dirt road to the yellow State Forest gates.) There are many nice, wide trails of easy terrain within this section of the Tioga State Forest. And even though there were heavy, recent rains, except for some side trails, these trails were high and mostly dry. It can be easy to get disorientated in this section as there are many loops of trails and there are little, if any, markings. Some trails have orange blazes indicating they are the snowmobile trails. Occasionally, there are intersections with dirt roads and signs, but not many. The lack of signs also makes it difficult to tell where the State Forest land ends and where private property begins. When in doubt, we returned to the dirt roads until we saw a yellow gate marking the State Forest land. However, we were glad we didn't miss this sector of trails as they were some of the nicest.

Despite the fact that our first visit was on a bright, sunny June weekend, we did not find the Pine Creek Rail-Trail, Colton Point, or the outlying trails to be crowded. Our second visit was in late October, in less than ideal weather, and there were more people on the rail-trail than on our first visit. But at no time did it feel crowded, and the separate paths for horses and bikes made for a very relaxing ride. On the surrounding mountain trails, you can ride for hours and hours and not encounter anyone.

Many of the State Forest roads also seem ideal for carriage driving. Check with the DCNR office as to where carriages are permitted, and to obtain information on the grade of the roads. Commercial wagon rides are often seen along the rail-trail. We were told that carriages might be permitted on the Pine Creek Rail-Trail; permission and a key to the gates must be obtained prior to arrival. There are also many other locations to ride throughout the State Forest. Many of these can be seen on the map. We will return to this wonderful area as it offers some of Pennsylvania's finest scenery, and there is so much area to explore.

We thank DCNR, who was very helpful by providing general information and maps on the area and for permitting horseback riders to enjoy this wonderful place. If it were not for the permitted equestrian usage, many individuals would not be physically able to cover and enjoy this large area on foot. We also would like to thank Judy Drake, a longtime rider of these trails, who offered to map out many of the equestrian trails for us and was very generous with her time in helping us locate some of the nicest trails. We are also appreciative of Fred Turner, who rode with us and was kind enough to send us the map printout from his GPS of our rides along some of these trails.

**EQUESTRIAN CAMPGROUND:**
As indicated above, motorized camping is permitted within the State Forest along, but off of, the forest roads. The challenge is to find a suitable location, as there aren't any designated or cleared areas for camping. Instead, we stayed at Woodlands Campground (formerly Fromes) on U.S. Route 6, which is conveniently located near the trails. The entrance is wide enough for large rigs and enters through a potpourri of businesses. But past this entrance, heading toward Pine Creek, there is camping with hookups and bathroom and shower facilities on one side of the bridge, and primitive camping on the other side of the bridge. The other side of the bridge is in a

rugged, high grass field in a low-lying area where the horses can be picket tied or electric fencing can be set up. On our first visit, we chose to stay with our horses in the field, but it was challenging to find a dry spot due to recent heavy rains. On our second visit, we stayed at the not too distant "other side of the bridge" in the main camping area which offers higher, dryer, level areas to camp with hookups. Some of the sites in the main camping areas do provide enough visibility to keep an eye on the horses in the nearby field section, and the horses do like the abundance of grass in the field. Pete Johnson, from the Pennsylvania Equine Council, managed to find what we considered the most scenic primitive site. He drove over the bridge into the field and headed out toward the right. There was a lovely, secluded spot next to the river with two trees to picket tie his horse. (With no rain or storms predicted, there was no need to be concerned about flooding. However, as the site is next to the river, this is not where you want to be if heavy rains are coming!)

To reach the trails, ride directly out of camp. Travel a short distance on the old railroad bed, which travels behind the campground office and Fromes Restaurant, and briefly passes some housing before heading for the forest. As indicated above, the railroad bed does get a lot of water but that is only for a short distance and we found it passable. Once at the bridge, make a left. Make another left after the bridge crossing, head down the back dirt road, pass the cabins, and head into the forest. There are many trail offshoots. Except where they were logging, we found them all to be very pretty. (We reminded ourselves that those loggers establish many of the trails we will enjoy in the future.) To reach the trails north of Route 6, we crossed over Route 6 and continued as described above. To reach the Pine Creek Rail-Trail, we trailered to the trailhead that is just a few miles down the road along Route 6.

## HISTORICAL INFORMATION:

Tioga is derived from the Indian word Tyoga, which was the name of the tribe of Seneca Indians who once dwelled in this region. Later, lumbering companies acquired much of the land. Various railroads carried timber to the sawmills via the Pine Creek rail corridor in the late 1800's into the 1900's. The railroads continued to carry freight and use this system until 1988. In the early 1900's, purchases of sections of the State Forest were made with the intention of protecting the Pine Creek water resource.

In the 1930's, the CCC began work constructing roads, bridges, and recreational facilities. Recently, the old rail line that traveled through the Pine Creek Gorge, also known as the Grand Canyon of PA, was converted to a rail-trail for hikers, bikers, and horseback riders to use.

Through the years, additional land was acquired comprising today's large Tioga State Forest region. The Tioga State Forest contains three State Parks: Colton Point, Leonard Harrison, and Hills Creek. There are campgrounds (non-horse) and facilities in the State Parks. Colton Point is on the western rim of the PA Grand Canyon; Leonard Harrison

State Park is on the eastern rim of the canyon; and Hills Creek State Park is located northeast of the gorge and Wellsboro. Also, within the forest, are the following natural and wild areas: Pine Creek Gorge, Reynolds Spring Natural Area, Black Ash Swamp Natural Area, and ASAPH Wildlife Area.

There are numerous lookout areas offering scenic views, such as Cushman Vista in southwest Tioga and the Pine Creek Vista on the West Rim Road. Waterfalls can be seen from Fallbrook in southeast Tioga County, and at Campbells Run near Tiadaghton.

## THINGS WE LEARNED THIS RIDE:
- We equestrians must work with and help DCNR to organize some of these beautiful trails. DCNR can use our assistance as they have limited resources, and this is a large trail system. Currently, parking and locations suitable for equestrian camping within the forest are not easy to find. Markings and equestrian trailhead parking is needed. Equestrians who can volunteer time or resources need to contact DCNR to see if they can be of service. These are gorgeous trails with mostly non-rocky terrain and lots and lots of forests. We can't wait to return.
- We were reminded how much logging can contribute to our trail system. So many of these nice trails were formerly logging roads.

## NEARBY AREAS OF INTEREST:
- Town of Wellsboro, a cute, quaint town with lots of interesting shops and restaurants. Wellsboro Chamber of Commerce (570) 724-1926

## NEARBY OUTFITTER WITH DIRECT ACCESS TO THE TRAILS:
- Mountain Trail Horse Center, Inc., Wellsboro (570) 376-5561, (877) 376-5561, website: www.mountaintrailhorse.com. Want to experience the PA Grand Canyon or the Tioga State Forest wilderness on horseback but do not have your own horse or can't bring yours? Try the Mountain Trail Horse Center. They have trail rides, overnight trail expeditions, canyon wagon rides, and various other activities. *Please note that the Mountain Trail Horse Center is an outfitter who provides the horse and is not a facility for camping with one's own horse.*

## NEARBY AND SURROUNDING AREA CAMPGROUNDS:
- Woodlands Campground (formerly 'Fromes'), Wellsboro (814) 435-8279. Woodlands Campground permits camping with horses in an open field. There are no corrals or stables, so bring a tie line, electric fence, or some other means of securing horses.
- Tanglewood Camping, website: www.tanglewoodcamping.com, Covington (570) 549-8299. Tanglewood Camping does permit camping with horses.

**NEARBY VET SERVICES:**
- Troy Veterinary Clinic, Troy (570) 673-3181
- Dr. Sullivan, Tawanda (570) 265-5071

**NEARBY FARRIER:**
- D. Saunders, Mansfield (570) 662-7524

# 45. Bald Eagle State Forest
# DCNR
### (Department of Conservation & Natural Resources)

**Lasting Impression:**   Huge, beautiful, rustic, alternating gentle and rugged terrain, nice primitive camping, plenty of wildlife, lots of potential and still developing.  Ride and explore where buffalo once roamed!

**Location:**  Bald Eagle State Forest is located in central Pennsylvania in Snyder, Mifflin, Union, Centre, and Clinton Counties.

**Length:**   The Bald Eagle State Forest is a sizable area consisting of almost 200,000 acres of State Forest land.   There are miles and miles of riding and equestrians are permitted to ride on this State Forest land, except for designated hiking trails such as the Mid State Hiking Trail (MST), natural areas, and other prohibited areas.  The MST trail, marked by orange blazes, is a hiking trail and is not suitable for horses.  The forest contains over 300 miles of dirt and gravel roads. Most of the state roads and trails permit equestrians; however, some trails are not suitable or passable due to rocky conditions.    A multi-use trail shared by equestrians is the Central Mountains Trail, which consists of 120 miles of trail. The Central Mountains Shared-Use Trail System, located near Route 192, spans from Bald Eagle State Forest to Tiadaghton State Forest.  The trail is marked with red blazes and varies from easy to difficult.

**Level of Difficulty:**   Easy to difficult.   (Some sections are difficult or not rideable due to rocky terrain.)

**Terrain:**  Terrain varies greatly, from wonderful wide, easy grassy stretches and old dirt logging roads, to gravel forest roads, to trails with an extremely rough to impassable rocky surface.  It helps to know where to ride.  Trails are mostly in forested areas but there are also some open areas.  The selections of trails that we rode were very gradual, not steep.   However, this trail system is large and mountainous so it is likely that there are some steep areas in the sections that we did not cover during our visit.

**Horse Camping:**   Yes, motorized and non-motorized camping is permitted within the State Forest at designated locations.

**Non-horse Camping:** Yes

**Maps and Info:**  DCNR, Bureau of Forestry, Bald Eagle State Forest, P.O. Box 147, Laurelton, PA 17835-0147, (570) 922-3344.   Maps for the Central Mountains Trail can be obtained from this office.

**Activities:**  Fishing, Boating, Swimming, Hiking, Biking, Picnicking, Horseback Riding Trails, Hunting (during season), Camping, Snowmobiling, Sledding, Ice Sports, and X-C Skiing.  *There are miles and miles of dirt and gravel roads through the forests that would appear to be ideal for carriage driving.  Check with the office prior to arrival.*

**Permits and Fees for Trail Use:** None
**Permits for Camping:** Yes, but no fee. Call (570) 922-3344 for permits.
**Comfort Station:** Not in the camping area, however, facilities including potable water are offered at the State Parks, including nearby R.B. Winter State Park

## DIRECTIONS:

There are many equestrian campsites at Bald Eagle located in distant locations throughout the forest. A map and directions to each of these should be obtained from the ranger station prior to arrival. To access the day use area in the central portion of Bald Eagle, take Route 192 west from Lewisburg for about 19 miles. Upon seeing R.B. Winter State Park signs, look for signs to the R.B. Winter campground. This is a sharp right where McCall Dam Road and Sand Mountain Road meet. Immediately after making this hard right, bear right onto Sand Mountain Road. Travel a short distance on Sand Mountain to a large lot on the right (directly across from the dump station, which is on the left.) Equestrians can access many of the trails by riding along Sand Mountain Road.

Easy access, central locations, and sizable camping spots are at Sites #11 and #12. To access Site #11, follow the above directions and continue along McCall Dam Road. It is just off McCall Dam Road. To access Site #12, do not turn off onto McCall Dam and Sand Mountain Roads, but instead continue on Route 192 until you see Tunis Road (about a total of 20 miles from Lewisburg) that is marked by a short brown post on the right. Make a right onto the dirt/gravel Tunis Road. Continue a short distance and make another right onto the dirt/gravel McCall Field Road. Cross over a small stream and travel a short distance to an open, grassy loop with a post indicating Site #12.

## THE TRAILS:

The Bald Eagle State Forest is situated in a setting of valleys, ridges, and gorges with the Allegheny Mountains to the northwest and the Limestone Valley to the southeast. The terrain varies greatly and includes many streams crisscrossing the forest. The Central Mountains Trail System is marked by red rectangles or blazes on the trees and various other objects such as gates.

Due to the extensive trail system and immense area of Bald Eagle, maps and camping site lists should be obtained from the Forester (at the above number) prior to arrival. There are many permitted camping areas, however, look for the camping areas which are close to the Central Mountains Trail system, logging roads, or forest dirt/gravel roads so you can ride out from camp. When we requested a map, the ranger was very helpful and marked the Central Mountains Trail system on the map. He also highlighted the main equestrian trail on the map, indicated adjoining camping areas, and specified which areas could accommodate large rigs or groups. There are additional favorites of equestrians; we were told a new map is currently being developed, and should be available in the future, which will provide even better detail than the current map.

The trail system is extensive and the Bald Eagle State Forest is beautiful. There are lots and lots of heavily forested areas with periodic clearings that serve as feed lots for the local wildlife. And there is much wildlife everywhere. We arrived to find a deer standing at our campsite; only later to see more deer, turkeys, owls, an assortment of interesting colorful birds, and many piles of bear droppings (that's close enough to a bear for me). There are some really gorgeous trails but the terrain is diverse, and rocky sections crop up frequently even after riding on easy terrain for long distances. But don't let this deter you. Not all trails have these major rock clusters. There are excellent easy, wide grassy stretches, quiet logging roads, and connecting State Forest dirt/gravel roads (most with wide shoulders) where you can ride for hours. It depends on where you choose to ride. Horses should have shoes for traveling on gravel roads or on rocky sections.

Due to the large size of this forest, we could only visit a portion of the trail system. These are the trails we liked and also some of the trails we would rather avoid until the footing is improved. *It should be noted that it appeared work was being done on some of the more rocky trails with wood chips being placed on the surface. If improvements to the rocky sections continue, there can be some additional excellent trail riding available and this could become one of Pennsylvania's premier destinations to camp and ride.*

**Trails we liked:**
- We found this to be a nice, short loop to start the horses on. It will help to have the equestrian map to see this trail. From Site #12, head out of the entrance to McCall Field Road, ( you will pass a stream and you can water your horses), make a left on Tunis, head a short distance toward Route 192. Cautiously cross Route 192. (During our visit, there were vehicles but this was not heavily traveled. There was good visibility, and we did not have a problem crossing this road.) Immediately on the other side, ride down the side of the gravel road, make a right, go around the pole and support wire (not under), and pick up the trail following the orange ribbons and red blazes. You will be riding on a wide, wooded trail. This trail, which parallels Route 192 (which we found to be a comfortable distance from Route 192), did not appear to have a name but was well marked. Continue through the wooded trail. Pass a brown cabin on the left and come to where you can go straight or left. Make a left, which is Dotty Mill Run Trail. It looks to be a dirt driveway accessing cabins but you will see the red rectangles marking the trail indicating it is rideable. *Most of the cabins are 99-year lease arrangements with the Forest and many share access roads with the Forest.* Pass the cabins, cross a stream to the right, and continue through the pine forest and

201

woods following the red markers. There is plenty of water for the horses along the way. After the stream crossings, the trail forks; bear right. *Dotty Mill Run Trail is very pretty with some short sections of rocks but not too bad. (If you were to continue left along Dotty, south of Brush towards Fallen Timber, Dotty becomes **much** more challenging in sections.)* After bearing right, there is a short, wet, grassy section that we bypassed by riding to the right side. Then continue and make a left through the feed lot. (This is where we came upon the mother turkey and her chicks; see below.) Come to a grassy T intersection and make a right, following the wide grassy stretches. The trail will again approach the vicinity of Route 192. Take the wooded trail parallel to Route 192 until you return to where you originally crossed Route 192, directly across from Tunis. Travel a short distance on Tunis and make a right on McCall to camp.

- Another nice warm-up loop is from a different direction out of Site #12 (opposite end of where you came into camp). (You can pick this up from Site #11 also.) Travel out McCall Field Road in the direction of Site #11 near Black Gap Road. Loop around, returning on either Black Gap Road or Black Gap Trail to Engle to Tunis to McCall Field Road back to Site #12.
- Cooper Mill Road is a gravel road with a nice shoulder in most places, offering a leisurely ride, and a nice scenic overlook. The overlook is located on the maps obtained from the ranger office.
- We really liked Bake Oven Trail but there were some rocky sections that we found passable. Mountain laurel trimmed the trail and was just busting out in bloom during our visit. There was an abundance of berry bushes at the top with evidence of bears that had recently helped themselves to the berries!
- Other roads we liked were Sand Mountain Road, Tunis Road, Boyer Gap Road, and Boiling Springs Road. We liked portions of the Cracker Bridge Trail, but there are some rocky sections that require navigation.
- Also, many of the trails and gravel roads intersect with power lines that also have some rideable trails. Certain areas could have a steep climb or descent, but other power line trails were very leisurely. It seemed that there was good visibility along the power lines so that you can see what you were getting into before you proceeded.

**Trails we prefer to avoid until better footing is laid due to extensive rocky sections:** *(These trails were all in really pretty settings, clearly marked, and should make very nice trails once the rock terrain is minimized.)*
- Fallen Timber Trail- This trail extends over the top of the mountain. We traveled a significant portion of this trail but turned off as we found it much too rocky for our enjoyment.
- The Old Tram Trail- We began riding along this and found the beginning of the trail to be great, with wood chips covering the rocky sections. Unfortunately, funding for wood chips throughout the trail had not yet been

obtained and we had to head back due to the rough terrain. We are looking forward to returning to ride this trail once the surface is improved.

We enjoyed traveling on some of the State Forest road system. We normally do not favor riding roads, but the Bald Eagle State Forest road network is mostly dirt/gravel and offers a very nice leisurely scenic ride with views of the forest and mountainsides. We visited on Memorial Day weekend and were surprised to find that the State Forest roads were not busy, and traffic was infrequent. Even when a vehicle did pass, due to the dirt/gravel surface, they proceeded slowly. (On the holiday weekend, the paved roads in the central R.B. Winter State Park section did have lots of activity but trail riders can avoid that area.)

Note: In regard to the road system, this area appears to be an excellent area for carriage driving. Some of the logging trails may be more rugged than drivers prefer, however, there are miles and miles of dirt/gravel roads nicely graded. We are not carriage drivers but we believe they would be very suitable for driving. Check with the ranger station first, however, to determine where or whether carriage driving is permitted.

It should be noted that, since our visit, we were informed of many additional trails in the northern section of the forest that are very nice for riding. We will have to return to locate and explore those trails in the future.

**EQUESTRIAN CAMPING:**
The Forest Office can provide a list of camping sites with a corresponding map for location reference. There are numerous equestrian camping sites throughout Bald Eagle; ask the ranger to indicate on the map which sites could accommodate your size rig, with easy access to the better equestrian trails. (Check to see if the new equestrian map is completed and available; this should be very useful.)

Camping is primitive; there are no facilities or water at the equestrian campsites. Often, there are nearby streams to water the horses. However, we found potable water, a dump station, and facilities available at the centrally located R.B. Winter State Park. This was available for campers with a permit to camp at the State Forest. R.B. Winter can be accessed off of Route 192 by entering the park and following signs to the camping area. There is a pull-off section with the dump station at one end and the water spigot at the other end. (The Forest Office indicated that the water was good for drinking.) Note that large equestrian rigs with living quarters will not have sufficient room to access the dump station and water faucet. We disconnected our trailer and drove over to fill our water containers.

The forest is grouped into four districts or divisions: Eastville, Hickernell, New Lancaster Valley, and Troxelville Divisions. The Eastville Division, consisting of

Sites #1 through #14, is located near the Central Mountains Trail. In this section, there are three designated group areas that require a special request in advance in order to use them. The camping areas recommended for larger equestrian rigs were Site #1, Five Points; #11, Black Gap Road; and #12, McCall Field Road. Five Points is located north of I-80. We did not ride to check out this site, as it was quite a distance from our campsite. Black Gap Road is situated close to McCall Field Road and both are a short distance off of Route 192. While obtaining a permit, ask the ranger for his recommendations. Site #12, where we stayed, had only recently been designated for equestrian camping and we felt that it was one of the more ideal sites.

Other than a few passerby's, we had Site #12 to ourselves. We liked this site as it had a remote private feel yet it was close enough to the access roads. The site is an open, grassy loop, with easy access, bordered by trees for picket tying with trails leading directly from camp, and with a nearby stream from which the horses can drink. (You pass over the brook as you turn onto McCall Field Road to approach the campsite.) We had our large rig and could turn around easily. The loop can hold about 5-8 rigs comfortably, depending on their size. There are lots of trees to picket tie to but be careful not to block the three dirt roads/paths linking to the site. Occasionally, hikers or all terrain vehicles travel these trails. A jeep, truck, and dirt bike did (slowly and cautiously) pass during our stay but, overall, there was not much activity, especially for a holiday weekend. Certain old logging roads are still open to vehicles and many have gates. During our visit of 4 days, we did not find any fast moving or loud activity that concerned us; in fact, it was pleasantly quiet.

Site #11, smaller than site #12, has sufficient space for one large or two medium sized rigs, and was just a short distance off McCall Dam Road. It also has trees to picket tie to, shade, and easy access to the trails.

## HISTORICAL INFORMATION:

The Bald Eagle State Forest derives its name from the Indian Chief "Bald Eagle". Mountain buffalo once roamed this region and this location was the last area in Pennsylvania to have buffalo. In the late 1700's, this area was settled. Many of the property owners served in the Revolutionary War and received their land grants as a result of their service. In the late 1800's, logging companies purchased much of the forest. Later, the land was sold to or acquired by the state.

The Bald Eagle State Forest is included in the "Multiple-Use Concept" plan for managing environmental factors and recreational use. The Forest is in a public watershed so special regulations as to usage apply. Many of the State Forest's and State Park's roadways and facilities were developed by the CCC in the 1930's. There are several State Parks within Bald Eagle State Forest including Bald Eagle State Park, Reeds Gap State Park, Poe Valley State Park, and R.B. Winter State Park. In addition, the State Forest contains several natural and wild areas to visit. An interesting attraction is at Snyder-Middleswarth. This natural area contains the largest section of virgin timber in the State Forests of Pennsylvania, totaling 500 acres. This area, which can only be accessed by hiking, was saved from logging in 1902 due to a stop-cutting order issued by the state.

Many thanks go to the friendly, helpful staff at the Bald Eagle State Forest ranger station and the local equestrians, including Pete Johnson, for their generosity of time and commitment toward the establishment, design, and marking of these trails.

## THINGS WE LEARNED THIS RIDE:

- On a beautiful, non-windy day, while riding in a forest of trees, we learned how well our horses could perform fancy, western reining maneuvers when they felt the vibration of a tree's roots tearing from the ground, and heard the thunder of a full sized tree fall to the forest floor directly in front of us. (Wasn't too far from 'Fallen Timber Trail' either!) We also learned our horses were much better at determining, in that split second, which of the many trees was falling and in which direction to run. (We sure didn't know!) This was one of those times that it was best the horse did not spook in place, but rather quickly exited the area of danger.
- We are lovers of wildlife and, during the excitement of a mother turkey and her chicks popping up around us in high grass, we sadly learned that young turkey chicks do not always run, but sometimes play possum and lay blending in with the ground leaving themselves vulnerable to being stepped on. In the future, we will dismount and walk carefully to avoid the baby chicks.

## NEARBY VET SERVICES:

- West Branch Mobile Veterinary Clinic, Lewisburg (570) 524-4500
- Middleburg Vet Service, Middleburg (570) 837-1212

## NEARBY FARRIER:

- S. Sims, Loganton (570) 725-3910

# 46. Wyoming State Forest
# DCNR
### (Department of Conservation & Natural Resources)

**Lasting Impression:** We loved this one! Clean, green, serene equestrian campground and outstanding trails to ride, plus nearby recreation to interest the whole family.

**Location:** The Wyoming State Forest is located north of Bloomsburg in western Sullivan County. The Wyoming State Forest District extends to Luzerne, Sullivan, Columbia, Northumberland, and Montour counties.

**Length:** Wyoming State Forest consists of approximately 42,000 acres with 50+ miles of horse trails. There are a few days of riding, with two main 25-mile loops plus many sub loops so riders can decide how long they want to ride. Additionally, there is riding on adjoining scenic State Forest dirt/gravel roads.

**Level of Difficulty:** Mostly easy to moderate. There is lots of easy, leisurely riding at Wyoming State Forest.

**Terrain:** Varied terrain, some flat, some gradual, some more challenging climbs, mostly wooded with some open areas, many wide grassy stretches, dirt trails, State Forest dirt/gravel roads, scenic overlooks, streams, waterfalls, and overall not a lot of rocks on the trail.

**Horse Camping:** Yes, with permit. Camping is permitted at the trailheads for motorized rigs or large outfits, and along the trail if staying in a small tent. There is a large designated equestrian camping area or loop off of SR 3009, which is marked by a brown State Forest Bridle Trail sign (opposite the large Wyoming State Forest sign). Horses are not permitted to be tied to trees or where they can have access to chew or rub the bark off the trees. Horses may drink from streams where there is a rocky bank, but not where there is a soft, dirt bank where they can cause erosion.

**Non-horse Camping:** Yes. There are various locations for camping in the State Forest; call the State Forest office for more information. Camping and cabins are also available at the nearby World's End State Park (fee).

**Maps and Info:** DCNR, Wyoming State Forest, 274 Arbutus Park Road, Bloomsburg, PA 17815, (570) 387-4255; or Hillsgrove Forest Headquarters, Dry Run Road, P.O. Box 75, Hillsgrove, PA 18619-0075, (570) 924 -3501. The DCNR website is www.dcnr.state.pa.us. Camping permits can be obtained at either of the above numbers. Although maps were stocked daily at the bridle trailhead during our visit, do request a Wyoming State Forest Bridle Trail map in advance as this is a large area and the maps are very useful. It is helpful to also get a map of the World's End State Park, Forksville, (717) 924-3287, to see where the water, facilities, and swimming area is located. Reminder, (at this writing) pets are not permitted in the

State Parks, however, we recently were told that dogs may be permitted in the future on a test basis.

**Activities:** Boating, Swimming, Hiking, Biking, Horseback Riding Trails, Fishing, Camping, Sledding, Picnicking, Snowmobiling, X-C Skiing, and Hunting (some sections may permit during season)

**Fees for Trail Use:** None

**Permits for Day Trail Use:** None

**Permits Required for Overnight Camping:** Yes. There is no charge for equestrian camping in the State Forest but permits are required and checked. The ranger advised that holiday weekends are busy and campers should call in advance.

**Comfort Station:** Yes, at the equestrian trailhead and also at the nearby World's End State Park *Under the "Governors Growing Green Initiative", a new shower house and flush toilet facility is being constructed at the nearby World's End State Park. There is a possibility that this facility may be made available to equestrian campers at Wyoming State Forest for a fee. (The World's End State Park campers pay a fee for their camping and the use of facilities so others will also need to pay a fee for this same privilege. During peak demand times, the facilities may not be available to those not camping in the State Park.) Inquiries should be made and approval received from DCNR or at the World's End State Park office prior to attempting to use the accommodations.*

## DIRECTIONS:

To reach the camping area, proceed as follows: From the north, take Route 87 to Route 154 (Forksville). Take Route 154 south for about 3 miles (passing the World's End State Park campgrounds and the Sullivan County fairgrounds) to a Y in the road. You will see a small, white SR 3009 sign on the left that points to the road on the right. (Please note: do not make a left, instead bear right onto SR 3009.) Travel on SR 3009 for about 2 miles. Look for a large Wyoming State Forest sign with a map on the right, and a smaller brown Wyoming State Forest Bridle Trail sign on the left. Make a left into the equestrian camping loop.

From the south, take I-80 to the Buckhorn Exit #232 Route 42 (old Exit #34). Follow signs on Route 42 north toward Eagle Mere. Route 42 winds through many quaint small towns. At Muncy Valley, follow the signs to World's End; do not take the truck Route 42. There is a climb after Muncy Valley but we did not find it too bad; it was not switchbacks where it was difficult to gain speed to climb. After traveling a total of 31 miles on Route 42 north, before Eagle Mere, look for State Route 3009 to the left. (SR 3009 is also called Double Run Road.) Make a left onto SR 3009 at the World's End State Park sign. Go about 2.5 miles and you will see the brown Wyoming State Forest Bridle Trail sign on the right. The one-way loop entrance is at this sign and exits at the next road on the right. While heading north, if you reach Shanerburg Road, you have passed the entrance and are at the exit location. The entrance is clearly marked. The dirt/gravel road is a large loop. We found that there was plenty of room for large rigs and there was no problem driving through the whole circle. The trailhead is in this loop and is marked by a #1.

Day parking is permitted along the road in the State Forest. Day users may access the trails by parking at the many roadside-parking areas within the State Forest. (See below for info on one convenient location for the east loop at the corner of Route 154 and Shanerburg Road.)

## THE TRAILS:

These trails are nice and there are lots of them. Maps are available and can be obtained upon making reservations. Just ask the office to send the map with your permit. There are two 25-mile trail loops, the West Loop and the East Loop, which start and finish at the same trailhead. The two loops are described and marked on the Wyoming State Forest Bridle Trail map that can be obtained from DCNR. The trailhead begins at the equestrian campground location off of SR 3009 near Shanerburg Road, although trails can be accessed at other locations within the State Forest. The equestrian trails are marked by orange blazes on the trees, which we found to be very helpful. Often, there are other colors on the trees but equestrians should follow the orange. There are signs and markers at the head of the trails. The trailheads and trails are well marked; however, first time visitors may find some sections confusing due to many crisscrossing trails. But, there is usually a State Forest dirt/gravel road not too far away to help orient oneself. New equestrian maps were published in the summer of 2002, which are very useful. DCNR is considering further enhancements by changing to numbered intersections to correspond with numbers on the map. Recently, many other DCNR locations have made this improvement. We like the numbered intersections with corresponding numbers on the map as we find it easier to follow.

Mature woods of birch, ash, beech, poplar, hemlocks, and others species line the trail. The trail is diverse with canyons and vistas. For the most part, the trails are wide. We did not encounter any narrow, "on the edge" sections as we rode the equestrian trail. There are a few good climbs and descents, which should be expected, as this is mountainous country. There are some trails that are high and look down a significant slope through the forest. But there is a dense forest offering a physical barrier and possible comfort to people who do not like heights. I do not like to ride where the edge of the trail drops sharply, but did not have a problem with any of these due to the nice wide trails and the trees lining them. There are also lots of easy, gradual stretches to ride for horses or riders who may not be suited to climbs. Riders will pass areas cleared for timber or "timber management". There is abundant wildlife including deer, turkey, porcupine, and bear, which may be seen. Sections of the equestrian trails pass within close distance of World's End State Park, but this park is basically a day use, non-horse area. Riders are requested to stay on the designated equestrian trails as they ride near this area.

Due to varied terrain, climbs, and descents, we found the West Loop of the trails to be more challenging than the East Loop of the trails. However, we did not find it difficult, and it was a pleasure to ride along the many scenic vistas. While riding the West Loop, do visit the High Knob Overlook. The view from High Knob offers panoramic views of the mountains and awesome beauty, especially in the spring when the flowers are in bloom and in the fall with the colorful foliage. The trail also passes by the Kettle Creek Gorge Natural Area. The natural area is closed to horseback riders but open to foot travel. It is in the southern section of the park. The West Loop was hit by a tornado in the spring of 1974, changing sections of the landscape as it once appeared. Time is repairing much of this damage and the forests are full of new growth.

As nice as these trails were, and even on the weekend, we saw very few people out on the trail. We met several bicyclists that were extremely courteous of the horses and helpful too. There seemed to be a good relationship between the bikers and horseback riders at Wyoming State Forest.

Our favorite loop was a section of the East Loop which consists of wide, leisurely stretches of grassy trails, trimmed by ferns (must be really pretty in the fall), with very little rocks if at all. The trail meanders down by the stream in the Shanerburg Run valley with a wonderful cooling effect on a hot summer day, and we found the terrain easy to ride. On the last day of our visit, we planned to ride for just a few hours, so we utilized a day parking area. This site is on Shanerburg Road where Shanerburg Road and Route 154 meet. We traveled along Route 154 and backed into the site on Shanerburg Road. (Shanerburg Road is a long, dirt, two-way road of narrow width and may have presented some challenges for our bigger trailer so we chose to back into the parking area from Route 154.) This lot can accommodate one large sized trailer with living quarters or two 2-horse trailer rigs comfortably, assuming no other users are there. We then rode for a short distance down Shanerburg (in the direction away from Route 154) and took the grassy stretch to the left. You can also ride to this loop from camp if you have more time. On a hot day, we rode this cleared section in the morning as the wide open grass stretches get a lot of sun and are much nicer to travel while it is still cool. But once you return to the wooded area and descend down to the valley by the river, the ride becomes much cooler due to the stream crisscrossing the trail. Just remember to follow the orange circles and don't miss seeing the scenic eastern loop in the vicinity of Shanerburg Run and Pole Bridge Run.

We visited this trail in mid July during a heat wave. We still found this an ideal area to visit in the heat of the summer. The trails were mostly canopied, plus we would

209

leave in the early morning when the woods were cool. One word of advice, though- do bring fly protection. On the hotter days, the flies are very active. Once it cooled down, we did not find flies to be a problem. On those hot muggy days, spray wasn't enough for those persistent bugs. We brought fly blankets, fly masks, and fly leggings for when the horses were tied. For trail, we kept fly masks with ear protection and spray on the horses. And, we used a (people rated) insect repellent spray on us and put a small can of the spray in the saddlebag as a mid-ride refresher. We sprayed this on ourselves and on the surface of our saddle pads, making for a more enjoyable ride.

The trails loop around nearby World's End State Park but there are no equestrian trails or equestrian camping within the State Park. However, World's End State Park and the surrounding area offer a selection of nice places to go for a swim after a hot day's ride, along with recreation for non-equestrian family members.

## COURTESIES:
Thank you to Joe Montgomery of DCNR for answering all my questions, and to Richard Sparks and Brian Valencik of DCNR for stopping and visiting with us and sharing some of their knowledge, and especially for indicating their willingness to work with equestrians. Volunteers are welcome. We were told that we may be able to have more facilities, and materials could be made available, but dependable help is needed. If you would like to assist DCNR with putting up corrals and tie rails, or with trail maintenance, etc., do contact the above number. Please note it is important that volunteers not only volunteer, but also be reliable and show if arrangements have been made. DCNR is welcoming equestrians to help and provide their input. (Please be constructive.) All we need to do is help and we can positively affect and preserve this beautiful place to camp and ride.

Also, our thanks to Craig Shambough, whom we met out on the trail (we were impressed and appreciative of how courteous he was to the horseback riders). Craig runs the Eagles Mere Mountain Bike Shop and bikes this area almost daily. He told us which were some of the "must see" trails. He recommended the eastern most loop that we accessed at Route 154 and Shanerburg Road near Pole Bridge Run. We absolutely agreed with his choices and were grateful for his guidance. Also, thank you to Jim Eves and the Twin Tier Trail Riders, real nice folks, who personally rode with us and showed us around some of the trail systems. Both Craig and Jim work on maintaining these trails and have a wealth of information to share.

## EQUESTRIAN CAMPING:
Tent camping and roadside camping (with a trailer, large tent, van, etc.) is allowed. Motorized campers must camp next to roadways or in the designated equestrian loop off SR 3009. Dogs are allowed in the State Forest, however, check in advance for a limit. Currently, picket tying is allowed, and there are

some tie rails in the equestrian campground at the sites. Other options, such as covered tie rails or corrals are being considered. As with anywhere, the limits and rules for camping will likely change over time, and should be obtained and read prior to arrival. The trailhead can accommodate several large rigs.

The campground off of SR 3009 has outdoor toilets located at the turn of the equestrian loop. There is no water at this equestrian camping area. We were told that, at one time, there was water but inconsistent usage affected the quality. However, there are many streams along the trails and equestrians are permitted to use the frost-free hydrants at World's End State Park. Refer to the World's End State Park map, which indicates where water is located. There are both hand pumps and frost-free hydrants located throughout the park. The more convenient water sources (more easily accessible by vehicle, do not take the trailer) can be reached by traveling into World's End State Park and crossing over the Loyalsock Creek, then traveling toward the cabin area and sites #1, #2, and #3. The frost-free hydrants are located by the comfort stations in the small oval loop. We checked with DCNR and they confirmed equestrian State Forest campers could use the water at the State Park and there is no fee. Within the Wyoming State Forest equestrian camp there are picnic tables, including a group, covered area. The covered area is ideal for a nice group dinner get-together. You pass this site as you enter the loop; it is on the left.

We arrived early on a Thursday and had our choice of camping sites. Our favorite pick (here goes, we probably won't be able to get it in the future) is the campsite at the turn in the loop. It is in a roomy, nice setting off the camp road, with a convenient tie rail, table, lots of picket tying in the woods, a far away feel, and just a really nice, scenic location. A few rigs can fit at this site, and the trailhead and maps are directly next to it. (The trailhead is within a close distance from the other sites as well.) This site, as with the other equestrian sites at the Wyoming State Forest bridle trailhead, is grassy and not just a gravel parking lot like so many other campgrounds for equestrians. We loved it, plan to share it with our friends, and we are looking forward to returning in the near future. We were told that, at one time, the area was not as attractive and had become disused and overgrown. As you read below, under the history, many factors did not work in the Forest's favor. However, during our visit, it appeared that equestrians had a renewed interest in the Wyoming State Forest, and the area is making a return. This is with good reason as, during our visit, we noted the sites were very clean, the grass was cut, the area was well maintained, the trails were superb, and there was no evidence of careless campers. We were also told, that now, more government-funded resources are available to the equestrian campground. And what a nice job they are doing with those resources! We had a very positive experience and were glad to see the rangers checking the campsite each day and re-stocking maps. Their friendly presence was welcome and their attentiveness and concern explains the exceptional appearance of the campground.

As for the horse tie area, well we must have been following those same nice folks (could it be Ken, Candi and friends?) who leave the horse area very clean and then lightly spread orchard grass on top. (The scattering of orchard grass greatly improves the appearance and seems to protect the surface of the picket tie area.) We met the above folks at Green Lane, arrived at Tuscarora after they departed, and probably just came into Wyoming State Forest after them. Their signature is a clean horse area with green orchard grass spread over the area. The orchard grass seems to weather and appear better than timothy or straw after rains, and is an easier footing to clean up. We will try to bring some on our future trips and pass on that same courtesy to other equestrian campers. We really appreciate folks who clean up the manure, rake the divots out of their horses' tie areas, and leave no piles for others to pick up. Responsible camping and this type of consideration will help keep the campgrounds open to horses.

## HISTORICAL INFORMATION:

Wyoming State Forest ("Wyoming" from the Wyoming Valley of the North Branch of the Susquehanna River) is a result of the "Total Resource Plan" which mixes recreation with environmental management, including water regulation, water quality control, wildlife protection, and forest timber production.

In the 1930's, the state purchased the land from the Central Pennsylvania Lumber Company after the land was cleared for lumber. Now, second-generation hardwoods populate the State Forest. Some of the nearby areas that do not have their own equestrian trails, but are of interest, are the World's End State Park, Kettle Creek Gorge Natural Area, and the Jakey Hollow Natural Area. In 1936, the World's End State Park evolved as a result of the work of the Department of Forest and Waters, and the Civilian Conservation Corps (CCC). The park originally came under the Forest District but is today run by the Pennsylvania Bureau of State Parks. In 1970, the Kettle Creek Gorge Natural Area was established as a natural preserve. In the 1990's the Bureau of Forestry purchased the Jakey Hollow Natural Area in Mt. Pleasant Township (just north of Bloomsburg) which has been designated as a natural preserve area. The uniqueness of this area is that the upper half has first-generation virgin hemlock, white pine, and hardwoods. Also nearby is Bear Wallow Pond and Sones Pond. In the 1930's, these ponds were made as a result of the damming of streams when the park roads were constructed.

Per conversations with various individuals, the equestrian campground and trails enjoyed lots of use about 10+ years ago. Then their popularity decreased, possibly due to downed trees on the trails due to a fungus outbreak, insect damage, and destruction from tornadoes. Resources were limited and the trails and campground were not at their best. Now, much effort has been made to return this special campground to its former beauty. The trails are nicely maintained and the campground is clean, clearly marked, and the grass is cut.

Plus, DCNR rangers stopped to visit and to get our feedback. During the week, we had the campground totally to ourselves. Other campers arrived on Friday but the campground never felt crowded. It was big enough to absorb the people. Although there was a good sized group during our visit, the ranger said they were still not getting as much regular usage as they would like. Let's spread the word because, if we don't use it, we will likely lose it. And this is one campground worth keeping and traveling to!

**THINGS WE LEARNED THIS RIDE:**

- The rangers at Wyoming State Forest were very friendly and asked what they could do to improve the equestrian area. This is when they indicated they might be able to put up 12x12 or 20x20 corrals if equestrian volunteers would assist. They are also considering covered tie stalls. We are sending them pictures and videos of other equestrian campgrounds' facilities for their reference. I asked what **we**, equestrians, could do to cooperate and maintain a good relationship with the State Forest. They complimented equestrians on how they left the campsites clean. But they asked that when equestrians visit the public overlooks and central vistas, they not leave manure at these sites. When the horses leave droppings at these sites, the Forest Office receives angry complaints from non-equestrians. These other visitors often are very upset and vent it, putting pressure on DCNR. To avoid this, the ranger asked that riders dismount at the overlooks and scatter their horse's manure. This would be considerate of the non-equestrians at those locations, keep a better image of horseback riders, and also help keep these scenic overlooks attractive and open to equestrians. During one of our other rides at another location, I did see an equestrian riding drag and checking that the vicinity of a popular overlook area was left clean by a group of riders. We learned from his actions; and we felt he was considerate, responsible, proactive, and smart. We will try to be more mindful of these important public areas for both ourselves and the groups we are riding with. Since our visit, we have seen parks that have tie rails for the horses near the overlooks. (See the Susquehannock chapter.) This may be something for parks to consider as it may resolve many issues and concerns for the riders, the park personnel, and other trail users. One of the rangers also asked that horses avoid wet areas and bypass them if possible.

- The ranger indicated a strong concern about horses chewing or damaging trees. Although sometimes this is not easy to find, we look for tie areas that permit horses to be a sufficient distance from the trees. If there are no better choices and the trees are close; material can be wrapped around the tree to protect from damage. Duct tape or hay string (the kind horses can't hurt themselves with) can be used to secure the material. John and I discussed this and thought, for extreme circumstances, a muzzle might be a possible answer for bad offenders, or even for those horses who brutally attack other horses at

213

the public (straight) tie stalls. We have also seen where riders, during a lunch break, tied two sets of leads to center their horses between two trees so that the horses could not have access to damage the trees. These ideas reflect a respect for the environment and a positive, proactive approach to keeping equestrians welcome in the forest. Please be advised that one occurrence, where a horse does damage to a tree, can result in heavy fines. We have heard of a few individuals who have recently been fined at different State Forest locations. If equestrians aren't careful in this matter and permanent damage occurs, equestrians could lose their right to camp and enjoy the State Forests on horseback.

- We thought this to be a resourceful idea: One of the other campers put their awning at a tilt with a bucket at the end. When some heavy rains came, they had extra water for their horses.

## NEARBY:
- Sullivan County Chamber of Commerce (570) 946-4160
- Twin Tier Trail Riders, e-mail: jroot@npacc.net
- Covered bridge near the intersection of Route 87 and Route 154 in Forksville
- Diesel at the intersection of Route 87 and Route 154

## NEARBY STABLES:
- Drake Hollow Stables (feed, hay, overnight stabling, trailer parking, and motels nearby), Dushore (570) 928-7101
- D&L Equestrian Center (boarding, training, and emergency *only* overnight stabling), Hughesville (570) 584-2571
- Spotted Horse Riding Stable (boarding, lessons, guided trail rides, and emergency overnight stabling), Dushore (570) 924-3210

## NEARBY VET SERVICES:
- Troy Veterinary Clinic, Troy (570) 673-3181
- Dr. Sullivan, Tawanda (570) 265-5071

## NEARBY FARRIERS:
- R. Minnier, Dushore (570) 924-4606
- D. Treaster, Dushore (570) 924-3210

# 47. Trails in Progress & Possible Future Equestrian Trails

These trails were in the construction phase or under discussion at the time of this writing. Contact the below numbers for more information, or do an online search to determine their status and completion.

## THE THUN TRAIL
**Location:** The Thun Trail is mostly in Berks County, near Reading, and runs from Reading to Stowe.
**Description:** When completed, this rail-trail is expected to be 15 miles in length. This trail is part of the large plan to have a connected network linking Brandywine trails, the city of Philadelphia, and Reading.
**Maps and Info:** PA Rails-to-Trails Conservancy, call (717) 238-1717, website: www.railtrails.org. The Schuylkill River Greenway Association is active with the management of this trail. They can be reached at info@schuylkillriver.org or (484) 945-0200.
**Activities:** Hiking, Biking, and Horseback Riding Trails
Many thanks to Keith Swenson for his professionalism and dedication to the establishment of excellent multi-use trail systems, his openness and willingness to consider multiple users' needs, including equestrians', and for his support in the search and establishment of additional future trail systems. Keith has been a great resource of information and I am very appreciative.

## THE SLATEDALE TRAIL
**Location:** Northern Lehigh County, from Slatedale to Emerald to Slatington
**Description:** Ultimately, this rail-trail may be part of the larger, connected network of trails
**Activities:** Hiking, Biking, and possible Horseback Riding Trails

## ENDLESS MOUNTAIN RAIL-TRAIL
**Location:** Alford to Montrose, Susquehanna County
*Note:* Unfortunately, we were informed that the future of this trail is uncertain. At this writing, we were told it is not being maintained and there isn't an access point for trailers, however, rail-trail groups are striving to save it. This rail corridor travels through some very nice countryside so, hopefully, it will be preserved in the future.
**Length:** 14 miles

**Info:** For general rail-trail info see website: www.dcnr.state.pa.us/rails/endlessmrt
Also: Endless Mountain Riding Trail, Bridgewater Riding Club, P.O. Box 21, Montrose, PA 18843
- Pocono Mountains Vacation Bureau, (800) 762-6667, website: www.poconos.org
- PA Rails-to-Trails Conservancy, (717) 238-1717, website: www.railtrails.org

## Talk of Others:

### GOD'S COUNTRY SHARED TRAIL SYSTEM
**Location:** Tiadaghton State Forest
**Info:** Contact Jim Hyland at DCNR; see the Tiadaghton chapter for phone numbers.
**Length:** This is expected to be a very large trail system.

### OWL CREEK
**Location:** Tamaqua
**Info:** At the time of this writing, further information was not yet available to the general public.

# 48. State Gamelands Trail Information

At the time of this writing, there was much uncertainty as to the permitted uses, including horseback riding, on State Gamelands. Due to the changes being considered and implemented, and due to the already large volume of trails in this book, I decided it would not be effective to cover the many gamelands at this time. However, the information is or will be available for readers and riders to obtain from the Pennsylvania Game Commission website. The Commission can also be called to obtain information.

Each gameland has its own regulations, limitations, and authorized uses. Some may be open to horses and some may not. At certain times of the year, riding may not be permitted. Since the initial writing of this article, I have been informed that, basically, riding is allowed on trails only if they are posted as open to riding and only during certain times of the year. Trails are closed to riding unless indicated otherwise. It is important to note that assumptions should not be made. Ask the gameland you are interested in if riding is permitted, and if there are any restrictions. Check the website or request the information if you are planning to ride State Gameland trails.

**Maps and Info:** A map of the state of Pennsylvania, reflecting the numbered gamelands, is available. If you specify the gameland number, the Commission can send a detailed, local map of that gameland along with the related guidelines and accepted uses. Maps can also be downloaded from their website.

*For general trail info:* Pennsylvania Game Commission, 2001 Elmerton Avenue, Harrisburg, PA 17110-9797, (717) 787-9612 or for state headquarters (717) 783-8164. The website is www.pgc.state.pa.us.

*For land management:* (717) 787-6818

*For additional info:* Northeast region (877) 877-9357, southeast region (877) 877-9470, northcentral region (877) 877-7674, southcentral region (877) 877-9107, northwest region (877) 877-0299, southwest region (877) 877-7137

*For a State Gamelands map:* Call (717) 783-7507 (small fee) or access the State Gamelands website.

# 49. OUR TRAIL & HORSE CAMPING QUESTIONNAIRE:

**Date of planned trip, place, address, contact person, phone, website, e-mail address? How many miles of horse trails?**

**Terrain and difficulty of trails?** (i.e., rocky, sandy, well marked, narrow, wide, on the edge, any road riding, trail obstacles, etc.)

**Are the trails multiple use, if so what type of use?** (i.e., bike, motorized, ATV)

**What is the best month to visit the trails?** Ask for recommendations. (Considerations: ideal temperatures, trails not muddy, insects [flies, mosquitoes, ground bees], flowers in bloom, fall foliage, not crowded, hunting seasons, any special events taking place that would interfere with trail enjoyment, etc.)

**Ask for maps and information on the trails.**

**Do they have horse camping? Cost of camping, stalls, and hookups?**

**If no horse camping, any nearby places to camp with or to board a horse?**

**Can the trails be accessed directly from the camping area or do you have to drive to the trailhead. Is road riding required? Any there any major road crossings to access the trails?**

**Can the facility accommodate a large rig?** State full size of your unit. (How many feet are the sites?) Are the sites pull-through or is backing necessary?

**Are the sites primitive; do they have electric or water? Is there shade?**

**If there is no water at the sites, is there water for the horses? Is it potable?**

**Is a farrier or veterinarian available if needed?**

**Do you have box stalls?** If you choose box stalls, mention you will bring your own buckets and ask for their buckets to be pulled prior to your putting the horse in the stall. Horses using community buckets can catch various ailments. Check with your vet as to recommended vaccinations. We bring both a spray disinfectant for areas the horse may have contact with, along with an anti-chew spray to discourage or minimize nose contact with surfaces. Sometimes stalls are not as nice as they sound on the phone, or transmission of ailments can happen at the best of places due to transient traffic. Often, our preference is to picket tie or place them in an open corral. If there are no stalls, and if traveling with an extra horse, ask if there is anywhere an extra horse can be left securely. Can other horses get at him? **Hay and bedding available?**

**Picket tie lines or portable electric fences permitted? Tie stalls? Are they covered?**

**Do they have full dividers between horses** (so horses can't bite or kick each other)?

**Coggins needed? Health certificate needed or any other item? If dogs are permitted, rabies or other info required?**

**Toilets, showers, dump station?** (Can your size camper reach the dump station?)

**Any (additional) nearby horse trails? Ask for any other info & maps to be mailed.**

**Specific directions to equestrian trailhead and to campground if applicable:** Remind them you are hauling and need sufficient clearance. Ask about any extreme climbs, tight turns, construction, or rough roads.

**Do they take reservations? Deposit required? Cancellation policy?**

# 50. OUR TRAVEL CHECK LIST

***Horse Trailer/Camper:*** *(This is why we have a big camper! It's a big list!)*
- Maps, directions, overnight trailering guides in case of a breakdown (see chapter 52)
- Portable waste water caddy for campers
- Folding table, folding chairs
- Buckets, feed trays or feed bags
- Hose, water, feed, hay (we always bring extra hay if there is room)
- Hay bags to hang from picket line (preferably material/canvas kind, not string bags as horses' legs can get caught in those especially if tied low)
- Bungee cords to tie horse to picket line (we like the right sized bungees better than tying with lead ropes as we find them easier, and horses are less likely to get tangled. We do not use the emergency release kind on the tie line as we find they release too easily. Bungee ties can be found in catalogs and at tack stores.)
- Manure fork, broom, manure bucket or portable wheelbarrow
- Picket tie line (1+ inch thick nylon rope, allow 25'/horse, 100' helps if trees are spaced far apart.) Also, burlap to wrap around trees to prevent damage from horses chewing the bark.
- Ladder to place tie line high in trees and "come along" pulley to secure line
- Wood shavings or straw bedding for horses (straw helps in wet weather, and helps prevent erosion to the tie area)
- Saddles, bridles, saddle pads, girths, breast collars, helmets, chaps, spurs
- Lead ropes, halters, brushes, hoof picks
- Horse blankets, fly sheets, fly masks
- Leg wraps, shipping boots
- Horse papers, Coggins, dog papers (if applicable) including rabies certificate, etc.
- Horse fly spray and human insect repellent
- First aid items including bute, mineral oil, gall salve, iodine, medicated ointment
- Poultice, mineral ice (for you and the horse) or liniment
- Electrolyte powder or paste
- Disinfectant spray (if stalled or if public buckets not removable)
- Large containers of water, if water is not available when camping (we always travel with a few 5-gallon jugs in case of breakdown or traffic jam)
- Check horses' shoes- We bring 2 extra shoes, made up ahead of time, for our one horse who has a unique style of shoe, so it can be matched in the event of losing one. We also use borium. For quick fixes, we keep a used shoe, which is a good spare for our other horses.
- Paper goods, towels, dish detergent, camping utensils, stove, etc. as needed
- Flashlight, citronella candle, lantern, radio
- 'No chew spray' for bad behavers (useful around stalls, fences, tree wraps)
- Propane (or charcoal), grill, wood for fire

## *Along with other clothes items:*
- Sunglasses, hat, helmet, riding shoes
- Swim wear (after a long, hot day of riding, a dip in the creek is wonderful)

## *For cold or bad weather:*
- Muck or rain shoes
- Long johns, sweatshirts
- Jacket, raincoat, and umbrella
- Wool sweater, warm socks
- Riding gloves

## *For the saddlebags:*
- Trail map and extra copy (if one bounces out of the bag), topo map, glasses to read that map (for us middle-aged folks)
- Cellular phone, compass, and GPS (we have to get one of these)
- Water
- First aid kit including any prescription medication if applicable, antibacterial crème, iodine, alcohol swabs, Band-Aids, bandages, tube of electrolyte paste, Banamine (consult with your vet first), bee sting/insect bite lotion, small can of insect repellent spray, moist antiseptic towelettes, tissues, and Benadryl or allergy medication. (If you run into ground bees, allergy medication can be very helpful. Check with a physician first.)
- Canister of bear pepper spray (it's better than nothing!)
- Snacks (i.e., cracker packages [extra food is important if you get lost])
- Extra lead and halter to tie horse
- Extra strands of leather in case something breaks
- Extra Chicago screws if applicable
- Trail marking tape. (We prefer orange. We also use a few strands to block off danger zones on trails and warn others of bees.)
- Sunscreen, rain coat, camera, film
- Vet wrap, bandanna (handy for many uses)
- "Easy Boot", duct tape to secure the boot, hoof pick, knife
- Treats for the horses (can be used as a coercion or reward)
- Small flashlight (if you get lost and are returning at night)

*We actually do get all of this in our bags, plus lunch!*

# 51. Useful, Interesting, or Informative Websites

**www.bbonline.com/horse** B&B Online for Horses, Inns with accommodations for horses

**www.cr.nps.gov** National Park Service

**www.crossroadstrailers.com** Crossroads Sundowner Trailer Sales (This is where we got our horse trailer with living quarters, and we are very happy with it.)

**www.dcnr state.pa.us/forestry/stateforests** DCNR State Forest info

**www.dcnr state.pa.us/stateparks** DCNR State Park info

**www.dcnr.state.pa.us/rails** DCNR info on PA rail-trails

**www.dermafas.com** Veterinary wound healing crème (including aural plaques)

**www.equisearch.com** Equisearch, equestrian trail links

**www.elcr.org** Equestrian Land Conservation Resource

**www.endurance.net** Endurance and Distance Riding

**www.experiencePA.com** Places/Outdoors/Activities in PA

**www.gaitsofgold.com** Works of Brenda Imus & Gaited Horse Resources

**www.garthandkathy.com** Garth and Kathy Rumsmoke ride trails coast to coast and are regularly featured writers in Trail Rider Magazine.

**www.giddy-up.com** Trail riders' portable mounting aid

**www.horseandmuletrails.com** Horse and Mule Trail Guide USA

**www.horsetrails.com** Trail Blazer Magazine

**www.merckvetmanual.com** The Merck Veterinary Manual, reference guide on diagnosis, treatment, and prevention of animal disease *(consult with your veterinarian first)*

**www.nepa-rail-trails.org** Northeast Pennsylvania Rail-Trails

**www.pennsylvaniaequinecouncil.com** Pennsylvania Equine Council

**www.pgc.state.pa.us** Pennsylvania Game Commission

**www.railtrails.org/field/pennsylvania** Rails-to-Trails Conservancy Pennsylvania Field Office

**www.ridepennsylvania.com** Ride Pennsylvania Horse Trails website

**www.rvclassified.com/campgrnd/cg-pa/htm** Pennsylvania Campgrounds

**www.showhorsepromotions.com/pa/htm** Pennsylvania Show Arena and Hotel Directory

**www.tmacc.org/info/exitnumbers.htm** Penn Dot's Exit Numbering System

**www.topozone.com** Topo Zone recreational and professional topographic maps

**www.traillink.com** Rail-trail information

**www.trailridermagazine.com** Trail Rider Magazine

**www.willowbrookdev.com** Willow Brook Farms Horsemanship Clinics

**www.woodalls.com** Woodall's Camping and RV'ing website

*Other websites are listed in related chapters.*

# 52. Other Helpful Sources of Information and Publications of Interest

*We use a few of the following books when we are in need of an overnight stabling facility for the horses. Although most stable listings are not campgrounds of the traditional sense, often they have adequate facilities or will permit equestrian travelers to park their camper overnight while stabling the horses. Others only have overnight stabling but can recommend a nearby camping area or motel. Several of these books we keep with us while traveling in case of an emergency, or in the event of a vehicle breakdown while on the road with horses. Regarding publications that are updated annually, we do not always dispose of old issues because they may still have good information that the new ones may not, as advertisers do not always renew their ads. We find, while traveling with horses, especially far from home or out of state, the more resources you carry with you, the better. We also keep and carry an address book of equestrians we have met or know so that if we do have a breakdown, we have a contact that is local to that area. We have found fellow horse enthusiasts to be a great help in a jam, and those in the vicinity would likely be able to accommodate us or direct us to where we could get assistance, and recommend local vets, farriers, etc., whatever is needed. It helps to innovate while taking to the road with horses. A good source of these types of resources is the advertising sections of trail publications such as Trail Rider Magazine and Trail Blazer Magazine.*

**AAA** (for both information and for recreational vehicle hauling)
1-800-JOINAAA
Website: www.aaa.com

**Hawkins Guide, Horse Trailering on the Road** (features Federal Regulations, Vehicle Registration and Guidelines, Horse Trailer Manufacturers and Dealers, Trailer Repair, Individual State Information, Scale Locations, Weight and Size Factors, Towing, Vet Services)
Bluegreen Publishing Co.
P.O. Box 1255
Southern Pines, NC  28388
1-800-316-8863

**Nationwide Overnight Stabling Directory & Equestrian Vacation Guide**
Equine Travelers of America, Inc.
P.O. Box 322
Arkansas City, KS  67005-0322
(620) 442-8131
Website: www.overnightstabling.com

**North American Horse Travel Guide**
By Bruce McAllister
Roundup Press
P.O. Box 109
Boulder, CO  80306-0109
1-800-460-9166
Website: www.horsetravel.com

**Pennsylvania Atlas & Gazetteer**
Topographic maps of the entire state
DeLorme Mapping Company
P.O. Box 298
Freeport, ME  04032
(207) 865-4171

**Pennsylvania Equine Industry Directory**
Pennsylvania Equine Council
P.O. Box 21
Dallas, PA  18612
1-888-304-0281
Website: www.pennsylvaniaequinecouncil.com

**Pennsylvania's Rail-Trails**
Rails-to-Trails Conservancy
Northeast Regional Office
105 Locust Street
Harrisburg, PA  17101
(717) 238-1717
Website: www.railtrails.org/pa

**The Paper Horse** (features coming trail events in Pennsylvania), see ad
HCR 67, Box OH 95
Mifflin, PA  17058
(717) 436-8893
Website: www.thepaperhorse.com

**The Trail Rider Magazine, LLC** (see ad)
P.O. Box 5089
Alexandria, LA  71307
(318) 487-8608
Website: www.trailridermagazine.com

**Trail Blazer Magazine**
4241 North Covina Circle
Prescott Valley, AZ  86314
(928) 772-9233
Website: www.horsetrails.com

**U.S. Stabling Guide**
Balzotti Publications
5 Barker Street
Pembroke, MA  02359
1-800-829-0715
Website: www.jimbalzotti.com

**Western Horseman** (see "Trail Riding" section covering trails from the east to the west)
3850 North Nevada Ave.
Colorado Springs, CO  80933-7980
(719) 633-5524
Website: www.westernhorseman.com

**Woodall's Eastern Campground Directory**
Woodall Publications Corporation
13975 W. Polo Trail Drive
P.O. Box 5000
Lake Forest, IL  60045-5000
1-800-323-9076
Website: www.woodalls.com

**BLOOPERS**
Cows holding up bridge

**BLOOPERS**
If the sign says "Fallen Timber Trail", think twice!

**BLOOPERS**

Uh, honey, I think we are off the map. (Men never say "lost".)

**BLOOPERS**

Hmmm, if we're going down stream, this must be the wrong way.

**BLOOPERS**
John & Moonshine ponder how to descend a steep flight of stairs on what we had thought was an equestrian bridge.

John and I with our good friend (and great chef) Steve Luoni (center)

# HAPPY TRAILS!

234

235

# PLEASE PROVIDE YOUR COMMENTS!

**Note to the Reader:** Trails are always changing. If you find any of the described trails have significantly changed, new trails have opened, or you know of Pennsylvania trails not covered in this book, please notify the publisher and author at the below address. Any comments will be considered in future editions of books and are appreciated.

Send to:
Hit The Trail Publications, LLC
P.O. Box 970
Cherryville, PA 18035